A COURSE IN INDIAN PHILOSOPHY

A COURSE IN INDIAN PHILOSOPHY

A.K. Warder

MOTILAL BANARSIDASS PUBLISHERS
PRIVATE LIMITED • DELHI

Second Edition: Delhi, 1998
(Earlier edition published under the title:
"An Outline of Indian Philosophy")

ISBN: 81-208-1244-1 (Cloth)
ISBN: 81-208-1482-7 (Paper)

MOTILAL BANARSIDASS

41 U.A. Bungalow Road, Jawahar Nagar, Delhi 110 007
8 Mahalaxmi Chamber, Warden Road, Mumbai 400 026
120 Royapettah High Road, Mylapore, Chennai 600 004
Sanas Plaza, Subhash Nagar, Pune 411 002
16 St. Mark's Road, Bangalore 560 001
8 Camac Street, Calcutta 700 017
Ashok Rajpath, Patna 800 004
Chowk, Varanasi 221 001

PRINTED IN INDIA

BY JAINENDRA PRAKASH JAIN AT SHRI JAINENDRA PRESS,
A-45 NARAINA INDUSTRIAL AREA, PHASE I, NEW DELHI 110 028
AND PUBLISHED BY NARENDRA PRAKASH JAIN FOR
MOTILAL BANARSIDASS PUBLISHERS PRIVATE LIMITED,
BUNGALOW ROAD, DELHI 110 007

CONTENTS

PREFACE TO THE SECOND EDITION

The course for which the *Outline of Indian Philosophy* was originally written has long ceased to appear in any university calendar, thanks to the universal cuts in support for education. Its content is of course completely irrelevant to the world of greed and money-making which has replaced the remarkably idealistic societies emerging from the crucible of death and destruction in the Second World War. Then, the survivors were glad to be alive and wanted to fill the mourning world with new joy, not with money. The greatest joy was that of knowledge in all its forms, of science, of art, of the human quest for enlightenment wherever records had survived. This knowledge was delightful in itself, but it might also enlighten our society and secure our freedom. The cultural hegemony of Europe having evaporated in the failure of 1938-40, the new knowledge might enhance our view of civilisation, giving breadth and depth to reflections on how the future might be better than the past.

That dream has now been shattered. This investigation of the philosophy of India, which was part of it, exists in a passive form, the professor who created it having retired. The publishers of the *Outline,* however, have resolved to renew the book, in the hope that such a prospect of sustained thought about the possibility of knowledge itself can still inspire fancy. They also wished to claim for it the status of an actual *Course in Indian Philosophy,* for private study.

The text has been kept to its original scope, since the first intention was just to photograph it, with revisions pasted over the old wording, occupying exactly the same space. These revisions, therefore, consist mostly of more exact translations substituted for the old ones, with here and there a substituted paragraph or some sentences added in the available space at the end of a chapter. No additions could be made to the Bibliography except by deleting existing items. Now the publishers have re-set the text, which greatly improves its appearance and clarity, but without having allowed the author to take advantage of the flexibility.

A translation can never be made perfectly accurate, but only to focus more sharply on the source, like a better telescope. As Diṅnāga might have said, we can gradually exclude inaccuracy. Some examples here are: 'sensation' for 'perception', which should have been obvious before because it is 'to the sense' (*pratyakṣa*); 'perception' is now restricted to the mental activity (*saṃjñā*). 'Own-being' instead of 'own-nature' is consistent with other kinds of 'being' (*bhāva*). 'Principles', instead of 'elements' or 'phenomena', for *dharmas* is far better because it does not suggest eternal substances nor on the other hand an unlimited vagueness not yet analysed, without observed regularities. It may also show how its homonym came to be used for a doctrine. Sanskrit (and Pali) distinguishes many kinds of 'object', especially the real (*vastu*, 'in itself' or 'out there' as some would say), the 'sense datum' (*viṣaya*) and the 'support' (*ālambana*, the mental 'object'). There is the object aimed at, which is also the meaning (*artha*), we might call it the 'objective' (see pp. 92, 180), but has not yet been clearly focussed. Sense 'entrance' (*āyatana*) is much better than the vague 'sphere'. 'Base' instead of 'element' is historically correct as well as clearer, since the *dhātu* is also the 'ore' from which a metal springs, its source. For *vedanā* we have travelled from 'sensation' (rejected because that belongs to *rūpa*, matter or the physical) via 'emotion' (but not in this book, rejected because it overlaps into the 'forces') to 'experience' (thus it is the same as *vedayita*, experienced or experiencing). *Nāmarūpa* is still obscure, but it is *nāma* which gives form to inchoate matter (*rūpa*, originally the 'appearance', see pp. 18-9 and 50-1).

The longest revision concerns Diṅnāga, especially on his *Pramāṇasamuccaya*, of which it is at last possible to obtain a sufficiently comprehensive view in its original Sanskrit terms, thanks to Professor Katsura's article on the Apoha Theory of its fifth chapter. There is a substantial addition on the Bahuśrutīya School of Buddhists on p. 96, also derived from the research of Professor Katsura. Also substantial is the insertion on pp. 192-3 on the Sthaviravāda philosophers Ānanda, Dhammapāla and the anonymous author of the *Gaṇṭhipada* on the *Paṭisambhidāmagga*.

So we try again to break through the limitations of Eurocentric prejudice and ignorance and misleading translations, which exclude the analytical philosophy of India, as well as her ancient sciences, from due notice and useful provision. People still think Indian philosophy must be 'spiritual': not philosophy but religion, irrational and mysterious. But on the whole Western philosophy is more 'spiritual' and mystical:

for a thousand years it was totally subordinated to dogmatic theology, whilst earlier Plato and others used myth to expound some of their supposed insights. Even recently, the struggle for independence from 'revelation' and faith has been hard and protracted. By contrast India, until the ravages of Western inquisition and the argument of the sword in the form of Islam, enjoyed two thousand years' steady development of free thinking investigations of epistemology, logic and language. Who can better show the harmony and continuity between science and philosophy than the free Indian thinkers? Who now has the better understanding of the interaction between mind and matter, or between language and the incessant storms of radiance and molecules it tries to comprehend? In Lokāyata and Buddhism mind is living matter itself, variously explained. In all Indian philosophy, with the partial exception of Navya Nyāya, language speaks only of classes, cannot reach particular events. Neurology now appears to confirm the Buddha's hypothesis of the unreality of the 'soul' or 'self' and to establish a Lokāyata-like view of consciousness as a property of matter, suitably arranged. The quest for knowledge continues; perhaps a new dream of the future will take hold of humanity.

This *Course*, however, makes no comparisons, except that it necessarily translates Indian concepts into a foreign language. The aim here is simply expository: better communication from the vista of a past civilisation.

A.K. WARDER
January, 1994

PREFACE TO THE FIRST EDITION

This *Outline* is intended to serve as an introductory textbook for Indian philosophy. It indicates the scope of the subject, providing essential basic material for the study, chronologically arranged, and giving references for further reading. The 'material' here provided is taken direct from the original sources, i.e. the works of Indian philosophers, and translated by the author of the *Outline* in all cases: its authenticity can always be checked by anyone who cares to look up the original, provided he can read the original language.

Much that is found in books purporting to be on 'Indian Philosophy' is of doubtful authenticity or else not on philosophy at all. Students should reserve judgment until they can verify the precise statements of Indian philosophers in the original sources, having first discovered which the relevant texts are. In no other subject have the subjective views of modern authors been so whimsical and arbitrary. As far as writings in English are concerned, the view seems to prevail that in fact India has had no philosophy in the strict sense of a discipline. Most English books contain only religious dogma and speculation, very various in content but agreeing in missing the problems of philosophy itself. It is as if every man is born knowing what 'philosophy' is, having his own 'philosophy', and accordingly able to select from Indian literature and write on 'philosophy' without having studied the subject itself. Of course, this is using the word 'philosophy' in a different sense from the discipline proper. The misfortune here is that those who are concerned with philosophy proper are put off by most of the books they may pick up on Indian 'philosophy' and misled into thinking India has nothing to offer in the way of philosophical investigations. The present book is merely a general survey, allowing no room for detailed exposition and discussion, which requires monographs on individual philosophers and problems. As a general outline it also traces the origins and is arranged chronologically, though it hardly contains any history beyond this arrangement. This is meant to facilitate the placing of a philosopher to some extent in the development and study of the problems, in other words in his philosophical environment. Despite its brevity and the limitations of an attempt to survey an entire field of human enquiry from its origins, it is hoped that this introduction will help to dispel misconceptions and to bring to the attention of contemporary philosophers investigations of interest and value.

In general the author has here sought for philosophy in the strict sense of the discipline of philosophical analysis and criticism, as explained in Chapter I. Metaphysics or 'speculative philosophy' is regarded as peripheral, bordering on religion. Ethics and aesthetics have been omitted as special philosophical enquiries which require separate study. Thus the main direction of the present study is epistemology, which includes logic.

University of Toronto

A.K. Warder
1967

I PRELIMINARY DEFINITIONS

It is difficult to define 'philosophy'. In fact the nature and scope of the subject is one of its primary problems and is a highly controversial matter. If we here adopt a particular standpoint and pursue our survey from it, it must be in the awareness that others who use the same title 'philosophy' have had very different points of view. Students who have followed courses in Western Philosophy will be well aware of these problems.

Our standpoint here is that the central and characteristic business of 'philosophy' consists of an enquiry into the credentials of what purports to be 'knowledge'. To adopt the usual philosophical terms, we are taking 'epistemology' or the 'theory of knowledge' as the essential part of philosophy, holding that other branches of philosophy are dependent on this and presuppose something known as a starting point. Of course, the various sciences, from astronomy to linguistics, offer much that is 'known', as data from which one might develop 'philosophical' investigations or speculations. The philosopher, however, will wonder why such data should be relied on as true or 'known'. He will compare the offerings of astronomy with those of 'revealed' religion and consider which has the best title to be relied on. He will also wonder about the reliability of any kind of 'historical' statement or record. Though in principle somewhat sceptical, he may be inclined to attach considerable weight to some statement because it was made by some great philosopher whom he admires. Whilst the scientist may be remarkably successful in accumulating 'knowledge' by the exercise of common sense, some acquired habits and methods of work and a certain amount of intuition or guesswork (afterwards put to some practical test), the philosopher may wonder why he should believe even the direct evidence of his senses, let alone any construction deduced from this.

Philosophy according to this standpoint involves a critical attitude to any kind of authority or tradition. It develops into the analysis of statements and of concepts, of our means of acquiring knowledge. Faced with arguments, demonstrations and 'proofs', it analyses these and tries to determine whether any confidence can be reposed in them. It tends to interact with the sciences which offer data and 'knowledge', and itself to be empiricist in outlook. In tracing the origin and development of philosophy in India we shall use criteria of this kind in selecting our subject-matter.

In India in particular, there is a certain overlap between philosophy and religion. It has in fact been denied that there is, or should be, any distinction between them. This denial reflects a point of view very different from that which we have adopted here, and we attempt to make a clear distinction. The basis of this distinction is the methodologies of the two subjects: religion takes its stand on revelations, including 'mystical' intuitions of ultimate, preferably supernatural, 'reality', and seeks to establish absolute authority which cannot be questioned by merely this-worldly means such as empirical science; philosophy as outlined above deals critically with the pursuit of knowledge and admits no absolute authority.

It is nevertheless a feature of Indian religions that they have often enlisted philosophy in their defence and justification, seeking what we may call philosophical respectability, and in this way they have made interesting and sometimes valuable contributions to the philosophical exercise itself, even on occasion throwing off philosophical schools which concerned themselves more with philosophy proper than with the religion they were intended originally to support. We also find the opposite process in India: a tradition which began as a philosophical enquiry may later be turned into a kind of religion by some of its followers, who tend to regard the earlier texts as some kind of revelation and authority, even in defiance of the apparent meaning of those texts themselves.

In the area of overlap between philosophy and religion we find a number of what may be called 'metaphysical' systems, heavily speculative in that they make it their main business to go beyond empirically accessible data into the construction of transcendent or supernatural worlds of 'knowledge'. In this outline we shall not devote much time to the study of such systems.

It will be very useful to look at the history of science in India, on account of its close relationships with philosophy and influence on philosophical methods. In very ancient times, before philosophy can really be distinguished as an independent subject of study, science itself was hardly distinguishable from religion. All human knowledge was bound up with myth and ritual. The methods of, say, agriculture, which we nowadays are accustomed to think should be based on scientific knowledge, seem then to have been as magical and ritualistic as the means by which one was supposed to be able to attain a happy state in the next world. Gradually, however, the various sciences became better understood and large areas of human activity which had formerly been governed by religious conceptions were detached more or less completely and carried on according to their own principles. Philosophy grew independent in much the same way at about the same time, indeed it is sometimes hard to distinguish philosophy from science, particularly in this earliest period.

II SUMMARY

Origins. The pursuit of knowledge in ancient India was, in the earliest period now intellectually accessible to us, i.e. in the oldest extant literature, the Vedic tradition, carried on within the framework of religion. *Veda* itself means 'knowledge' and represented an accumulation of knowledge handed down among the priests. This 'knowledge' consisted largely of myths and descriptions of the gods, a good deal of ritual for securing desired ends and some admixture of human historical traditions in process of being assimilated to myth. 'Philosophy' as opposed to myth can perhaps be traced from certain expressions of doubt, suggesting the possibility of more rational methods of enquiry than the poetic intuition which creates myths, in these Vedic texts. Doubts are expressed about the existence of some of the gods, and especially about the origin of the universe (cosmogony), concerning which there are several conflicting accounts already in the *Ṛgvedasaṃhitā*, the oldest part of the *Veda*. The origin is explained in terms of myth, or of ritual, or of more abstract and rationalistic speculation beginning with 'nothing', 'neither being nor nothing', etc. These more abstract speculations are developed further in the later parts of the *Veda* and especially in the latest part, the *Upaniṣads*, where a great variety of views is expounded more systematically, providing starting points for the various schools of Brahmanical philosophy. All the Brahmanical schools start from the *Veda* as accepted tradition or scripture, whence they are also known as Vaidika (Vedic) schools, though they differ in their attitudes to it. (It must be emphasised that the properly Vedic *Upaniṣads* are only five in number, probably representing the period about 900 to 600 B.C.; all other *Upaniṣads*, and there are many, are later than this and are spread over many centuries of time, reflecting all kinds of later schools of philosophy.)

The Mīmāṃsā can be called the most Brahmanical (or 'orthodox' from the Brahmanical point of view), most Vedic school, since its professed aim is simply to systematise the doctrine of the *Veda*, not to add to it nor to argue independently of it. As it later clarified its position it held that the *Veda* is the only source of the kind of knowledge that really matters, the application of which can lead to happiness and freedom. Though it assimilated all the varied speculations of the *Upaniṣads* to a single position it could not achieve this simplification for the *Veda* as a whole: it remained with two departments of study, (1) the ritual as a system of actions bringing about desirable results and (2) the knowledge of *brahman*, the ultimate reality or 'being', as by itself enough to lead to supreme bliss and liberation from transmigration. Eventually the students of *brahman* broke away to form a separate school or schools known as the Vedānta. Later still, with the growth in popularity of theism and especially of belief in a personal God during the Middle Ages, and the tendency to syncretism between the different religious traditions of India, the later schools of Vedānta occupy themselves more and more with theology and the question of the relation between the individual soul and God. The Mīmāṃsā proper remained basically atheistic, though some of its later writers proposed to make a place in it for God. (The many gods of the *Veda* are for it little but the servants of the ritual, which is the supreme power; they do not differ essentially from men.)

The Sāṃkhya continued the speculations of the *Upaniṣads*, and could be regarded as more faithful to their tradition in spirit than the Mīmāṃsā is, in that like the Upaniṣadic thinkers it sought not to systematise old materials but to improve on them. Though it seems to have started out from some of the data of experience, like some of the early Upaniṣadic philosophers, its main conclusions appear purely speculative, and in its later theory it stresses the importance of its doctrine of inference as the means of establishing its speculative principles. It sets up two ultimate principles, soul and matter, and explains our experience in the world, and our possible liberation from transmigration, in terms of the interaction of these principles and of a theory of the evolution of the material principle. God is optional, the theistic Sāṃkhya schools being later named 'Yoga' schools. The souls are in essence passive, though liable to seduction, and God being a model soul is equally passive in the universe, though a source of inspiration to others. As a Brahmanical school the Sāṃkhya admits the authority of the *Veda* but puts forward its own system as the knowledge required to achieve liberation. Some of the later Vedānta schools borrow heavily from the Sāṃkhya for their doctrines of matter and evolution, demonstrating that it is not difficult to harmonise the Sāṃkhya with the *Veda*.

All this 'Vedic' philosophy is in principle traditionalist, or at least, if Upaniṣadic speculation was originally more or less free, it became increasingly traditionalist. All its philosophical achievements are subordinated to certain dogmas, though the understanding of these may vary greatly. The brahmans believed that they were in possession of some very special knowledge which had somehow been revealed to their ancestors and which could not safely or sensibly be abandoned: there was no substitute for it, at least for the higher aims of life, and apparently no immediate possibility of a new revelation or of any other means of checking its validity.

More interesting philosophically are the schools which rejected tradition and dogma and unverifiable assertions on authority and set out on the basis of independent enquiries into the nature of reality, the way to happiness and freedom and the means of knowing anything.

The various Śramaṇa schools of the Buddha's time rejected the Vedic tradition and produced a variety of philosophies, partly empirically based and partly speculative.

The Lokāyata was materialist, disbelieved in transmigration, recommended seeking happiness in this life while it lasts. On the problem of knowledge it held that sensation was the only means we have of acquiring knowledge and it took up a completely sceptical position as regards attempts to construct out of our sense data any generalisations about the universe. Thus it was not prepared to admit the universality of natural laws, the uniformity of nature. Everything was spontaneous and there was completely free will.

The Ajñāna or 'Agnostic' school maintained a total scepticism, holding no doctrine at all as to the nature of reality or the possibility of knowledge but merely recommending friendliness and avoiding argument as a way to happiness.

The Ājīvaka school was diametrically opposed to the Lokāyata in that it maintained determinism against their free will. The universe consisted of the interplay of elements, or rather atoms, entirely subject to Destiny and giving no scope for any other agent. It is not surprising that they seem to have specialised in predicting the future, believing it to be already unalterably fixed.

The Jainas rejected this determinism and broke away from the

Ājīvakas, to which their founder had originally belonged. Transmigration, they held, could be ended by asceticism and did not have to continue according to Destiny until all the preordained millions of lives the soul had to undergo had run out. Transmigration was caused by one's own actions, which could be balanced out by opposite actions, resulting in liberation or *nirvāṇa.* Asceticism if severe enough could bring about this result quite quickly, cancelling out bad actions through the suffering of their agent. As regards knowledge the Jainas held a doctrine of points of view, according to which various opinions could be simultaneously true, in fact relatively so in different schemes. This position had something in common with that of Agnostics, but was not completely negative. It led the Jainas later to maintain an attitude of extreme toleration in religious matters.

The Buddhists proved to be the most important of these Śramaṇa schools and the most productive of further developments in philosophy. Their extant texts give us a far richer picture of the Śramaṇas generally, as well as of their own school, than has been preserved by any of their rivals. Their position was in one way close to that of the Jainas, in that they accepted free will, as opposed to the Ājīvakas, and also effective causality (free will limited by natural laws, which operated universally), both physical and moral, as opposed to the Lokāyatikas. Happiness is to be sought within the limits set by the laws of nature, final happiness or *nirvāṇa,* however, by avoiding further proliferation of the causal process, having thoroughly understood this. As opposed to the Jainas, however, the Buddhists maintained the very significant position that understanding alone could bring about non-attachment and the ending of the causal processes bringing about transmigration. It was not necessary or even helpful to practise severe asceticism to balance out past bad actions. Moral causality was fully accepted and future good or bad experiences in transmigration as arising according to it, but liberation was to be attained not by working within the relative ups and downs of transmigration (which meant still being attached to it) to achieve a balance, but by breaking out of the whole process through understanding, by an act of complete renunciation.

The Buddhists based their doctrine on the evidence of the senses. They argued from experience and doubted all tradition. The early Buddhists accepted the world of experience as 'real' in the everyday or common sense meaning of that expression. Accordingly they accepted their observations as establishing the existence and the activities of numerous separate elements or principles (*dharmas*) as the realities of which the universe consists. They sought to give a satisfactory account of these, especially in so far as they were relevant to the quest for happiness or liberation. Beyond these principles they saw only their regularity or principle-ness, not any more ultimate reality such as the *brahman*. In fact they were sceptics in that they avoided postulating metaphysical entities beyond experimental verification. Their principles and their principle-ness were regarded as discovered by empirical investigations and as in principle verifiable by anyone interested, otherwise they would not be real. It was not the authority of the Buddha or anyone else which made anything true. Even transmigration was supposed to be a matter of experience, since claims were made of the memory of previous lives. The empiricist limitation of entities to what was strictly necessary for an account of experience excluded the concept of a 'soul' as one of the elements or principles or as existing in any form. This sharply distinguished the Buddhists from the Jainas and Ājīvakas as well as from the Brahmanical schools, and seemed to bring them into line with the Lokāyata. But they maintained 'rebirth' against the Lokāyata as strongly as the Jainas and others, only giving a quite different account of its mechanism. There is in fact nothing which transmigrates, or rather no entity which transmigrates, hence no transmigration in the literal sense; only there is very definitely a transmission of forces from life to life, a working out of causal laws and production of future experience as an effect of old actions. It was objected to the soul theories that an eternal soul, as described by those schools, could not consistently be said to participate in changing experience. The assumption of such an entity explained nothing. In general the Buddhists thought it unwarranted to suppose anything beyond simple qualities ('quality' is later, at least, a meaning of *dharma*, a principle) occurring in the universe: it did not explain anything to allege that beyond, or underlying, these qualities there were substances, whether a 'soul' as a substance underlying consciousness or any other kind of substance underlying the principles of the physical world. So-called 'transmigration' was thus a mere sequence of momentary 'consciousnesses', related to one another as causes and effects but not containing any continuing entity. There is no experiencer, but just experience.

These positions of the Buddhists were rather promising for the future development of philosophy. They retained ever after their interest in the theory of knowledge: how can we be sure of what we are supposed to know, how can we bring our ideas into closer correspondence with reality? On the question of the nature of that reality, however, of principle-ness, some Buddhists moved away from the conception of a plurality of real principles. First they argued that since they were always changing, transient, they were in a sense not quite 'real', did not really 'exist'. This line of thought carried further an older idea of there being two levels of truth, or of statements, the strictly philosophical (description of principles and causal laws) and the everyday or popular (ordinary usage about 'self' and 'persons' as if such concepts corresponded to entities). Now this new Buddhist trend, the so-called Mahāyāna, and on the other hand the reformist philosophical school of the 'Intermediate' Madhyamaka, went further and held that even the elements or principles could be called 'real' only at the level of everyday usage and appearance, which was known as the 'concealing' level. Philosophically, at the 'ultimate' level where one attempted to speak not of superficial appearances but of ultimate reality, the principles were unreal, had no real being, no existence of their own, because they were not independent entities but entirely dependent on causes and conditions, were nothing in themselves. The only ultimate reality was then the fact of principles being conditioned, their 'conditioned origination', the causal law of their nature.

Some Mahāyāna Buddhists then went still further and arrived at a position of philosophical idealism. This was the Vijñānavāda or 'Consciousness (Only) School', also known as Yogācāra. From principle-ness they moved on to an absolute idea underlying nature, which they identified with consciousness in some sense. There existed an ultimate, absolute, undifferentiated reality. In its undifferentiated state it could not actively be conscious because being conscious means being conscious of something and presupposes a duality, a differentiation. Thus as soon as active consciousness became differentiated a stream of transient experience was generated. From the ultimate non-duality, the non-dual ultimate reality, there was differentiated subject and object and further divisions, all dependent on consciousness and thus no more than relatively real, or even purely imaginary. Thus the universe of transmigration was generated.

The Indian Buddhists as empiricists for the most part rejected any idealist position, which could hardly be distinguished from some form of later Vedānta (the ultimate reality, which is pure consciousness, is *brahman*) if it asserts an ultimate eternal being, and reworked their theory of knowledge. The Madhyamaka doctrine of the principles having no own-being had produced a very thorough and comprehensive critique of all philosophical concepts, leaving nothing but empirical experience. A new epistemological school, the Sautrāntika of Diṅnāga (Dignāga), very cautiously tried to establish a more positive doctrine of the theory of knowledge and of logical demonstration (inference) which might escape this critique. They set up a pragmatic criterion of truth. Afterwards some philosophers combined features of the Madhyamaka and Sautrāntika doctrines and produced various hybrid trends.

Parallel to the study of the theory of knowledge among the Buddhists there runs a development of scholasticism and also of the practice of debating, beginning with the Abhidharma studies of the early schools. This scholasticism is not, as a rule, empiricist, but rather deductive and systematising from accepted premises (in principle the statements of the Buddha), for which reason it was severely criticised by the Madhyamakas as contrary to the spirit and intentions of the Buddha. It made substantial contributions to the theory of definition and deduction.

There remains a school which at least through most of its history has been Brahmanical or Vedic, though possibly it was not so at its origin. This is the Vaiśeṣika, of which the Nyāya was for eight centuries an independent branch, after which they reunited. This school originated as an investigation of reality similar in outlook to the Śramaṇas, not depending on authority but on empirical observations. Either originally or later, however, it admitted the authority of the *Veda*, as a source of information on moral questions, yet practically it ignores the *Veda* and bases its whole system on independent enquiry. Inference is more important for it than sensation as a means of knowledge, and the enquiry begins by working out the doctrines of inference and induction. Applying these methods to the data of experience the Vaiśeṣika establishes a number of categories or classes of object to which words refer, and the members of these classes. These categories are: substance, quality, action, universal, particular, combination. The atoms constituting most substances are held to be eternal, whilst their combinations are transient. The soul is assumed, as a substance which is the basis of experience and which is eternal. The Nyāya branch specialised in debate and logic. After centuries of criticism by the Buddhists of their somewhat metaphysical concepts (especially of the 'universal'), and vigorous polemic against these philosophical opponents, the new, reunited school, which came to be known as the Navya Nyāya, carefully re-worked its whole doctrine as in principle a theory of knowledge (cf. the Buddhist Sautrāntika school), as a preliminary (but practically endless) enquiry into our means of knowing anything and into our use of language. The Old Nyāya and the Navya Nyāya were both theist, in strong opposition to the Buddhists, whereas the Vaiśeṣika at least in the early period was atheist.

With the Turkish conquest of much of India in the 13th and 14th centuries Buddhism and several other schools were obliterated in India and Indian philosophy led a very restricted and precarious existence in the regions still under Indian rule. For Indians this was a period of return to their most ancient traditions, of defending what seemed to be the essentials of Indian civilisation. On the whole there was little of the free thinking which is so characteristic of ancient India, little quest for what was new. The most interesting school of philosophy which survived in this dark age was the Navya Nyāya established in Tīrabhukti.

In conclusion it should be noted that this outline omits to discuss Indian ethics and other branches of philosophy, being limited to the central problem of knowledge.

III ORIGINS

The origins of philosophy in India can be traced in the literature of the *Veda*, the earliest Indian literature now available to us. This literature spans a considerable period, from about 1500 B.C. onwards over about a thousand years, allowing us to see the gradual development of ideas. Its language is an ancient form of 'Sanskrit' and it represents the tradition of the Aryan people settled in India after their conquest of the earlier non-Aryan civilisation centred on the Indus River. Little is known of the thought of that older Indian civilisation, since the language of the documents (inscriptions) which have survived from it has not yet been deciphered. We cannot therefore know whether they had developed 'philosophy', though it seems probable, if merely on grounds of analogy with other bronze age civilisations (in Mesopotamia, etc.), that they had not and that their thinking remained at the level of religion, of myth and mystery. The earliest Vedic literature certainly reflects such a 'mythopoeic' outlook.

The earliest parts of the *Veda* are the *Saṃhitās* ('Collections'—of traditional material) and the earliest of these is the *Ṛgvedasaṃhitā* ('Collection of the Veda of Hymns'), though its contents represent compositions over the whole period from approximately 1500 to 1000 B.C. It consists of poems and songs of many kinds, but mostly in the form of hymns to the gods: whatever the origin of the poems, they happen to have been preserved because they were given a place in a collection of texts used as a repertoire of hymns in the performance of sacrifices to the gods. Since the gods were connected with such fundamental ideological matters as the origin of the world and the order of nature, the poems addressed to them sometimes tell us how the ancient Indians thought about these questions and how their reasoning about them developed. Cosmogony or the theory of the origin and development of the universe turns out to be of crucial importance in the historical development of philosophy out of myth and speculation.

Cosmogony. The ancient mythology regarded various gods or divine beings as the creators of the world. Thus we find the widespread ancient idea of Heaven and Earth, a god and a goddess, as the parents of all creatures and of the other gods (I.159, 160, 185, VII.97, etc.). But in one of these poems (I.185) the question is raised, and not answered, where Heaven and Earth came from. Elsewhere, perhaps in poems which are on the whole later, they themselves are said to have been created by various gods (VI.30, VIII.36, X.29, 54—Indra; X.81—Viśvakarman; X.110—Tvaṣṭṛ). It is quite characteristic of the *Veda* that its statements are inconsistent; it is not a systematic text, whatever the later ritualists may hold, it is basically poetic and is of course the work of many authors who might hold very different views, in particular the poems addressed to different gods tend to exalt each god at the expense of the others. Sometimes the gods are thought to have built Heaven and Earth (i.e. the universe) like a house (X.81, cf. II.15, X.149, VI.49, etc.), and this leads to the question what was the wood which they used in building them (X.81—the answer given in a later Vedic ritual text is that it was *brahman*: *Taittirīya Brāhmaṇa* 2, 8, 9, 6). The idea of measuring occurs in several of these poems as an essential part of the work of constructing the universe (see also V.85—by Varuṇa with the Sun).

In the later parts of the *Ṛgvedasaṃhitā* (especially Book X) these mythical explanations are supplemented or superseded by speculations of a more rationalistic character concerning the ultimate origin of the universe. Thus one theory (X.72) is that originally there was nothing or 'non-being' (*asant*), and out of it 'being' (*sant*) evolved. Another theory tries to go further and suggests (X.129) that originally there was neither being nor non-being, continuing to speculate in a philosophical atmosphere of doubt as to how the ultimate being of the universe, its supreme being or God, as we may try to interpret it, might have evolved. Here is a translation of the main points in the poem:

> At first there was neither being nor non-being, (but somehow) the One, a living being, came into existence through the influence of heat (apparently from its own heat), embracing everything in itself. Then from desire there arose mind. Then a measuring line was stretched across horizontally, dividing what existed into male and female principles. (At this point the speculation breaks off, but with a question:) Who really knows? Not the gods! (They

did not exist at first and so cannot know.) Only he who surveys the universe from the highest heaven perhaps knows, or perhaps he too does not know.

In the male and female principles separated horizontally we should probably recognise here the ancient conception of Heaven and Earth, but it has been transformed into a phase in a rationalistic explanation of evolution. Most impressive and most philosophical here is the admission that we do not know the origin of things (despite all the old traditions of the *Veda*) and that perhaps even the highest of the gods does not know. Such a statement surely marks the birth of philosophy, of a critical approach to all supposed 'knowledge'.

In this poem it may appear that 'heat' (*tapas*) is the ultimate cause of the evolutionary process, a kind of ultimate element out of which everything is generated. This term *tapas* is in later centuries used for the ultimate principle of asceticism, in a rather different system of ideas, which is thought to have creative power (and destructive power). Here its action is followed by that of 'pleasure' or 'desire' (*kāma,* also 'love'), generating mind (*manas*).

Another and very ancient idea of the ultimate principle or element of the universe is that of the primaeval ocean or waters, anciently deified as the 'mothers' (feminine and plural) of everything (VII.47, VI.50—of all that is fixed or moves, X.9, 17, 30). This conception develops into that of a kind of primaeval chaos out of which the universe evolves. Thus in one poem (X.82, cf. 121) an embryo is born in the waters, an embryo which is the highest deity, which then creates all things (and is known an Viśvakarman, Creator of All). In the later Vedic literature (after the *Ṛgvedasaṃhitā*) this embryo is identified with the ultimate or absolute being, or the highest deity (*brahman,* neuter nominative *brahma* as abstract principle, masculine nominative *brahmā* as a person), creative power or the creator, etymologically the 'great one'.

At the end of the period represented by the *Ṛgvedasaṃhitā* (say, about B.C. 1000) religion in India was dominated by ritual. The ritual actions, or sacrifices, were alone considered important and significant, the gods were merely the servants of the ritual (they were needed to receive offerings, for example, but the efficacy of an offering lay in the correct performance of the act itself, not in the propitiation of the god who received the offering), the universe and everything in it was explained in terms of the ritual, as simply a grandiose ritual process, instead of in terms of myth. Philosophical speculation such as we have just noted seems to have occupied a peripheral place, cultivated by a few thinkers who were not satisfied with ritual and symbols, with the ritual performances which provided a lucrative living for the expert priests who officiated at them. In a poem (X.90) which is believed to be among the very latest in the *Ṛgvedasaṃhitā* we can see the ritualist conception of the origin of the universe. It begins with a primaeval being or person called Puruṣa ('Man'): the gods sacrifice him, creating the universe out of the parts of his body. (In the later literature this Puruṣa is identified with the ultimate *brahman* of which the universe is made.) Of course this is not an ultimate origin since Puruṣa and the gods already existed, though perhaps it satisfied some ritualists. When later the ritualists worked out their cosmogony more carefully, they adopted the view that at first the sacred words (of the *Veda*), which from the earliest Vedic literature on were called *brahman* (sic!), existed, had in fact eternally existed, and that with them as blueprints the material objects of the universe arose out of them. This view will be discussed below in its chronological place, but we may perhaps see an anticipation of it in a poem of the *Ṛgvedasaṃhitā* (X.125) describing the Goddess Speech (Vāc), who supports the highest gods, through whom alone men eat, see, breathe and hear and with whom they live, who makes strong the man she loves, who extends over all existing creatures and whose power encompasses Heaven and Earth and what is beyond them. In connection with *brahman* we may note here that etymologically it meant originally 'great' and that its meanings in the *Veda* probably derive from the idea of power. Besides the regular meaning of a sacred utterance it is remarkable that in some contexts it means 'food', at least according to the early lexicographer Yāska. The link between these two apparently very different meanings is perhaps the idea of something which sustains or gives strength.

An important concept in the early *Veda* which, with a change of verbal expression, remains a basic idea in later Indian philosophy is that of *ṛta*, the 'order' or simply the 'way' or 'truth' of the universe, or sometimes rather the 'true order' or 'proper way', with moral implications. It is extremely difficult to determine the original idea underlying this term, and the difficulties are hardly resolved by comparison with the obscure meaning of the Avestan cognate *aša*, a fundamental religious concept in Zoroastrianism about which scholars are unable to agree, although there it appears strongly moral in content ('truth', 'justice', etc.). Since the term appears in both the Vedic and Avestan traditions in generally similar religious contexts, it must be very ancient in this kind of meaning among the Indo-Iranian peoples before they were divided, and have a prehistory inaccessible to us. In the Indian tradition we find that the term *ṛta* is at the end of the Vedic period replaced by *dharma* in similar or wider meanings, and we shall have to discuss this new term at length in due course. (In the *Veda* it appears very rarely in the form *dharman*, apparently synonymous with *ṛta*.) Its root means 'hold', 'maintain'.

In the *Ṛgvedasaṃhitā ṛta* is used for the way of Heaven and Earth (X.121), the movements of the Sun (I.24) and the right path for men (X.133, verse 6). The basic idea may be the 'course of things' (the root being *ṛ*, to go or move), either the natural course or the proper course. In the latter sense, with moral implications, *ṛta* is sometimes said to be upheld by the gods, especially by Varuṇa, or by Mitra and Varuṇa together (I.23). Varuṇa is especially connected with justice and Mitra with legal contracts in the earliest mythology accessible to us. Thus the meanings of *ṛta* seem to vary from the way things are (natural law) to the way they should be (moral law), but possibly we should always think of the latter, with the idea that Heaven, Earth and the Sun might deviate from the right course but for their perfect virtue as high deities.

Doubt. Apart from the philosophical doubt we noted above in one of the later poems in the *Ṛgvedasaṃhitā*, there are occasional expressions of doubt concerning the gods, even in earlier poems. There are doubts whether the gods exist, particularly whether Indra (on the whole the most conspicuous and popular of the Vedic gods, almost a national or rather tribal god of the Aryans, who leads them to victory in war) exists (II.12, verse 5, VIII.100, verse 3). There were at any rate some men who doubted the assertions of the priests, and sometimes the priests themselves seem to have doubts about their traditions, which of course would encourage the freer development of speculation and of philosophy.

Science and philosophy are intimately related, but both in ancient times grew up under the dominance of religion. At about the same time, it would seem, both began to break away as independent disciplines, in method if not always in application. To a great extent in fact early philosophy in our sense is 'natural philosophy', i.e. the beginning of a critically established science of physics and of other branches of investigation of the natural world. Cosmogony becomes an attempt to study the natural universe. Apart from physics thus growing out of mythology through the development of rational thought, certain other branches of science are found in applied forms as branches of Vedic study, since they were used for the ritual (it should be borne in mind that whatever was not used for such purposes has disappeared from the extant literature, since for the early Vedic period the only text preserved is the *Veda* itself). The ritual itself was obviously studied as a kind of technology, believed to promote good crops, fertility, etc., amongst other desired aims. It incidentally as it were, but essentially in fact, incorporated some genuine science: astronomy for its calendar, grammar and phonetics for the analysis and correct pronunciation of the sacred texts, geometry for the construction of its altars. In such a tradition it is perhaps not surprising that linguistics became the most advanced of the sciences at an early period, and remained a model for all the other sciences thereafter. Mathematics (first arithmetic and geometry) also was well developed at an early period, with elaborate calculations concerning such things as the numbers of words or syllables in certain texts and in certain metres, or the numbers of bricks used in building altars; fairly soon it advanced to the conception of positive and negative numbers, i.e. abstract number. In geometry we find the study of triangles and quadrilaterals, *pi*, "pythagoras' theorem", etc. Medical science grew out of the originally magic rites of the *Atharvavedasaṃhitā*, part of which seems to be as ancient as the main parts of the *Ṛgvedasaṃhitā*, part rather later.

The development of both science and philosophy, if or when they can be distinguished as separate, corresponds to the development of a rational, critical, analysing trend of thinking, replacing in successive areas of study the ancient mythopoeic framework within which all 'knowledge' was interpreted. Their methods are similar, contrasting with those on which religion is based.

Following the *Saṃhitā* period of Vedic literature, but overlapping it, we find the *Brāhmaṇas* of the *Veda*. Whereas the *Saṃhitās* are collections of the sacred words, the *Brāhmaṇas* in principle deal with the ritual, describing this in great detail, including the use of the sacred words in it. They represent the period probably mainly after B.C. 1000, and lasting some centuries, when the ritual dominated the religion of India, the old theology was merely incidental to it and everything tended to be explained in ritualistic rather than mythopoeic terms. The time of their final redaction was certainly a good deal later than that of the great elaboration of the ritual (it is hardly possible, however, to determine exact dates in the growth of these texts), and the *Brāhmaṇas* incorporate as their final sections the latest parts of the authentic *Veda*, the *Upaniṣads*, often spoken of as if they were independent texts on account of their different, speculative and philosophical rather than ritualistic, content. The ritual texts proper thus represent a period of transition between mythology and the speculative-philosophical *Upaniṣads* which we shall discuss later. In them we find a continuation of the cosmogonic speculations of the *Ṛgvedasaṃhitā*, keeping alive the trend towards philosophy through this period. The most important *Brāhmaṇa* is the *Śatapathabrāhmaṇa*, a *Yajurvedabrāhmaṇa* (The Vājasaneyin recension). It gives a variety of evolutionary speculations: in the beginning there was nothing but water, or rather the waters (plural); they desired to reproduce, generated heat and produced the (golden) embryo, from which all creatures were born, the further detailed account being ritualistic in its explanations (IX.1.6); or in the beginning there was neither being nor non-being of the universe, but mind existed, which created from itself fire and speech, from which in turn other things were produced (X.5.3); or in the beginning the *brahman* (neuter, the abstract principle or ultimate being) existed, created the gods in the worlds (three worlds, Earth, Air and Heaven, constituting the universe), went beyond these worlds but then returned into them by means of *nāmarūpa* (a term of obscure origin, later meaning a living body, literally 'name' and 'appearance', or 'speech' and 'matter', or 'name' and 'sight', apparently here the combination of intelligibility and matter which makes the universe as we know it possible, 'sight' is what is visible)—as far as *nāmarūpa* extends this whole (universe) extends (XI.2.3); and so on. The main new development here as compared with the *Ṛgvedasaṃhitā* is the concept of *brahman* as the ultimate being. The central meaning of *rūpa* seems to be 'appearance', the visible, aspect, but it implies the physical, matter. 'Name' probably implies understanding and control, classifying, organisation; not mind itself but the action of the mind especially through language.

IV UDDĀLAKA

Of the numerous *Upaniṣads* extant, five are ancient and authentic as parts of the Vedic Canon, closely associated with, or incorporated in, their respective *Brāhmaṇas* and in the same prose style. All other *Upaniṣads* are later and show new trends in thought which must be recognised as different from those of the Vedic period proper, however interesting they may be in their own right. These new trends are those of the period of the origin of Buddhism and of later periods (in fact the composition of apocryphal *Upaniṣads* is probably still continuing). The five ancient *Upaniṣads* are the *Chāndogya, Bṛhadāraṇyaka, Aitareya, Kauṣītaki* and *Taittirīya.* They contain the teachings of roughly a hundred different persons, mostly named and the majority, though not all, priests. From their interrelationships, often as teacher and pupil, it can be calculated (see Ruben) that they represent about five generations in time, covering very approximately, so far as the historical traditions and archaeological evidence allow us to guess, the century B.C. 850 to 750. A good many of these teachers appear in the *Brāhmaṇas* as well, making evident the considerable overlap of Brāhmaṇical ritual-based speculation and Upaniṣadic speculation tending to free itself from any ritual connection. The process was gradual and to a considerable extent the two trends coexisted as alternative and equivalent exercises performed by the initiated, if not by the Aryan society at large. We must further bear in mind that we have little guarantee that newer doctrines were not ascribed to famous ancient teachers: some of these Upaniṣadic theories may be somewhat later than the period suggested above, although on the whole there is nothing in them to indicate a date as late as the period of the Buddha (6th and 5th centuries B.C.) for the ideas expressed.

The earliest of the teachers who appear to have had their views recorded in the *Upaniṣads* were mystics or interpreters of the symbolism of the ritual and the sacred texts and of the cosmos. We have in effect the macrocosm or the universe itself, in which the symbols are writ large, and the microcosm or ritual paraphernalia, in which they are miniaturised—and can be manipulated by the priests. There should be complete parallelism between the two. As for the sacred texts, for example, we are told that the *ṛc* (*Ṛgveda* or collection of sacred hymns) is the stars, whilst the *sāman* (*Sāmaveda* or collection of sacred melodies to which the *ṛces* are to be sung) is the Moon; alternatively the sky is the *ṛc* and the Sun the *sāman*. These ritual equations are of merely negative interest to us, as a sample of ritualistic thinking. Among this early group of *Upaniṣad* thinkers, however, Raikva in the *Chāndogya Upaniṣad* of the *Sāmaveda* (*adhyāya* IV) developed the cosmogonic speculations: here we find a theory which is probably very old though perhaps not clearly represented in earlier Vedic texts, that of air as the ultimate or original element. Air or wind (*vāyu*) and breath (*prāṇa*), are the two ultimate elements in the universe, or probably two aspects of the one ultimate element (we may perhaps identify the wind as the macrocosm and breath as a microcosmic aspect in living beings). Everything else develops out of these two and in due course vanishes back into them again. Fire, the sun, water, etc., vanish into the mind, the self of a person vanishes into breath, as do his senses when he is sleeping.

The greatest of the thinkers of the *Upaniṣads* is Uddālaka, who may be slightly later than these mystics though still relatively early among the hundred or so teachers there represented. He was perhaps the first real philosopher, unless we are to count such pioneers as the poet of *Ṛgvedasaṃhitā* X.129 (who according to tradition was the Creator Prajāpati or Brahmā himself). Uddālaka is methodical and systematic.

Uddālaka is mentioned in the *Śatapathabrāhmaṇa* as going from central-northern India to the Northern country (probably Gandhāra) and challenging the priests there to a discussion (XI.4.1). Such discussions (in the period of the *Brāhmaṇas* usually about tricky points in the ritual) were always popular in the tradition of the Indian priests and in wider circles, there were in fact contests in learned competence, sometimes for rewards in the form of wealth, sometimes to settle that the loser should become the pupil of the winner, in other words to determine their relative social prestige. In the present case, however, we are told that Uddālaka was highly impressed by the learning of one of the Northern priests, Śaunaka, and immediately asked to become his pupil in order to learn the answers to some strange facts of life. These answers are all ritualistic in character. Thus men are born without teeth because a certain rite is performed without prayers, and acquire them only later, on account of various prayers recited in following rites. In other words Uddālaka studied the ritual traditions and speculations of his day. All the more striking is the contrast when we read his own ideas in the *Chāndogya Upaniṣad* of the *Sāmaveda* (*adhyāya* VI). In a philosophical spirit he doubts received traditions and rejects them in favour of careful observations of nature, carried further by experiment, thus tries to find out what causes things to appear as they do and offers generalisations of a rational and scientific character.

In his exposition in the *Chāndogya Upaniṣad* (in the form of a dialogue with his son), Uddālaka first rejects one traditional account of the evolution of the universe found in the older *Veda*, namely that originally there was non-being, nothing, and being evolved out of it. He asks how being could have come out of nothing, and concludes that there must have been being even at first. There must be some original being, from which everything in the universe has come. He proposes, and tries to establish scientifically, a series of natural stages of development, explaining how all realities have come out of being. First being produced heat (*tejas*). Then heat produced water. Then out of water came *anna*, 'food' in its ordinary sense but here probably including all solid matter. From heat, water and food everything in the universe arises, including man and mind. We note that Uddālaka conceives of his original being as already alive and capable of forming wishes. It wished to become many things, and thereby produced heat. The three elements heat, water and food likewise are living, are indeed referred to as 'divinities', and wish to produce the multiplicity of realities. Everything therefore is alive from the beginning, the matter of the universe is alive and desires to grow, and this is why evolution takes place. Everything again reverts in time to the three elements and ultimately back into the original being: thus at death man reverts to that being from which he ultimately came. Here there is no room for gods creating anything or for any other outside agency working on matter: the matter of the universe itself, its own original being, is the creative agent and everything arises through natural processes to be explained through the nature of this being itself and then of the elements it generates.

In order to justify these conclusions Uddālaka gives the following observations, intended to illustrate the relationships between his realities. When a man (thus a living being) is hot, he sweats, thus heat generates water. Food is dependent on rainfall, therefore ultimately arises from water. Among the later derivatives from the elements are the components of the human body (flesh, blood, bone, breath, etc.), including mind (*manas*). In order to prove the dependence of mind on matter he proposes an experiment (which his son is said to carry out, being thereby convinced). If a man fasts, abstaining from food but taking water, for fifteen days, he becomes incapable of remembering the texts he previously knew. This shows that mind depends on food, or rather originates from food. Breath on the other hand arises from water, according to Uddālaka, and therefore remains despite the fast. The experiment is even quantitative in intention, since Uddālaka maintains that man consists of sixteen parts or fractions, equivalent to a day each: on the fifteenth day of the fast he is almost exhausted. On taking food again mind and memory return and Uddālaka's son is able to remember the texts.

In order to introduce his doctrine of ultimate elements out of which the whole universe is constituted, and of the still more ultimate being, Uddālaka points out how things superficially different may be essentially the same. From any lump of clay, he says, everything made of clay can be known; from one copper ornament whatever is made of copper can be known; from one pair of scissors everything made of iron can be known; the different names used for different objects made from these same substances are mere conventions of speech, for in fact the substance is the same. (This perhaps is Uddālaka's understanding of the distinction of *nāman*, 'name' or verbal distinction, and *rūpa*, 'matter' or real distinction.) One can thus generalise about the nature of things by disregarding superficial differences, and ultimately one can study the ultimate elements or element of the universe by looking for a common substance.

A conception of causality is found in Uddālaka's reasoning about the relations between the elements and the realities which arise from them. He uses the term *mūla*, originally 'root', for a cause and *śuṅga*, originally 'shoot', for an effect. Thus water is the cause of food, food is the cause of 'man' or of mind. Further observations are added to show the necessary connections here: thus water is necessary for the assimilation of food (food depends on water). Many analogies are added to show how everything is supposed to go back into'being' (at death). Being is (like) a very fine substance present in everything though not directly visible in itself. The very popular phrase 'thou art that' (*tat tvam asi*) is here used by Uddālaka to his son: you are (ultimately) that same being. (The modern Vedāntins understand this in their special way, of course, as part of their doctrine of *brahman*, combining Uddālaka's statements with those of various other thinkers, whereas Uddālaka himself shows no acquaintance with this kind of mysticism, or rather pursues his enquiry along quite different lines. The process of going back into the ultimate being is apparently automatic, a natural process, in Uddālaka's theory; it does not depend on any knowledge or striving on the part of an individual to 'attain' a higher state.)

The basic characteristics of science and of a critical and rigorous philosophy are clear in Uddālaka's exposition. A critical approach to tradition. Development of a method of observation and experiment and induction from evidence. The idea of universal natural laws (as, everything made of iron can be known from one iron object; universal elements as ultimate constituents of the entire universe). Investigation of 'causal' relations, embracing mental as well as physical realities. The idea of a quantitative experiment. The elimination of any supernatural cause or forces working on the universe and the attempt to explain it out of itself through the interrelationships of the realities within it. The law of the gods is to give way to natural law. The attempt to distinguish between more real or ultimate substances and less real modifications or derivatives (this again is an aspect of generalisation).

V ŚĀṆḌILYA, YĀJÑAVALKYA AND OTHER UPANIṢAD SPECULATIONS

The trend which became the basis of orthodox Vedānta (of various sub-schools), i.e., the mystical speculation about *brahman*, seems to begin with Śāṇḍilya. In the *Śatapathabrāhmaṇa* (X.6.3) in a passage on meditating on *brahman* he is represented as saying that one should meditate on the *ātman*, soul or self or most essential body of man, which is the *puruṣa* (or Puruṣa, the primaeval being, 'Man'), 'man' in the heart. This probably means that the *brahman*, the absolute, ultimate or primaeval reality, is the same as the individual soul. In any case in the *Chāndogya Upaniṣad* (III.14) the latter doctrine is stated clearly and attributed to Śāṇḍilya (once again we have the overlap between the *Brāhmaṇas* and the *Upaniṣads*, the same teachers appearing in both). Here he says 'my soul (*ātman*) is *brahman*' (III.14.4), and just before that the soul is the smallest thing (in the heart) yet also the largest, larger than these worlds (III.14.3). Again there is a similar, but not identical, wording in the *Brāhmaṇa* version. This equation of *ātman* and *brahman* was subsequently known as the Śāṇḍilya Vidyā, Śāṇḍilya's Knowledge.

Śāṇḍilya says practically no more than this in the texts available to us, but Yājñavalkya, a junior contemporary of Uddālaka (at the end of the *Bṛhadāraṇyaka Upaniṣad* he is even set down as a pupil of Uddālaka, though in fact he completely rejected Uddālaka's teaching) elaborates the thesis at considerable length, though unsystematically (in sharp contrast to Uddālaka's systematic exposition of his ideas). Yājñavalkya is presented as a master of all the doctrines of the ritualistic speculation, as invincible in contests of learning on such matters. In the *Bṛhadāraṇyaka Upaniṣad* of the *Yajurveda* (it is in fact the concluding part of the *Śatapathabrāhmaṇa*), III and IV, answering the questions of other people, he explains that there is an immortal soul in every being, and that it is not distinct but the same in each being. For the most part he presents this as poetic intuitions, with many analogies but hardly any inductive reasoning. Probably this poetic element in his discourses helped to make them popular. For example when asked (IV.3) 'What is man's light?' he answers first the Sun. The questioner pursues this asking what is his light when it has set. He answers the Moon, and then successively fire, speech and the soul (*ātman*). When asked what soul he replies the *puruṣa* (man) which is the light in the heart, consisting of consciousness (*vijñāna*) in the breath, which becomes dreams and goes beyond the world. It goes in two worlds, 'this' and the 'other'. Yājñavalkya then elaborates a theory of dreams and of a higher state of deep, dreamless sleep, free from all desires. At death the *puruṣa* (man) goes back into breath and is subsequently reborn. Here (IV.4) an analogy is used: the soul passes from one body to another as a caterpillar comes to the end of a blade of grass and climbs over onto another. This soul is *brahman*, it consists of consciousness, mind, breath, sight, hearing, earth, water, air, space, heat, non-heat, desire (*kāma*), non-desire, anger, non-anger, *dharma*, non-*dharma*, everything. Rebirth takes place through desire, the soul makes itself a new *rūpa* (appearance) as a goldsmith changes the shape of a piece of gold. He who is without desire, however, is *brahman* and goes to *brahman*.

In these discussions we meet probably for the first time with the conception of rebirth, direct transmigration of a soul from one body to another, and at the same time with the idea that by becoming free from desire, on the other hand (not automatically as with Uddālaka), the soul can revert to the primaeval *brahman*.

However, Yājñavalkya goes on along a somewhat different tack. The soul is 'not born' (*aja*), presumably not (really) of this world. It is the lord and master of all, of all beings. It is indescribable (*na-iti, na-iti,* one cannot apply any expression or indication to it, it is not anything which can be pointed out), inconceivable, imperishable, not attached, does not suffer. It is not worried by the thoughts 'I have done what is good, I have done what is bad'—it has gone beyond both. It is ageless, deathless, immortal, fearless. It is *brahman*. He who knows this becomes *brahman*.

None of the things of this world are desirable in themselves (IV.5): they can be dear to us only on account of the soul (*ātman*). When the soul is known, everything is known. But after death there is no perception (*saṃjñā*): where there is duality (*dvaita*) there is perception and being conscious (*vi-jñā*), where there is no duality there can be no perception and no being conscious, since there is nothing to perceive or be conscious of.—This last conclusion is for once a logical deduction, consistent with the ultimate unity in *brahman*, but is represented here as bewildering to Yājñavalkya's questioner (in this case his wife). The later Vedānta, however, maintains that *brahman* is conscious (*cit*—'thinking') and happy (allowing it to be conscious of itself).

We may note here very briefly a few other doctrines stated in the *Upaniṣads*. In the *Aitareya Upaniṣad* of the *Ṛgveda* there is a cosmogony beginning with the soul (*ātman*), rather than with *brahman*: the *ātman* first existed and nothing else whatsoever. The *Taittirīya Upaniṣad* (of the *Yajurveda* school of that name) is closer to the usual Vedānta ideas of later times, but whilst stating that *brahman* is all things it particularly stresses that *anna* ('food', cf. above, III and IV) is *brahman*; the idea probably is that the power of growth is *brahman*, and this may be a very ancient and primaeval conception of *brahman*. It is also stated that joy (*ānanda*) is *brahman*.

A strange doctrine is offered by Pratardana, a king (not a priest) of *Kāśi* (capital Vārāṇasī), in the *Kauṣītaki Upaniṣad* of the *Ṛgveda*. (Later Vedāntins have neglected this text: going beyond good and evil, with Yājñavalkya, was all very well, but this apparently goes too far.) It is supposed to have been revealed to him by Indra, the God of War and (later) King of the Gods, certainly among the most popular gods until the latter part of the Middle Ages. Indra points out (as indeed we can read for ourselves even today in the Vedic texts) that he has committed all sorts of sins, especially murder, and yet has come to no harm, not a hair of his head has suffered. 'Know me!'—He says, 'He who knows me comes to no harm whether by theft or murder or by any other sins!' He continues that he who meditates on him obtains long life in this world and eternal life in the next. Unexpectedly passing on to something more theoretical Indra propounds a theory of attention which is of interest as the prototype of several later theories in India: the mind must be 'present' for any perception to take place (later, the mind is sometimes conceived of as an atomic entity which moves among the organs of sense and may be absent from them all). Related to this is his idea that one cannot breathe and speak at the same time. 'Understanding' (*prajñā*) is the supreme power or faculty, controlling the other faculties and senses (speech, breath, sight, hands, mind, etc.). The enumerations given here bear a marked resemblance to those of the Sāṃkhya school which later continued the speculations of the *Upaniṣads.*

VI THE ŚRAMAṆAS

The development of philosophy outlined so far is known to us only from the texts preserved in the Brahmanical 'Canon' of the *Veda*. What has survived has survived because it found a place among these texts, was therefore presumably considered part of an orthodox tradition acceptable to the Brahmanical religion. It seems remarkable, indeed, that such a variety of views has been preserved, though later all are interpreted as aspects of a single view—or perhaps rather of two views, the ritualistic and the speculative (Mīmāṃsā and Vedānta), though these continued to be regarded as two aspects of a single world of truth. It seems a matter of chance that such thought as Uddālaka's should have found any place in a tradition which quite early became a system of dogma: a chance which perhaps depended on a fortunate circumstance that Uddālaka's 'being' could be assimilated to the *brahman*, also probably on his prestige, whatever its basis, which might have recommended the assimilation of his views to orthodoxy if it could be done. Whether there were other thinkers like him in their independence of tradition, but impossible to be assimilated to it later, we have no knowledge until we come to about the time of the Buddha (*c.* 500 B.C.). Philosophers, like other men, have to make a living, and perhaps it was in fact not possible for any to do so outside the tradition of the Vedic priests until social changes took place which deeply disturbed the Vedic or Brahmanical society (primarily that of the Paurava Empire in North India, from about the 13th century B.C. to the 8th century B.C.), shattered its unity and led new groups of rulers to an interest in new ways of looking at the world. Whatever the reasons, between the 8th and the 6th centuries B.C. the Paurava Empire, which formerly had claimed to unite Aryan-speaking India, broke up into a large number of independent states, states moreover which differed widely in their systems of government and in the degree of their adherence to the old traditions. A powerful factor by the 6th century, and perhaps the decisive one in the shattering of traditional values, was economic progress, especially the opening up of the Ganges Valley and the expansion of manufactures and trade, letting loose new forces in society through the circulation of new wealth, which generated a money economy. Tradition provided little or no guidance for governments struggling to control these forces, hence new concepts were in demand, moreover, the development of technology was certainly accompanied by a development of science and of theorising which would help to feed the speculations of philosophers, whilst providing new challenges to the critical analysis of phenomena.

By the 6th century B.C. we find in northern India alongside the hereditary priesthood of the brahmans another class of teachers and philosophers, who were not hereditary but recruited from all classes of society, who in fact repudiated the hereditary principle along with all the brahmans' pretensions to special traditions, special abilities and special privileges. They were known as the *śramaṇas* ('strivers', presumably after truth). Whatever their social origin, they abandoned their former life in society and became wanderers, making a livelihood by begging and teaching or by gathering food in the forests. They established organised schools and communities in due course and gradually found recognition in their function as philosophers and teachers from the society they had left. In general they claimed to teach men how to live, how to attain real happiness or how to attain some higher state of experience, either in this life or in some future life, considered as supremely blissful or peaceful or as perfect freedom. They rejected the Vedic tradition and the rituals of the brahmans (which they denounced as bogus and merely a means of swindling the public who had to pay fees for their performance) and offered other means than tradition of knowing the truths they claimed to teach. The means of knowing anything came to occupy an increasingly important place in all their investigations and discussions. In general they tended to be empiricists, appealing to experience as the source of knowledge, and to be in touch with science (particularly astronomy, mathematics and medicine, as well as physics). Their special views depended on their conceptions of the nature of the universe, which varied greatly. They agreed, however, in treating it as a natural phenomenon with ascertainable natural laws, not as the creation or plaything of gods or a God. It consisted of certain natural elements, whose properties governed its development. Various conceptions of causality entered into their accounts of the functioning of the universe and everything in it, and these might cover moral action by living beings as well as purely physical action. Man's destiny depended on himself, except for a determinist school which held that all men passed through an identical series of lives predetermined by 'Destiny' as a kind of supreme and unalterable law of the universe. The conception of man varied greatly: according to some he had an eternal soul, whilst others held that he had none, was simply a fleeting consciousness either bound by causal relations or completely free and spontaneous.

The origins of this *śramaṇa* movement are unknown. From the work of many individuals and groups of the 6th century B.C., at least five major schools grew up about B.C. 500 or a few years later, and came to dominate Indian philosophy for many centuries thereafter, setting the pace for the Brahmanical schools which tried to oppose them. Their ideas will be outlined in VII—IX below.

VII LOKĀYATA, ĀJĪVAKA AND AJÑĀNA PHILOSOPHY

Lokāyata. The name Lokāyata derives from *loka*, 'world', 'universe', implying a kind of natural philosophy (study of the nature of the universe). It might be translated 'naturalism'. There is also a traditional interpretation that the name means 'widespread in the world', i.e. a very popular philosophy or else the everyday 'philosophy' of ordinary people (not, therefore, a sophisticated philosophy, according to its critics). The debate among scholars about the name is not very important for us.

The early Buddhist texts (e.g. the *Dīgha Nikāya*, I p. 55) represent a *śramaṇa* named Ajita Keśakambalin as a famous contemporary of the Buddha, holding an objectionable doctrine which they call 'annihilationism' (*ucchedavāda*). The main points of his teaching are as follows. There are no such things as sacrifice (rituals) or (meritorious) giving, or results of good and bad actions. There is no distinction of this and another world (or simply, there is no 'other world', as heaven or a future life). There are no mother and father (probably meaning in any religious sense, or generally no special relationship and very likely referring to the *svabhāva* theory, everything has its 'own-being'). There is no transmigration of living beings. There are no priests (brahmans) or philosophers (*śramaṇas*) in the world who have gone into things rightly, practised rightly, and (so), having themselves known and observed this world and the other world, make them known. Man is compounded of the four elements. When he dies, the earth coalesces and amalgamates with the earth substance, the water with the water substance, the heat with the heat substance, the air with the air substance, the faculties pass into space . . . It is vain and false to speak of a future life: the fool and the wise man (alike) after the splitting up of the body are annihilated, perish utterly, are not after death.

(Such views were obviously objectionable to the brahmans; the Buddhists objected to the idea of complete annihilation, no continuity whatever between present and future allowing any basis for a doctrine of moral causality, results for the agent—in some sense—of good and bad actions.)

In modern terms this philosophy can be designated 'materialism'. Man (and everything) is a compound of the four material elements, his 'faculties' (conscious life) ultimately nothing, but presumably a property of the particular compound while it lasts. Those who claim to know something beyond this world (contrasting this with an other—to which men are supposed to go after death) speak falsely. Unfortunately none of the ancient texts of this school seem to have survived, except in quotations by their opponents, like this one, which naturally have to be treated with caution as likely to give a very imperfect and even inaccurate account. Other Buddhist texts (not this one) name the Lokāyata and connect it with 'natural history'. From numerous references we learn of the existence in ancient times of a *Lokāyata Sūtra*, usually ascribed to a certain Bṛhaspati, and of several commentaries on it. It existed in some form in the 2nd century B.C. (Patañjali, *Mahābhāṣya*, Vol. V, p. 210, Harayāṇā Sāhitya Saṃsthāna edition, on Pāṇini VII.3.45), when it already had at least one commentary, by Bhāguri. It is suggested that the Bṛhaspati saluted as a teacher in the *Arthaśāstra* (end of 4th century B.C.), which itself claims to follow the Lokāyata philosophy (as applied to political economy), was the author of the *Lokāyata Sūtra*. Though he is usually named in connection with it, at least one late text (*Tattvasaṃgraha* 1860-4 and its *Pañjikā*) names a Kambalāśvatara as its author. Perhaps this name is a form of Keśakambalin, and perhaps it is just another name for Bṛhaspati, but at present we do not know. With these reservations about the possible lack of authenticity of the fragments of the *Lokāyata Sūtra* available to us as quotations, we may now give the main ones.

According to the Buddhist philosopher Āryadeva (2nd century A.D., in his *Śataśāstra*, see p. 6 of Tucci's translation in his *Pre-Diṅnāga Buddhist Texts on Logic*), Bṛhaspati's book began by speaking of happiness and this subject underlay the whole work (presumably was its primary aim). His followers criticised the Buddhists for being concerned instead primarily with unhappiness. Āryadeva expounds the view further as follows (pp. 7f): happiness is happiness by its own-being (it is not produced out of anything else), just as salt is salt by its own-being; moreover (again like salt) happiness can impart happiness to other realities (is itself happiness and can make other realities have happiness, as salt can make other realities salt); a further parallel is a lamp, which illuminates itself and other realities (real objects).

'Own-being' (*svabhāva*) is a key concept of the school, which consequently is several times referred to as the Svabhāvavāda (see e.g. Aśvaghoṣa, *Buddhacarita* IX.58-62; *Śvetāśvatara Upaniṣad* I.2; *Mahābhārata* XII. 8035-55, 8529, etc.; *Śukra Nītisāra* IV.3.55—*sarvam svābhāvikam*; Candrakīrti, *Madhyamakāvatāra*, text preceding and following *Kārikā* 100—realities occur without 'causes', through their own-being, except that in some sense the four elements are the 'cause' of realities, since all realities are compounded of them; but there are no moral causes and effects, therefore enjoy yourself: what is past no longer exists and once your compounded body breaks up it will not come back again; *Tattvopaplavasiṃha* p. 88). Verses are quoted in the *Sarvadarśanasaṃgraha*, in Guṇaratna's *Vṛtti* on the *Ṣaḍdarśanasamuccaya* and elsewhere to the effect that it is own-being which makes fire hot, water cold, the wind refreshing, thorns sharp, animals and birds varied in character, cane sugar sweet and so on. The view apparently is that realities occur because it is their nature to do so, though they did not exist before (Āryadeva, p. 7), and the concept of causality is rejected (Candrakīrti loc. cit.; *Nyāya Sūtra* IV.1.22). (In the earliest Buddhist sources, such as the *Dīgha Nikāya*, the theory of realities originated without causes is generally known as *adhiccasamuppanna*, 'originated spontaneously', 'originated independently', and later this is explained as *yadicchā* (Sanskrit *yadṛcchā*), 'chance', 'spontaneity', 'at will'.) *Svabhāva* also = existent of itself.

Happiness (*sukha*), then, should be the only aim of men (*Sarvadarśanasaṃgraha* I). It arises when embracing a woman, etc. It should not be thought that it cannot be aimed at because it is mixed with unhappiness. For one should enjoy the happiness whilst avoiding the unhappiness, just as one avoids the bones when eating fish, removes the straw from grain, and so on. Thus one should not abandon happiness through fear of unhappiness. Men do not give up sowing rice because there are animals about (who may eat it), or abstain from cooking because there are beggars (who will ask for a share). Only fools will consider abandoning happiness because it is mingled with unhappiness: who would throw away rice because of the husks ?. . . A more succinct statement of this principle is found in a much more ancient source (*Nettippakaraṇa*, p. 110, date about 1st century A.D.): "Happiness is not attained easily (or 'by happiness', *sukhena*) but with difficulty (or 'through unhappiness')."

Next, probably, followed a section of text on the theory of the elements and the nature of consciousness. Here we reach common ground with the quotation from Ajita Keśakambalin given above. The realities (*tattvas*, really existing entities, also called 'elements', *bhūta* or *mahābhūta*) are earth, water, heat and air. In their union there is the body, the senses, the faculties and perception (*saṃjñā*). From these comes consciousness (*caitanya*, 'thinking'). Consciousness (*vijñāna*—a synonym) is like the intoxicating power which comes from the ferment, etc. (the ingredients used to make liquor). (Quoted e.g. by Guṇaratna, *Ṣaḍdarśanasamuccaya*, just before *Kārikā* 85, and by Bhāskara, *Brahmasūtra Bhāṣya*, III.3.53, the latter as '*Sūtras* of Bṛhaspati' and the former as 'Vācaspati', which may be taken as another form of the name; the former leaves out the last sentence, but it is well known from other sources.) After this probably followed the statement referred to as by Kambalāśvatara in the *Tattvasaṃgraha* (1864), mentioning the ancient conception (from the Vedic period) of five kinds of wind in the body (five kinds of internal movement, in fact, the first being breathing) and saying that consciousness (*caitanya*) arises from the body itself when moved by the five winds. A fuller quotation is found in Somadeva's *Yaśastilaka* (Vol. II, pp. 252-3, Kāvyamālā 1903 edition): consciousness arises through the own-being of the effects and qualities of that (body) itself, from the mingling of the five winds (the five are named here), from the mixing together of the maturing of the features of the body, and from the cooperation of the wind of the forest and the wind of the earth; like the intoxicating power from flour, water, molasses, the *dhātakī* plant, etc., and like redness from the betel leaf, lime and betel nut. And its course is begun as the embryo and ended at death: when it is past it will not grow again, like a leaf which has fallen from a tree. Since there is no other world and life has the own-being of a bubble on the water, the intoxicating power being adduced (to exemplify its nature), what is the purpose of this effort hostile to themselves which people make? (i.e. of religious exercises, asceticism, etc.) . . . One should be happy as long as one lives; no one is beyond the range of death, and of one extinguished in the ashes (of cremation) how can there be any coming back? Another simile for the perception of life (*jīva*) is the rainbow (*indradhanu,* Saṃghadāsa: *Vasudevahiṇḍi* p. 275).

Having argued that consciousness occurs only in the body, and lasts no longer than the particular body in which it is found, it seems that Bṛhaspati returned to the question of happiness and the aim of life, which depends on a proper understanding of the nature of consciousness (for the sequence of ideas see e.g. Haribhadra, *Ṣaḍdarśanasamuccaya, kārikā* 85 following the four element discussion and followed by discussions on happiness and pleasure). Since consciousness arises from the four elements and only in a body, it is the visible happiness experienced in this world which should be our aim, and to sacrifice this for an invisible, hypothetical happiness supposed to be experienced in another world (in the future, by this same consciousness after it is supposed to have left the body) is stupidity and ignorance. Those people deceive us who urge us to renounce the happiness which is in our grasp, in this world, in the hope of obtaining happiness in 'heaven' or 'liberation' (final beatitude) by means of asceticism, prayers, meditation, sacrifices, etc. In this connection there are a number of verses quoted in some of our sources, ridiculing the rituals of the brahmans and also suggesting they are simply a means of livelihood for the rascals who swindle the public with them. Some of these verses were perhaps in the original *Sūtra* (there are parallels for ancient prose texts on technical subjects, generally dry and terse in style, being occasionally relieved by verses in a lighter or more lively manner). It is the worldly way which is to be followed (quoted *Tattvopaplavasiṃha* p. 1). Since there are no subjects (souls) which go to another world (*paralokin*), no other world exists (quoted by Jayarāśi, *Tattvopaplavasiṃha* p. 45 in connection with the conception of a soul, *ātman,* supposed to go to another world: we have no knowledge of any possibility of a soul passing on without the body to some other or future life, therefore there is no such 'other world').

The *Kāmasūtra* (I.2.25-30) quotes as Lokāyata a series of succinct prose statements which may well have been from the original *Sūtra,* near the point we have now reached. 'Duties (*dharmas,* religious duties and rites) should not be observed, because their results are hypothetical and doubtful. Who but a fool would hand over what is now in his grasp for another (presumably for another world, for something in a future life)? A pigeon today is better than a peacock tomorrow. A certain (silver) *kārṣāpaṇa* is better than a doubtful (gold) *niṣka*.' In the *Ṣaḍdarśanasamuccaya* (*kārikā* 86 and *vṛtti*) we read that duty (*dharma*) is not superior to pleasure (*kāma*, explained as the happiness of enjoying the objects of the senses), or, alternatively, that pleasure itself is the highest 'duty'. The point of this is that the orthodox Brahmanical view from an early period laid down three ends of life, duty (or 'virtue', *dharma*), wealth (*artha*) and pleasure (*kāma*): all were to be pursued, but duty (as prescribed by the Vedic tradition) should take precedence over the others, which should give way to it in the event of any conflict of interests (pleasure should also be sacrificed to wealth). The Lokāyata thus opposes to this doctrine the view that 'duty' should not be pursued at all and that the only end of life should be pleasure. We may note in passing that there is evidence, as might be expected, of a special connection between the Lokāyata school and the 'science of pleasure' (*kāmaśāstra*), and also that Uddālaka's son (Śvetaketu) was one of the early pioneers of that science; though the *Kāmasūtra*, the earliest book on the subject known to be extant, is an orthodox version of the science as accepted by traditional brahmans, and before expounding it says that duty and wealth should be put first. According to Bṛhaspati (quoted by Sadānanda, *Advaitabrahmasiddhi*, and by Nīlakaṇṭha in his Commentary on the *Bhagavadgītā*, XVI.11), 'Pleasure alone is the single end of man'. With these sources we may compare two quotations (origin not stated) in the ancient *Nettippakaraṇa* (pp. 52 and 110): pleasures should be enjoyed . . . and multiplied, therefore abstention from pleasures . . . is immoral (*adharma*, contrary to 'duty'); he who indulges in pleasures enriches the world and he who enriches the world produces much 'merit'. The *Sarvadarśanasaṃgraha* account, besides mentioning 'happiness' as the aim or end of life, notes also 'wealth and pleasure' as the two ends. Perhaps this is from a different Lokāyata source, giving a slightly different view. Otherwise we must understand that wealth is necessary as a means to pleasure. The science of wealth (i.e. political economy), especially as represented by its most ancient available text, the *Arthaśāstra*, certainly draws inspiration from the Lokāyata philosophy. Pursuing the critique of religion, the *Sarvadarśanasaṃgraha* adds that the supreme 'lord' (*īśvara,* which means either 'God' or a rich man or earthly lord) is (only) a king successful in the world. 'Hell' is only unhappiness produced by thorns, etc. 'Liberation' (*mokṣa,* sometimes proposed as a fourth end of life, higher than duty or virtue) is (simply) the annihilation of the body. The *Veda* is only the incoherent talk of rascals.

The conclusion of this section of the *Sūtra* would appear to be that we are free to pursue pleasure or happiness and should spontaneously do so in accordance with our 'own-being'.

There is one other major point which is made in several of our sources, namely the nature of the Lokāyata theory of knowledge. It is doubtful whether any fully developed theory of knowledge had been elaborated as early as the time of the Buddha and Ajita Keśakambalin, since in the extant Indian philosophical literature we hardly find any such elaboration, though we do find some relevant preliminary discussions, before about the 2nd century B.C. However, the fully fledged Lokāyata theory is at least implicit in the earliest known Lokāyata doctrines, hence it should be mentioned here, although with the reservation that it may not have been clearly formulated in the terms standardised later. The Lokāyata theory, then, is that there is only one means of acquiring knowledge, namely sensation (*pratyakṣa* is the term used later). We should accept only what we actually sense directly and immediately through our senses. On the basis of this theory the Lokāyatikas were ready to refute all the doctrines of those schools of thought which maintained the existence of another world, not sensible through the senses but 'known' only in other ways, such as from revelation or through inference. The doctrines of moral causation, in fact of almost any kind of alleged causation, were rejected as going beyond the evidence of sensation. As opposed to such conceptions, the Lokāyatikas claimed that their doctrines were evident to all through immediate experience. Later on they developed interesting critiques of the theory of inference, on which so many of the doctrines of their opponents were based, and of the concept of causation, also important for most of their opponents, who argued back to 'first causes' and the like. We can leave these critiques until we come to the period when they were probably elaborated. The noteworthy point here is that we have a school of philosophy in India making a complete break with tradition and appealing simply to empirical evidence as the basis of its own view of the nature of the world and the aim of life.

Ājīvaka. The name Ājīvaka appears to be derived from the term *ājīva*, meaning 'way of life', in the sense of the special way of life of the *śramaṇas*, namely that of being a wanderer instead of remaining in the ordinary society. An organised school named the Ājīvakas was formed at the city of Śrāvastī, probably in B.C. 489, as the result of a meeting of a large group of *śramaṇas*, led by three of the most famous contemporaries of the Buddha. We may suppose that their idea was to unite all the wanderers (those of the *ājīva*) in a single organisation, having agreed on their doctrines and perhaps also having regulated their position in relation to the ordinary society and their rules of discipline. The three prominent leaders, each of whom contributed a characteristic doctrine, though one which harmonised with the others, were Gośāla, Pūraṇa and Kakuda. As in the case of the Lokāyata, the Ājīvaka school has not survived to modern times. All its texts appear to have been lost and we depend entirely on the versions of Ājīvaka doctrine given by its opponents. The main source is the same *Dīgha Nikāya* which gives us a version of Ajita Keśakambalin's teaching. Here we find (I pp. 52-4 and 56) versions of the doctrines of the three Ājīvaka leaders named above.

According to this Buddhist source Gośāla's doctrine, which it calls that of the 'purity of transmigration', is as follows. There is no cause or condition whereby beings are defiled: they are 'defiled' (i.e. undergo the experiences of transmigration, pleasant and unpleasant) through no cause or condition. In the same way they are 'purified' (eventually escape from transmigration) through no cause or condition. Men do not accomplish anything at all, either by themselves or through the efforts of others. There is no such thing as 'strength' or 'energy' (important factors in the 'striving' of the Buddhists), men have no vigour or courage. All beings, all life, all living beings, all souls, are powerless, without strength and without energy. They are changed in nature by the combinations of Destiny (*niyati*) and so experience happiness and unhappiness in six different classes of birth. Gośāla goes on to specify some of the countless forms of life which every soul has to experience in the course of its transmigration, powerless to influence its destiny in any way. In the end each soul comes to the end of its transmigration and so of its unhappiness, simply because it has run through the entire gamut of prescribed experiences, like a ball of string completely unravelled, and without having been able to alter the course of its experiences in any way through its (imagined) efforts and (supposed) actions. Apparently every soul runs through exactly the same course of experiences as every other and after an unthinkably long period reaches final peace at the end. This Buddhist source of Ājīvaka doctrine is confirmed by the evidence of Jaina texts, for example the *Uvāsaga Dasāo* (quoted by Basham in his *History and Doctrines of the Ājīvikas*, p. 218: his book is a convenient source of information on the Ājīvakas and their teaching, and contains almost all the relevant material known to be extant). The *Bhagavatī* (Basham p. 219) has a close parallel to the prescribed course of transmigration. It also agrees with the Buddhist source in stating that the total time a soul takes to complete its transmigration is 8,400,000 *mahākalpas*, but goes further in giving a calculation showing that this period of time is equivalent to nearly thirty million million million, multiplied by the number of grains of sand in the bed of the River Ganges, years. As to the sand in the Ganges, a Buddhist text (*Saṃyutta Nikāya* IV p. 376) says there is no mathematician able to calculate how many grains there are. Perhaps the Ājīvakas thought they knew better, and we are reminded that they had a tradition that the soul of Gośāla had inhabited the body of a mathematician, Arjuna, before becoming Gośāla: in other words the Ājīvakas were connected with contemporary science and their speculations on the scale of time were probably inspired by the development of mathematical calculations (for Arjuna see Basham p. 34). Since the entire period of transmigration is called a *mahāmānasa* (Basham p. 254), 'great heaven', it is possible there was also a connection with astronomy and the theory of the revolutions of the heavenly bodies (believed to repeat over a very long period of time). The main point of the Ājīvaka doctrine is evidently that everything is predetermined by Destiny and nothing men attempt to do can have the slightest influence on what happens, thus their imagined actions are entirely illusory if believed to be free: there is no independent action by living beings. Various stories have been handed down in connection with the Ājīvakas suggesting how a feeling that inevitable Destiny governed all things and rendered human effort futile impressed itself on them (Basham pp. 42ff., 38f.). The Jaina commentator Śīlāṅka (9th century A.D.) quotes a series of arguments designed to prove the fatalist thesis (Basham pp. 230ff.), which are probably taken from later Ājīvaka works though some of the arguments may be ancient in essence. Thus: we see people perform the same actions yet get completely different results, which must therefore come from some agency other than human effort; such conceptions as Time and God as agents cannot logically account for the variety and amorality (causing unhappiness) of the experiences we are subjected to; 'own-being' (*svabhāva*, the Lokāyata principle) no more explains man's ineffectiveness than just 'man' by himself, nor are his actions, conceived by some as moral causes, any better as an explanation than just that man is imagined to be an agent. Only he whose aim coincides with the power of Destiny will 'succeed', and only the conception of 'Destiny' can account for our arbitrary and unhappy experiences. In other words the Ājīvaka conception claims to be drawn from experience and to be an explanation of the nature of the universe and its motive power based on the experience of life. Destiny is the supreme, impersonal and inflexible, Law of nature, and it is absolutely regular in that all souls have exactly the same sequence of experiences, whilst the universe as a whole, at least according to later Ājīvaka conceptions (Basham pp. 236f.), is so absolutely regular as to be in a kind of 'steady state' (*avicalitanityatva*), since everything is already fixed and there is in effect no such thing as 'time', nothing new can ever happen.

It is noteworthy that the ancient Ājīvaka texts (described to some extent by the Jainas, Basham pp. 213ff.) included many books of portents and other ways of prognosticating the future. Since according to Ājīvaka ideas the entire future was already predetermined, it would seem to follow as a firm conclusion that through insight into various natural phenomena one ought to be able to read the future and make accurate predictions. As the object of the Ājīvaka philosophy was presumably to reconcile oneself to Destiny and accept everything with equanimity, it might perhaps help if one could be prepared for its blows and shocks in anticipation. There was also a practical application, however, for history records that Ājīvakas were sometimes employed by kings in ancient India to predict the future (e.g. by the Emperor Bindusāra, *Vaṃsatthappakāsinī* I p. 191).

The Jaina *Sūyagaḍa* seems to imply (is so interpreted by Śīlāṅka) that, after completing their transmigration and reaching a state of peace, the souls were destined eventually to repeat the whole process (Basham p. 259). Certainly some at least of the later Ājīvakas held this view (Basham pp. 260f.), thus the process of the universe was endless (cf. the 'steady state').

Consistent with the teaching of Gośāla is that of Pūraṇa, called by the Buddhists *akriyā*, 'inaction'. All the supposed actions of men, popularly regarded as good or bad, such as generosity on the one hand and violence on the other, are not really good or bad at all. This means that they produce no effects, are not moral causes, are not really actions at all (*Dīgha Nikāya* I 52f.).

Kakuda contributed a theory of elements or 'substances' (*kāyas*). There are seven of these: earth, water, heat, air, happiness, unhappiness and soul (*jīva*). They are uncreated, uncuttable, sterile, immovable and rigid. They do not change and do not affect one another in any way. Consequently such supposed actions as injuring or hearing or being conscious of anything, or causing other persons to do such actions, do not exist, since the supposed actions pass ineffectively between the uncuttable, unchangeable substances. This evidently is an atomic theory, of atoms of these ultimate substances to which nothing can happen and between which all 'actions' pass harmlessly. It is also a theory that the matter of the universe is eternal in its atoms, whilst their transient combinations are of no real significance (*Dīgha Nikāya* I 56). Probably later, the Ājīvakas worked out a more detailed theory of atoms and their combinations, in fact of the structure of matter in molecules: the atoms themselves were invisible, only their combinations visible; the different elementary substances had different properties and combined in fixed proportions to form particular types of molecule (Basham pp. 263ff.).

In the field of dialectics the Ājīvakas are known as having a system of argument peculiar to themselves but having much in common with that of the Jainas, which in fact appears to have been developed out of it. It is called the *trairāśika*, 'three-groups' or 'three-sets' (of possible statements). According to the Jaina sources (Basham pp. 175 and 274) they maintained that everything 'is', 'is not' and '(both) is and is not'. Thus everything is 'living', 'not living' and both 'living and not living'—evidently from different points of view. The presumable purpose of this method of argument is to be ready to refute opponents by adopting different points of view, from which their more categorical or dogmatic statements can be contested. A further method is that things can be considered according to three schemes *(nayas)*, as substance (*dravya*) or as modification (*paryāya*, or transformation) or as both (Basham p. 274). On the basis of this system the Ājīvakas were in the habit of taking up a non-committal and critical position in relation to any proposition put forward, and we are reminded of the famous remark *hupeyya* (=*syāt*, 'it may be!') of the Ājīvaka Upaka to the Buddha when the latter told him he had attained enlightenment (*Vinaya* I p. 8).

Ajñānavāda. The term Ajñānavāda, 'Agnosticism', is used by Śīlāṅka (Basham, *History and Doctrines of the Ājīvikas,* p. 174) for one of the ancient schools of Indian philosophy, and is so named in one of the earliest Jaina texts, the *Sūyagaḍa* (I.6.27, I.12, II.2.79). This ancient source (I.12) describes the school as one of the ignorant teaching the ignorant, of incoherence and confusion. The Jainas seem to have regarded these Agnostics as simple wandering ascetics who dismissed knowledge as useless.

The Buddhist *Dīgha Nikāya* (and parallel Buddhist sources) ascribes to a *śramaṇa* Sañjayin the following view, which it calls 'equivocation' (*vikṣepa*, also translatable 'confusion'). 'If you were to ask me', says Sañjayin, 'Is there another world?—Then if I thought there was another world I would explain it thus: There is another world. But I do not do so. I do not say it is true. I do not say it is otherwise. I do not say it is not so. I do not say it is not not so.' He goes on in exactly the same way to evade the questions whether there is not another world, whether there both is and is not another world, whether there neither is nor is not another world, whether there are beings who transmigrate, whether there is any result of good or bad actions (or is not, or both, or neither), whether the 'thus-gone' (*tathāgata*, in these contexts apparently any living being supposed to go beyond death) exists after death, does not exist or both or neither.

The same view, again called 'equivocation' but without mention of any teacher, is further elaborated elsewhere in the *Dīgha Nikāya* (I pp. 24-8) partly in the same words. Those who take up this position are called 'perpetual-equivocators', who, whatever question is asked them, resort to it in various ways. Some of them do not understand what is good and what is bad in their true nature. Consequently they think that to attempt to explain what is good or bad would arouse 'will' (strong feelings), passion, anger and aversion. These in turn would cause falsehood, that would cause remorse, and that would be an obstacle (to the best life). They vary in that some are deterred by fear of and disgust at falsehoods, some by fear of attachment and some by the fear of examination (of being argued with). All therefore resort to the same formula of equivocation 'I do not do so. I do not say it is true . . etc. . . not not so' as is given above. Other equivocators are said to be 'dull and extremely stupid', and one of them is quoted in exactly the same words as Sañjayin's given above. He apparently resorts to equivocation out of pure stupidity, whereas the others do so from fear of undesirable consequences.

From this scanty record we may perhaps conclude that the Agnostics held that no conclusions about any of the speculative questions raised by the philosophers were possible, that it is best to avoid discussing them, especially as argument tends to produce bad tempers and loss of peace of mind (which all were presumed to be seeking), and possibly that it is best to cultivate friendship. Their scepticism is shared to some degree by all the *śramaṇa* schools, and is an important element in the development of a critical philosophy, though of course they carried it to an extreme degree according to their opponents.

VIII THE BUDDHA

The Buddha was one of the *śramaṇa* philosophers. In the long run he was by far the most successful among them, in terms of the influence of his ideas, though in his own time the school he founded was probably very small in comparison with the widespread organisation of the Ājīvakas. This long term success has ensured the preservation of masses of texts purporting to contain his doctrine, and indeed much text-critical work is necessary to determine which parts of these texts are likely to be the most original, perhaps recording some of the actual words he spoke. Among the other *śramaṇa* schools only the Jainas have likewise endured until the present day and preserved a collection of ancient texts.

The term *buddha* is a title, meaning the 'enlightened', in the sense that the Buddha claimed to have discovered certain truths, on which he founded his teaching. Similar claims were made by several of the other *śramaṇa* teachers, though they used different titles. It appears that some of the Ājīvaka leaders claimed to have attained literal omniscience, including knowledge of all future events. The Buddha does not appear to have made any such sweeping claim, though eventually he came to be looked back upon by most 'Buddhists' as having attained a comprehensive intuition into all things, only a small part of which he passed on to his pupils.

The Buddha's doctrine may be regarded as a typical *śramaṇa* doctrine, with special features distinguishing it among the others. Thus the Buddha rejected all authority and appealed only to experience. He explained the universe as subject to natural laws only, by studying which one can hope to attain freedom and happiness (through recognising what freedom and happiness are in fact possible, in contrast to what is merely illusory or by nature impossible). The most important of these laws are causal laws, psychological and moral as well as physical. The aim is to attain true happiness or final peace (which is the same thing) or freedom (which is also the same thing), and a scheme of training and study leading to this attainment is offered. Like the Lokāyata, the Buddha rejected the concept of a 'soul', but unlike that school he argued in favour of a continuity through life and through successive lives, not through the persistence of any entity or substance but simply through the carrying on of effects from previous causes through the transient series of events popularly looked upon as a living being or person. This special theory of no soul and indeed of no 'substances' of any sort, in conjunction with a universal causality of events governing all experience, is characteristic of Buddhism and constitutes its most important contribution to philosophy.

The truths which the Buddha claimed to have discovered, and which formed the essential content of his 'enlightenment', are formulated as four in number: he understood in their true nature (1) unhappiness, (2) its origination, (3) its cessation and (4) the way leading to this cessation (*Majjhima Nikāya* I 17ff.). These truths are elucidated as follows (*Majjhima Nikāya* No. 141, in the Chinese version No. 31 of Taishō 26). (1) Unhappiness is all the pain and misery of life and eventual death, it is grief and depression and in general not getting what one wants; it is also 'birth', which is in fact 'rebirth' (not of a person but simply of the effects of past actions), leading to further unhappiness of the same kind; and generally the five 'groups' (*skandhas* of principles), which embrace all the events of the universe and provide the basis for 'attachment' (*upādāna*), in other words for any experience of living beings in the universe, constitute 'unhappiness' (this means that the Buddha did not believe it possible to find any true happiness among the changing principles of the universe). (2) The origination of unhappiness is that desire (*tṛṣṇā*) which leads to rebirth (not any desire, hence this English equivalent is not entirely satisfactory, but the thirst or drive for experience in the universe). This is a desire which is charged with pleasure and passion, pleased with whatever it encounters. (3) The cessation of unhappiness means the absolute cessation, through dispassion, abandoning, rejecting, getting free, not clinging, relative to that same desire. (4) The way to this cessation is a practical system having eight factors (the right theory, intention, speech, action, livelihood, exercise, self-possession and concentration).

The early Buddhist texts everywhere stress that the way to 'cessation' is a practical programme to be undertaken by each student, and that the truths are facts to be experienced and verified personally by them. There is no question of believing anything simply on authority, not even on the authority of the Buddha himself. In the texts he expressly disclaims any personal authority and directs his followers to realise the truth for themselves. The outlook is that of the making of a scientific discovery and announcing it to the world, whereupon others may investigate its truth for themselves. The critical attitude, the methods of science, an empiricist outlook, have here become firmly established in Indian philosophy. The point is emphasised in a text (*Aṅguttara Nikāya* I p. 189, also II 191, in Chinese cf. Taishō 26, No. 16) which lists arguments which are not reasons for coming to any conclusion on a doubtful or disputed matter. These non-reasons are tradition, a succession of teachers (handing something down on their authority), history, texts, reasons from logic (*tarka*), reasons from 'schemes' (*naya*, i.e. a predetermined or a priori system of ideas), reflection on features (as merely superficial aspects of things which do not show their real nature), approving through considering (mere) opinion, because (the person speaking) appears to be capable, and (finally) because our teacher is a philosopher (this last can also be understood as the Pali commentary takes it: because this philosopher is our teacher). Instead the Buddha urges his hearers to find principles out by themselves. A similar text (*Saṃyutta Nikāya* II 115ff., Chinese Taishō 99 section 14 No. 9) says that without confidence (*śraddhā*, trust or belief in what someone has said), without liking, without tradition, without reflection on features, without approving through considering (mere) opinion, one should find out, one should see, have personal knowledge of the conditions through which principles occur.

Shortly before his death (see the *Mahāparinirvāṇa Sūtra* in its various recensions, e.g. *Dīgha Nikāya* II 100, etc.), the Buddha, having rejected the idea that he has any jurisdiction over the community of his followers, and stated that it is open to anyone who thinks he has something to tell them to go ahead and 'promulgate' what he likes, says that his followers should live with themselves as islands or refuges, with no one else as a refuge, but also with the doctrine which the Buddha has taught as a refuge. As to this doctrine, it is described in a kind of formula which occurs several times in the texts as 'visible, timeless, verifiable (*aihipaśyika*, in Pali *ehipassika*), fruitful, to be experienced individually (personally) by discerning persons' (*Dīgha Nikāya* II 93 and at least thirty other places in the Pali Canon, *Mahāvastu* III 200, *Śikṣāsamuccaya* 323).

These references should be sufficient to establish the empiricist character of the Buddha's outlook and teaching, a character which pervades the early Buddhist texts. That there is unhappiness in life, and that it pervades life in such a way that happiness is not really to be found in anything connected with the world of transmigration and change, is supposed to be evident to everyone who cares to examine his own experience. If Buddhism spread and came to command a wide following, it was presumably because many people found themselves in agreement with the Buddha's findings. (Many who disagreed would of course follow the Lokāyata, which held that happiness was possible, on the whole, in this world.) What the Buddha found, in essence, was that the desire for any object of attachment in the world produced unhappiness in the form of that object. How? Because such objects, i.e. all the five 'groups' (matter, experience, perception, forces and consciousness) are 'not oneself' (not one's own, non-self or non-soul, *anātman*: this word for 'soul' being just a special sense of 'self'), since one cannot control any of them, saying 'Let it be thus . .' (*Vinaya* I 13ff., *Mahāvastu* III 335ff.). This non-soul doctrine leads into philosophical discussions which we will take up later: here the idea is simply the practical one that what one cannot control will give one dissatisfaction if one is attached to it, and none of the things of this world are under our control. Everything is impermanent, moreover, so that one cannot hold on to even what happiness there does appear to be in this life (again one cannot control it, there is this 'not one's own-ness'). Hence one should become indifferent to all the groups and seek dispassion, detachment. The fourth truth is the way to attain this detachment; the second truth is the study of the conditions producing experience in this world; the third truth is that the removal of the conditions will result in the cessation of the (undesirable) experiences they bring about. We may now take up the theory of conditions and causality propounded by the Buddha.

Many Buddhist texts deal with conditions and causes, and especially with what they call 'conditioned origination' (*pratītyasamutpāda*), the fact that principles originate through conditions (e.g. *Dīgha*

Nikāya No. 15/Taishō 1 No. 13/Taishō 14/Taishō 26 No. 97, *Saṃyutta Nikāya* II 22ff./ Taishō 99 sections 12, 14, 15/*Nidāna Saṃyukta* ed. Tripāṭhī, Berlin 1962). Ageing and dying, as typical of the unhappiness in life, have, as their condition, birth, which is understood to mean rebirth, and explained as birth as any kind of living being, anywhere. The condition for birth, in turn, is 'existence' (*bhava*), i.e. the existence of a sentient being, a living being, of some kind, in any of the possible forms of life. This is understood to mean the preceding existence, in effect a previous life, as a result of which rebirth and further future life is produced. One may ask how this is to be observed. The answer is that the Buddha, as part of his 'enlightenment', claimed to have recalled his own previous lives, and also to have 'understood' the transmigration of living beings according to their actions. It was in fact widely accepted in India that some people could remember their former lives, and that this memory could be improved by certain kinds of meditation or in other ways. The Buddha's enlightenment is described in the earliest texts as his acquisition of three 'knowledges' or 'sciences' (*vidyās*), namely (1) recollecting his former lives, (2) understanding the transmigration of beings according to their actions, bad conduct leading to misery and good conduct to a good (relatively happy) destiny, and (3) the four truths, including the possibility of ending transmigration (*Majjhima Nikāya* I 17ff./Taishō 125, k. 23, 665b-666 and Taishō 26, k. 25, 589c.).

For each condition the Buddha says that this is the 'cause' (*hetu*), the 'source' (*nidāna*), the 'origination' (*samudaya*) and the 'condition' (*pratyaya*) for the principle we are examining. If the condition did not occur, this principle would not happen. Continuing the investigation, we are given a series or sequence of conditions as follows, each item having as condition the one below it:

Ageing and dying
Birth
Existence (previous)
Attachment (*upādāna*, to pleasure, etc., also to belief that one has a soul)
Desire (*tṛṣṇā*, for sensual experience and for mental objects)
Experience (*vedanā*)
Contact (or stimulus, *sparśa*, of the sense organs with the mind)

A living body (*nāmarūpa*, the compound of matter and organisation)
Consciousness (*vijñāna*)
A living body (sic!—these last two are mutually dependent and neither can exist without the other)

The above seems to be the original form of the sequence of conditions (as in *Dīgha Nikāya* No. 15, agreeing with Taishō 14, the earliest Chinese version). In some texts up to three more items are added: the six senses (usual five plus the mind) between contact and the living body; the 'forces' (*saṃskāras*, physical and of speech and thought in a previous life) after consciousness as a further condition for that; finally 'ignorance' (*avidyā*, explained as wrong opinions, as not knowing the four truths) as the last condition, producing these forces (which will in turn create further consciousness in a suitable living body, and so on). These two final conditions in fact simply carry the pursuit of origins back into one further previous life: besides consciousness and a living body being mutually conditions for the experience of the life immediately under consideration, it is understood that these are the outcome of some former conscious experience, or more exactly of the actions then done, the forces generating more experience. The relationship of these forces to consciousness, spanning two lives, is in fact that of 'existence' to 'birth', also spanning two lives, given above, only it is looked at from a different aspect. There is no final, ultimate beginning, according to the Buddha; one can go on for ever tracing the cycle back from life to life, the same conditions will be found generating new life all the time: only knowledge of the four truths can lead to the ending of the process.

The texts note that there is no consciousness without a living body, and in fact consciousness is comprehended in consciousness of the six senses (the mind being the sixth, thus one can be conscious of the consciousness of the preceding moment in time), which exist only in living bodies. Presumably the Buddha held there was no experience of consciousness except in living bodies. As for the 'living body'; its 'matter' (*rūpa*) means the four elements earth, water, heat and air, together with the secondary matter which exists in dependence on these (the five physical senses and some other physical facts); its 'organisation' (*nāma*) is explained as experience, perception, volition (a 'force'), etc. A rather difficult passage adds that 'By whatever features (*ākāra*), characteristics (*liṅga*), signs (*nimitta*) or summarised descriptions (*uddeśa*) there is a concept (*prajñapti*) of the body of organisation, in the absence of these features, etc., there would be no contact (union) of the designation (*adhivacana*) with the body of matter. By whatever features, characteristics, signs and summarised descriptions there is a concept of the body of matter, in the absence of these there would be no contact of resistance (*pratigha*) with the body of organisation. In the absence of those features, etc., by which there is a concept of both the body of organisation and the body of matter there would be neither contact of the designation nor contact of resistance. In the absence of those features, etc., by which there is a concept of a living body there would, therefore, be no contact.' In other words, to explain the conditions for 'contact' there must be both matter and organisation, permitting both 'resistance' and 'designation'. Later on this text (*Dīgha* 15 and its parallels) concludes that to the extent that there is the living body with consciousness 'one may be born, grow old, die, pass away, be reborn, to this extent (also) there is a way for designation, a way for language, a way for concepts, scope for understanding,—to this extent the cycle (of the universe) revolves for the conceptualisation of this world.'

Such discussions lead naturally into the consideration of what it can mean to say that 'one may be born, be reborn' and the like: who is it that does these things, is it a 'soul' or what is it ? The Buddha was several times asked such questions (e.g. *Saṃyutta Nikāya* II 13/ Taishō 99 section 15 No. 10). Thus 'who' 'contacts' or 'desires' or 'is conscious' or 'dies' and so on? His reply is that the question is wrongly formulated, is 'not a sound question' (is 'loaded', we might say, tending to produce false answers). The proper form of the question is, he says, 'through what condition is there contact' or 'desire' or etc. In other words there is no person (soul, self, agent, etc., however described) 'who' does things, there is simply the process or event, and to state it accurately it must be put impersonally, otherwise there will be a bringing in of additional concepts (a 'person' or the like) unwarranted by experience and tending to be hypostatised as additional entities in the process. In the everyday language of ancient India, as everywhere, not only pronouns but also words such as 'a person' are used, and the Buddha himself often uses them in his discussions, especially when considering things from an ethical point of view and almost always when talking to ordinary people ('in the world') rather than to philosophers or to his followers. But the texts warn us that all such expressions are in effect to be treated as pronominal and as it were poetic (personification): exact statement requires their avoidance and in philosophical formulations the strict impersonal form must be used, so that non-existent entities are not accidentally brought in.

In another text (*Saṃyutta Nikāya* II 75f./Taishō 99 section 12 No. 18/Tripāṭhī 165-7) a brahman asks whether he who acts is the same as he who (subsequently) experiences (the result of the action, for 'himself', its moral result for him), or whether one (person) acts and another experiences (the result). The Buddha replies that these two conceptions represent two extremes which he avoids, giving an 'intermediate' explanation. The first alternative supposes an 'eternal' soul (or some such personal entity) which continues from event to event without change (since it always remains). The second imagines that there is a sort of soul, or person, 'who' acts, but that it is then 'annihilated' and some totally different person experiences the result. Instead of no change, there is no continuity at all. The Buddha by his 'intermediate' explanation means the sequence of conditioned origination. There is no soul or person, but there is causality or conditionality, whereby the preceding experiences (impersonal experiences, simple events, but living events) do condition those which follow. Nothing remains unchanged, yet the subsequent state of affairs is linked to, is the result of, the antecedent state, there is not a total separation, an 'annihilation' of what went before without any effect remaining. Similarly the Buddha's leading student of philosophy, Śāriputra, is asked by another of his followers (*Saṃyutta* II 112ff./ Taishō 99 section 12 No. 6/ Tripāṭhī 107ff.) whether each condition in the sequence is made by oneself, by another, by both oneself and another or without either (this fourfold formulation, a 'tetralemma', is interesting and was much used afterwards by the Buddhists, it may be compared with somewhat similar formulations by other schools, such as the Ājīvaka 'three-set' system). The answer is that none of the four alternatives is correct: the proper formulation is that each member of the sequence occurs through the condition of the next member. There are several other variants on this theme of the bogus 'oneself', 'yours', etc.

There are many other texts which take further the discussion about the theories of a 'soul' or the like put forward by some schools of thought. The usual term for a soul is *ātman* (in Pali *attan*). This is basically simply a reflexive pronoun meaning 'oneself', 'himself', 'herself', 'myself', 'yourself', etc., according to the context. In the genitive (possessive) case it may mean 'my own', 'your own' and so on. Brahmanical speculation in some of the *Upaniṣads* introduces the word in the sense of some kind of essential or innermost 'self', though in some contexts it refers to the body as 'oneself'. From this speculative use developed the concept of something other than the body, dwelling in the body, the subjective basis of experience which might be the real or essential self of a person, in other words a 'soul'. Brahmanical speculation further came to suppose that this soul was eternal, beyond the sphere of change and death to which the body was limited. In one of the texts we have used above (*Dīgha Nikāya* No. 15/ Taishō 14/Taishō 26 No. 97/Taishō 52) the Buddha reviews some of the theories of a soul which try to describe what it is. Thus it has been considered as either material or immaterial, as either finite or infinite, as transient (limited to the present life) of eternal, also as consisting of any or all of the 'groups' of principles known to us. For example some envisage the soul as experience. In this case, the Buddha argues, it may be happy, unhappy or neither, since an experience must be of one of these kinds. Moreover it can be only one of these three at a time. But all such experiences are impermanent, synthetic (*saṃskṛta*, produced by forces), originated through conditions, having the principle of becoming exhausted and ceasing. Hence one would have to say when experiencing such an experience 'This is my soul', but when the experience ceased one would have to say 'My soul has ceased to exist'. This conception thus leads to a 'soul' which is impermanent, a mixture of happiness and unhappiness (implying a compound, not an ultimate entity in itself) and which is produced and then ceases (through conditions). This contradicts the original theory (it may be noted that this critique bears on the Brahmanical and Vedāntic doctrine that the soul is pure joy or happiness). Then, the Buddha continues, let us suppose that the 'soul' is not experience, not any of our transient experiences. But in that case, if experience were completely non-existent (in the 'soul'), would there be the thought 'I am'? Surely not, so that the other alternative too is not satisfactory. If, finally, the attempt is made to describe the soul not as being experience but as having experiences, then if the experiences ceased would there be the thought 'I am this'? (In other words to envisage a 'soul' through any kind of experience does not give us anything beyond just that kind of experience, either we call experience the 'soul', which is not satisfactory, or we have nothing at all to describe as the 'soul'.)

Another text (*Saṃyutta Nikāya* III 46f./Taishō 99 section 2 No. 13=Vol. II p. 11b, 1ff.) rounds off this argument by declaring that all those who envisage a soul do so in terms of the five 'groups' or any one of them. They envisage matter, or experience, or perception, or the forces, or consciousness as a soul, or as being possessed by a soul, or in a soul, or having a soul in it. Clearly the argument given above in terms of experience applies mutatis mutandis to any of these theories. The whole argument reduces to a dilemma often stated in the Buddhist texts (e.g. in *Dīgha Nikāya* No. 9/ Taishō 1 No. 28), but generally using the term *jīva* (meaning the 'life' principle) instead of *ātman* for the soul, the two being synonymous, that (if one envisages a soul) either the soul must be the same as the body or it must be different from it. The 'body' here is equivalent to the 'groups' in the other discussions. Evidently to conceive a soul as the same as the body is futile, one would do better just to refer to the body. To conceive a soul as different from the body necessitates pointing out what that different thing is, apart from the body and any of its constituents (such as experience, perception, consciousness, all the 'groups' being included in the compound which is the body), and evidently no one could do this. As to the nature of 'consciousness', that is another question, discussed at length by the Buddha. Consciousness is changing continually and rapidly, it is even less stable than the body, therefore it is most unsatisfactory to imagine it is a soul (an essential self supposed to endure) (*Saṃyutta Nikāya* II 94f./ Taishō 99 section 12 No. 7/Tripāṭhī 115ff.).

It is insisted by the Buddha that consciousness cannot occur by itself, and we have already seen some statements to this effect. It is not like an independent 'soul'. The text we have basically followed above (*Dīgha* 15 and its parallels Taishō 14, etc.) has a section on the possible 'stations' of consciousness, which are simply the various kinds of living being with the scope of their possible experience.

Another text (*Saṃyutta Nikāya* II 65f./Taishō 99 section 14 No. 19) explains that 'That which one wills, determines, tends to do, is a support for a station of consciousness. When there is a support, there is a resting place of consciousness. When consciousness has rested there and grown, there is production of rebirth in future.' Thus though consciousness is transient it will continue to serve as a condition for more consciousness as long as the volition for such future experience occurs, or even just a 'tendency' (*anuśaya*) towards it. We should note, finally, that it is not consciousness which wills, etc., according to the Buddha, because according to his understanding of the situation 'volition' (*cetanā*) is a separate principle, one of the 'forces' group (along with contact or stimulus, reasoning, concentration, energy, understanding and many others, at least according to the classification of the schools of Buddhism which systematised the doctrine). There has to be a conjunction or compound of many conditions or principles, consciousness and volition among them, to make a mental event in the life of a living being possible. Consciousness is just one necessary ingredient in the event, which apparently serves to register and reflect the event forward, thus producing a further consciousness in the next moment which is aware of what has just happened. The schools of Buddhism later studied this question in detail, of the precise operation of the series of consciousness.

The schools of Buddhism, and other schools of Indian philosophy, were later much exercised over the problem of 'existence'. With their conception of everything as transient, continually changing, the Buddhists found it difficult to admit of anything that it really 'existed', this seeming to imply, as understood in India, an indefinite continuing something, an entity or as we might say a 'substance'. In Western terms, Buddhism was flatly against assuming any substance whatever, whether a soul or a material substratum, limiting its concepts in effect to the qualities which can actually be observed and seeing no need to posit any substance as a basis for such qualities. The Buddha already had something to say on the question of existence. 'The majority of people (*Saṃyutta Nikāya* II 17/Taishō 99 section 12 No. 19/Tripāṭhī 167ff.) have depended on the pair 'it-is-ness' (*astitā*, existence or existence-ism) and 'it-is-not-ness' (*nāstitā*, non-existence or non-existence-ism). One who sees the origination of the universe in its true nature (i.e. the occurrence of all principles through conditions), through right understanding, is not aware of non-existence with reference to the universe (may not be aware that the principles thus originated must cease, are transient). One who sees the cessation of the universe in its true nature, through right understanding, is not aware of existence (may think there is simple annihilation of everything, in effect nothingness, no continuity whatever) with reference to the universe . . . . "It exists" is one extreme. "It does not exist" is the second extreme. Not going to either of these extremes, the thus-gone (here this means one who has understood the truth, and the term is often used as a title of the Buddha) teaches an intermediate doctrine . . . (which is the sequence in conditioned origination).' The meaning of this text appears to be that there is nothing permanent or eternal in the universe, this conception being the 'It exists' extreme, the assertion of existence implying an absolute existence (cf. a 'substance'). On the other hand there is not an absolute destruction of all principles, such that one could say 'it does not exist', that there is in effect nothing, everything disappears without trace. This would be 'annihilationism', the other extreme. The real nature of the universe is understood to be that it consists of temporary principles, which 'cease', but not without serving as conditions for further temporary principles : there is a continuity though there is no continuous 'substance'.

Although he thus objects to the assertion of 'existence' in at least some sense apparently well established in his time, the Buddha nevertheless regarded the universe as some kind of objective reality. Each principle in the sequence of conditions is the condition for the next whether anyone discovers it or not at particular times in history (*Saṃyutta Nikāya* II 25ff./Taishō 99 section 12 No. 14/Tripāṭhī 148f.). When a particular 'base' (*dhātu*, explained by the Pali commentary as one of the conditions, with reference to the nature of that condition) is established, there is a station for (establishing of) principles (*dharmasthititā*), there is regularity of principles (*dharmaniyāmatā*), there is specific conditionality (*idaṃpratyayatā*). Śāriputra is praised (*Saṃyutta* II 56/ Taishō 99 section 14 No. 3) for having well penetrated the 'base of principles' (*dharmadhātu*). The Pali commentary explains this as the conditioned nature of principles, the 'base' then being their ultimate basis or source (*dhātu* was used in chemistry for the ores from which metals, etc., were produced, in linguistics for the 'roots' which were the irreducible meaningful elements in words). There is a further text in the Pali version (*Saṃyutta* II 56ff.) which says that any *śramaṇas* or brahmans who discover principles and their origination, whether in the past or in the future, must discover them to be the same as the Buddha has discovered them now, or as his pupils ascertain them to be: they are found to be true regardless of time. —This implies an objective reality, of the conditionality of principles and their regular origination according to it, according to certain fixed natural laws, regardless of our subjective experience. It is in the light of this that we must understand the controversy about 'existence' and 'non-existence' and the position the Buddha took in it. No thing (entity) exists permanently, but there is a regular and continuing origination of principles.

Some people asked the Buddha whether the 'universe' (*loka*) was eternal or not, or finite or infinite. The texts tend to bracket this controversy with that about the 'soul', to which the same predicates were variously applied (*Dīgha* No. 9/Taishō 1 No. 28; *Dīgha* No. 1/ Taishō 1 No. 21). The Buddha rejects such questions: apparently he regarded the 'universe' as no more an entity, which could continue for ever or be annihilated, a universal 'substance', than the 'soul'. Such questions, we might conclude, involve a hypostatisation of a word, giving rise to a concept of an entity (which seemingly must be either eternal or not eternal, infinite or finite), although the word referred only to a collection of principles. The Buddha held on the other hand that transmigration (*saṃsāra*), i.e. the process, was beginningless (*Saṃyutta* II 178ff./Taishō 99 section 34 and the end of section 33). No ultimate point of origin could be discerned.

It may be useful to add a note on the atheism of the Buddha. It should be clear from his conception of conditionality and natural laws that there is no place for a supreme supernatural being guiding (or creating) the universe. Some of the texts, however, take up the concept of 'God' (Brahmā) as creator, ordainer, father, supremely powerful, seeing everything, etc., and criticise it, in fact satirise it. It resulted from a misconception on the part of some brahmans who remembered a distant past, at the beginning of the present cycle of evolution. The living being who was then reborn first was lonely and wished for company. In due course others were reborn and he thought this was the result of his wishing, concluding he was God. They on their part, seeing him in existence first, equally accepted the error. Some brahmans remembering this situation in their past have circulated the error among men (*Dīgha* No. 1/Taishō 1 No. 21). The Buddha did not deny that there were 'gods', in the sense of living beings, with material bodies (however refined in nature), who might live in less unhappy conditions than men and in worlds other than ours, or in the heavens (sky) among the stars, etc. What he contended was that they were all subject to the universal laws of conditionality, just like men and animals, and that they had no power to interfere with natural laws: in other words they were not 'gods' in our (supernatural) sense but just living beings. As to Brahmā, there is a story (perhaps just a story and not meant to be taken as fact) that this first of living beings in our cycle is still alive in his highest heaven, with his devoted retinue of followers having very refined bodies like his own, but he has become painfully aware that his pretensions are empty, that he has no special power or knowledge. He carries on before his admirers as a mere fraud, afraid of being exposed (*Dīgha* No. 11/Taishō 1 No. 24).

The Buddha's conception of the universe is thus of natural and impersonal forces and processes, of conditions and principles, transient, with no enduring substances. It is not correct to speak of persons 'who' do things, but only of events which occur. It is enough to describe the 'qualities' (a possible translation of *dharma,* which we have otherwise translated 'principles') and the conditions under which they appear. There is no justification for assuming any substance, not definable apart from these qualities, in addition to the qualities we observe. This is a conception of the universe which is de-personified, de-anthropomorphised (but man himself is de-personified in any case), a collection of natural forces and principles to be described without postulating any unnecessary entities, or in fact any entities at all, only the minimum of observable qualities. It is a thoroughly empiricist conception. It implies a whole critique, an analysis of metaphysical concepts (such as 'soul'), worked out in detail by later Buddhist philosophers, and of metaphysical statements (such as 'the universe is eternal'). No doubt in many of the texts the language of the ordinary people of India is used, with its 'persons' and its popular conceptions of all kinds. But this is popular preaching for the sake of teaching moral precepts to ordinary people, in language they can understand; we are expressly told in the properly philosophical, or we might say scientific, texts, that to be accurate we must drop the personifications of everyday language: if taken literally, such personifications will lead to untenable metaphysical extremes such as an eternal, and therefore unchanging, soul, or the annihilation of a soul which persisted for a lifetime only. Nirvāṇa, finally, is not the annihilation of a soul, or the release of a soul, it is simply the cessation of a process, of a sequence of events.

The regularity of the conditions led to the hypothesis that there were principles which were real (*bhūta*) because they produced effects (other principles) in a regular manner. These principles were included in the five groups and were also without 'soul'. The same principles might happen as causes or effects of each other and as causes they are sometimes referred to as 'bases' (*dhātus*). They are all impermanent, but real for precisely that reason: they can participate in the causal process. Their regularity means that the same cause always produces the same effect: each principle has its own characteristics. The term 'principle' (*dharma*) is said to mean that it enters into causal relations (*Aṅguttara Nikāya* V 2ff./Taishō 26 [*Madhyama Āgama*] No. 43). A real (effective) practice is one 'stationed among the principles' (*Dīgha* No. 9, D I p. 190/Taishō 1 No. 28): the Buddha's way (to Nirvāṇa) is based on realities and therefore effective. Often principles are classed as good or bad from this practical point of view: ' . . . when you yourselves know these principles are bad . . . you should abandon them . . . or if they are good . . . you may adopt them' (continuation of *Aṅguttara* I 189ff., etc., referred to above). Thus the factors of enlightenment (self-possession, concentration, etc.) are good and the 'obstacles' to it (the will to pleasure, malevolence, etc.) are bad.

'Non-soul' is the Buddha's original critique of all philosophy, of all concepts of supposed entities which in fact are not entities, of all propositions about such entities. This leaves the impermanent and 'empty' principles as the only reality to be investigated.

IX JAINISM

The Jaina school appears to have originated through Mahāvīra, or the 'Jina' ('Conqueror', of the passions), seceding from the Ājīvakas (Basham's book on the Ājīvakas deals at length with the association of Mahāvīra with Gośāla and their eventual break) and founding a separate school. The disagreement was over the Ājīvaka doctrine of fatalism and the ineffectiveness of human action. Mahāvīra rejected this fundamental doctrine whilst apparently retaining most of the other Ājīvaka conceptions (an eternal soul in transmigration passing through a vast number of incarnations and eventually attaining release or final peace, a theory of elements and atoms, the dialectic of different schemes, etc., though our lack of information about the Ājīvakas restricts the possibility of comparison; much of the terminology of the two schools appears to be the same). Although Mahāvīra was a contemporary of the Buddha, the earliest Jaina texts now available appear to be substantially later than the early Buddhist texts. The Jainas themselves have traditions that their original texts (the *Pūrvas*) were lost (it is possible, however, that the *Pūrvas* were really Ājīvaka texts, out of which the Jainas gradually compiled their own selected and revised versions). However, some secondary texts (the *Aṅgas*) extracted from the original ones are supposed to have been codified towards the end of the 4th century B.C. Of the two later schools of Jainas, the Śvetāmbaras claim to be in possession of these *Aṅgas* whilst the Digambaras declare that the authentic old texts have been totally lost and rely instead on the traditions handed down by the teachers of their school and later codified in textbooks written by some of them. In fact the extant *Aṅgas* seem to cover many centuries of development: though the names were retained some of them were heavily revised to incorporate what were presumably new ideas. On grounds of language and metre, the *Ācārāṅga* and *Sūtrakṛtāṅga* appear to be the oldest texts and may be reasonably authentic copies of two of the *Aṅgas* codified at the end of the 4th century B.C. The former is a book of discipline for Jaina ascetics, the latter, though also largely devoted to the practical life of ascetics, deals to some extent with doctrinal matters. All the other *Aṅgas* as now available appear to be substantially later and to constitute very indirect evidence for any original Jaina doctrine (the next in date would be the *Sthānāṅga*, of perhaps the 1st century B.C.).

The *Sūtrakṛtāṅga* states its theme as the soul and its release. This is a doctrine of possible action (*kriyā*) (I.12.21) by which one can release one's soul at any time (not waiting to run a predestined course as the Ājīvakas maintained). This 'action', however, is more a matter of restraint, from the ordinary worldly actions tending to continue transmigration, than of positive action. The Jaina way to release consists of very severe asceticism, having no possessions, exercising complete self-control and avoiding (ordinary) actions (I.8, II.4). The most important point made in connection with avoiding actions is the insistence on non-violence (*ahiṃsā*) (I.1.4.10, I.11). The mechanism of release is to get rid of the 'influences' (*āsravas*), conceived as physical fluids which adhere to the soul and cause it to stick in transmigration. They are the result of former bad actions, which have to be counterbalanced by actions of the opposite kind, i.e. restraint and especially physical suffering, which seems to be regarded as somehow purging out the bad adhering to one's soul and purifying it. Energy (*vīrya*) has to be exercised to purge the soul of the influences which bind it (I.12.21). This physical mechanism of purification contrasts with the Buddhist practice which is essentially mental, understanding and meditation being the way to peace. The *Sūtrakṛtāṅga* criticizes various other schools, including the Ājīvakas, Buddhists, Lokāyata, Ajñānavāda and Brahmanism. Ritual is useless (I.7). There is no God (I.1.3.5ff.). Certain extreme views, such as that the universe is eternal or non-eternal, are to be avoided (II.5.2).

This does not give us much philosophy, for which we have to go to the later texts, which belong later in this survey. There is some probability, however, that the Jainas took up the following positions from practically the beginning of their school. One should avoid extreme views and bear in mind that most propositions can be both asserted and denied, depending on the point of view adopted (this is later the most characteristic Jaina doctrine; it is a modified scepticism to be compared with the extreme scepticism of the Ajñānavāda and the 'three-set' dialectic of the Ājīvakas, also with the Buddhist critique of metaphysical propositions). Linked to it is the conception of schemes (*nayas*), originally two in number, that everything can be considered as either substance (*dravya*) or modification (*paryāya*). There are five 'substances which exist' (*astikāyas*): 'matter' (under the unusual name *pudgala*), soul (*jīva*), space (*ākāśa*), activity (*dharma*, this seems to be a special Jaina use of *dharma*) and inactivity (*adharma*). Matter is (in the later Jaina texts) composed of atoms, indivisible and too small to be sensed, also eternal (whereas all their combinations as the matter we sense are non-eternal)—a doctrine apparently derived from the Ājīvakas, but modified to make compound matter real, though transient, permitting effective action. Activity and inactivity, or motion and rest, perhaps included, as originally conceived, merit and demerit in relation to the soul. On the other hand the conception of *dharma* as a natural activity (not some static quality or principle) may be ancient and may be used to illuminate the Buddhist concept of a *dharma*, suggesting that this meant an event rather than a quality.

X SĀṂKHYA AND MĪMĀṂSĀ

In Brahmanical philosophy two main traditions appear to have been established by the time of the flourishing of the Śramaṇa schools *c.* 500 B.C., the Sāṃkhya and the Mīmāṃsā. When these names became current is not known—perhaps only somewhat later. The Sāṃkhya represents a relatively free development of speculation among the brahmans, independent of the Vedic revelation and in some respects not unlike the thought of Uddālaka (but as we know it much more speculative and metaphysical, going far beyond the scope of observation and any kind of verification, on the basis of intuition and some reasoning). It has indeed been suggested that it was non-Brahmanical and even anti-Vedic in origin, but there is no tangible evidence for that except that it is very different from most Vedic speculation—but that is quite inconclusive; in the course of time it was found quite possible, perhaps with a little looseness of thought, to combine Sāṃkhya and Vedic traditional material into a hybrid philosophy of religion which proved very popular in Medieval India. The Mīmāṃsā on the other hand is strictly Vedic (is sometimes called simply Vaidika) and admits no other authority than the Vedic texts, eliminating even speculation, contrary to the spirit of the Vedic texts themselves; from the chaos of the tradition it seeks to produce order and absolute precision, final truth. Our sources for both schools in this period are unsatisfactory because after many further centuries of development they eventually became standardised in later forms and little but indirect evidence remains for their early forms. (For the Sāṃkhya we have E.H. Johnston's book *Early Sāṁkhya*, for the Mīmāṃsā there seems to be nothing comparable to outline the early sources for us.)

Speculations in the direction of the Sāṃkhya can be found in the early *Upaniṣads* used by us above. Apart from Uddālaka's theory of an original 'being' and of various elements evolving out of it, which may be regarded as the central idea of the Sāṃkhya (though its terms and its sequence of evolution are quite different), we find in other *Upaniṣads*, particularly the *Bṛhadāraṇyaka* (see Johnston pp. 19f.), various collections of the elements constituting human beings, their senses and faculties, consciousness (or intelligence, *vijñāna* or *buddhi*), the mind, etc., and as related to them the five types of sense object (the 'external' world as related to the 'internal'); the four physical elements (cf. Lokāyata, etc.) and space as a group are found in the *Aitareya* and *Taittirīya Upaniṣads*. This gives us most of the elements which were standardised in the Sāṃkhya as a set of twenty-four 'realities' (*tattvas*) evolved out of each other (there were however at least two different versions of the set). It is a much later *Upaniṣad*, the *Kaṭha* (probably *c.* 300 B.C.), which is the first known text to give us a version of the full Sāṃkhya scheme, with as first 'reality' the 'unmanifest' (*avyakta*) out of which all the other 23 are supposed to have evolved. Legend ascribes the foundation of the Sāṃkhya to a mythical sage, Kapila, whilst tangible evidence indicates an old Sāṃkhya system propounded by one supposed to have been a pupil of his, Pañcaśikha alias (Vṛddha) Parāśara (see *Majjhima Nikāya* III 298, *Mahābhārata* XII.308.24, Johnston p. 9). The *Majjhima* reference would seem to confirm a date in about the 5th century B.C. for Pañcaśikha. Other old Sāṃkhya teachers are named in various sources, and we find that there were many schools among them later, but Pañcaśikha's teaching may have dominated the tradition at first and is perhaps most likely to be that followed by the *Kaṭha* (not necessarily without modifications). Later he was followed by Patañjali in the extant *Yoga Sūtra* (probably 4th century A.D.), according to Vyāsa's commentary (Yoga is simply a school of Sāṃkhya) which often quotes him.

On the above assumptions the Sāṃkhya of Pañcaśikha, and in any case the earliest form of Sāṃkhya now accessible to us, proposes a scheme of evolution, or perhaps as yet simply a hierarchy of realities (but an evolutionary sequence seems probable), from the 'unmanifest' as follows. From the unmanifest arises consciousness, from that the 'great self' (*mahant ātman*; some sources suggest the soul or life principle, *jīva*, as a synonymous term in this place, whilst the 'self', *ātman*, may in the Vedic, including the Upaniṣadic, tradition imply the physical self as much as, or instead of, a spiritual self), from that mind (*manas*). Apparently also arising from the great self are the four elements and space, together with the objects of the five senses, on the one hand, and the five senses and five faculties (conceived as active, the senses probably being considered passive, these faculties are: grasping, walking or moving, speech, reproduction and elimination, the first two relating respectively to the hands and feet; this curious group is inherited from the *Bṛhadāraṇyaka Upaniṣad*) on the other. The exact original relations between all these items are not clear and the schools later revised them in various ways. The underlying idea is, as in Uddālaka, of successively coarser matter evolving out of the original subtle principle which is the basis of all.

At this point we come upon one further fundamental element in the system, sometimes said to be higher than any of the others (*Kaṭha*), otherwise simply something completely different in nature, namely 'man' (*puruṣa*), a term generally understood as and translated by 'soul'. As presented by the *Kaṭha Upaniṣad* the whole system looks more like a variant on the speculation of Śāṇḍilya or Yājñavalkya than the independent Sāṃkhya, and of course it is assimilated to the doctrine of *brahman* as ultimate reality. We are left wondering whether the Sāṃkhya proper, in its earliest period, maintained any 'realities' beyond the 24 physical ones based on the unmanifest, since these include a sufficiency of mental elements, consciousness, mind and even a kind of soul (the great self or life principle). The later system, however, developed the idea of the *puruṣa* as soul and made it a completely independent spiritual principle standing in opposition to the unmanifest, both being ultimates and neither evolved from the other. The conception then was that the souls (*puruṣas*, of which there were an infinite number) were in the habit of becoming entangled in the material world of the unmanifest, which meant unhappiness for them, and that the object of this system of philosophy was that they should free themselves from it, through understanding the truth. Possibly this 'dualistic' universe of spirit and matter was the original Sāṃkhya conception. We need not concern ourselves here with the obscure details of the mechanism of the souls' attachment to the material world and of their transmigration and experiences in it according to the proportions of 'goodness', 'passion' and 'darkness' (delusion) they assimilate from the unmanifest (whose nature has these three aspects). One final point on early Sāṃkhya: the name of the school means 'enumeration'—presumably, of the elements or realities set out in its doctrine.

Mīmāṃsā means 'investigation', and in the case of the school the investigation of the proper interpretation of the Vedic texts. The Vedic texts appear to have become pretty well fixed, as a 'Canon' of scriptures, by about the 7th century B.C., including the five most ancient *Upaniṣads* (apocryphal *Upaniṣads* such as the *Kaṭha* were added later but kept as distinct texts). It must be noted, however, that there were several schools of oral tradition among the Vedic priesthood, each with its own recensions of the texts it remembered, though the details of these traditions and texts hardly concern us here. Between about the 7th and the 3rd centuries B.C. the priests produced many systematic works ancillary to this *Veda*, namely lexicons, grammars, geometries, astronomies, law books, etc., and works on the ritual (*kalpasūtras*): these are called *Vedāṅgas*. Interpretative works on the ritual, etc., had probably during most of this period been confined to the particular schools, with their own recensions of Vedic texts, in different parts of India. From about the end of the period (though the exact date is quite uncertain: one might think of the 2nd century B.C. as a time of Brahmanical reaction against the ascendancy of the Śramaṇa schools, competing also with the universalistic outlook of these rivals by producing a universally valid Brahmanism) these local and variant traditions began to be replaced by, or at least subordinated to, a universal Mīmāṃsā code of interpretation claiming acceptance by all. A *Mīmāṃsā Sūtra* was accordingly elaborated (probably over a very long period), which eventually superseded almost completely the older *kalpasūtras* of the local schools. It was claimed to be based directly on the statements of the Vedic texts themselves, whose correct interpretation it laid down, whilst whatever was found in the *kalpasūtras* was at best an accurate reproduction of Vedic injunctions but at worst a corruption or contradiction of them. Local traditions and customs were to be rejected, according to the later Mīmāṃsā school: if there is such a thing as an injunction as to what we have to do, it is a universal one and should be followed everywhere. The *Mīmāṃsā Sūtra* in its final form belongs to the 1st century B.C. or later (and will therefore be considered below: XV), but it was ascribed to an ancient sage, Jaimini, who, if historical at all, would have lived in about the 9th century B.C. It seems at first to have included sections on the doctrine of the *brahman* (from the *Upaniṣads*), which were afterwards detached and elaborated as the now independent *Brahman Sūtra* (datable *c.* 200 A.D.) of the separated Vedānta school and ascribed to Bādarāyaṇa (an equally ancient and legendary sage).

The main topics of discussion among the Mīmāṃsakas as they developed into a philosophical school appear to have been the following. First the enquiry into *dharma* as laid down by the *Veda*, the supreme authority. The idea underlying *dharma* here seems to be that of one's 'duty' enjoined by the *Veda* (perhaps including 'law', as religious or sacred law derived from the revelation) or of the 'virtue' attainable by doing it. It came to mean whatever 'good' is attainable by carrying out the Vedic injunctions (especially performing the rituals) and to be carefully distinguished from any 'goods' knowable by means other than Vedic revelation (such as experience; these other goods would be worldly and inferior to the transcendent goods). The Mīmāṃsā doctrine in fact developed into an interesting and completely consistent system of metaphysics, by definition untestable by any experience possible in the world: if a thing could be known by worldly means it could not belong to Vedic revelation, which in principle revealed only what was not knowable by any means other than the *Veda* itself. These discussions naturally were related to those on the nature of the *Veda*, and on why it must be accepted as authoritative, which led to the conclusion that the truth of the *Veda* has to be taken as self-evident, because no empirical evidence can conceivably bear on it: but for the Vedic revelation we would be completely ignorant of the important matters made known by it. The very words of the *Veda* came to be regarded as eternal and uncreated (which led later to a variety of speculations).

The problems of interpretation of the Vedic texts, which were found in part to be exceedingly obscure, led to much study of philosophical interest, and the Mīmāṃsā became a kind of discipline, intermediate between linguistics and logic. The different types of text were classified (in such a way as to make them all relevant and necessary within the limitations of the emerging systematic metaphysics), the most important being the injunctions. Apparent inconsistencies in them had to be resolved, by formulating rules of interpretation which would eliminate them. Where the direct statements of the *Veda* seemed not to cover necessary points, rules had to be formulated for extending them by implication, consideration of context, etc., and about the relative weight of such devices in order to decide conflicts between them. A definition of the 'sentence' had to be established, in order to determine a method of dividing the texts into sentences, since in part this might be done in different ways with different results for the injunctions derived from them. The Mīmāṃsā study thus overlapped both linguistics and logic, especially the former.

XI DHARMA AND ARTHA

The word *dharma* has an exceptionally wide range of meanings. The (relatively) most original and basic meaning in the time of the earliest of our texts seems to have been something like 'way', as the way things are, or perhaps maintain themselves, or possibly are maintained, or should be maintained, by whatever or whoever is responsible for maintaining the order of the universe. The word is very rare, and therefore very obscure, in the earliest texts, where we find instead another term, *ṛta* (see III above), covering some somewhat similar meanings. In both words there seems to be a certain ambiguity hesitating between a conception of the way things are, as the course or nature of things, and one of the way things ought to be. We should probably conclude from this, and from a study of the Vedic religion, that the universe was conceived not as something completely objective and impersonal in the sense that conscious beings were powerless to influence it and had no responsibility for the course of events, but that on the contrary the natural order depended on men (and gods) working to maintain it. Any natural force or movement was probably felt to require some kind of conscious effort, as in living beings, otherwise it would cease: movement seemed to imply life. Further, life would seem to imply a degree of freedom and choice: the effort to maintain the universal order might be relaxed, or a wrong, abnormal direction might be given to things; a standard or proper way of doing things and having things seems to be envisaged, based on past experience, and men ought to work to maintain it.

As we have seen (in X), the Vedic and Mīmāṃsā tradition crystallised as a revelation and study of *dharma* in the religious and ethical sense of men's duties, including a system of law or jurisprudence, the latter also called *dharma* and eventually codified in 'institutes' called *dharmaśāstras*. In this *Course* we shall not pursue the ethical discussions which developed in connection with the theories of duties and law.

Buddhist texts also sometimes use *dharma* in the sense of virtue or justice, though they read into it their own conceptions and ideals in the field of ethical and social thought. On the other hand, in accordance with their conception of the universe governed by regular natural laws, by objective conditions which may be discovered or not discovered by living beings but cannot be altered by them (they can only work within them, if they understand them, in so far as they have the power and the will to perform or not to perform certain actions), the Buddhists in their philosophy developed a meaning of *dharma* in the sense of something which regularly does happen, under given conditions. A *dharma*, in this sense, came to mean a 'regularity', a 'natural principle', as any of a number (a finite number in most schools of Buddhism) of elements of which the universe, or of which all experience, consists. Since the Buddhist conception precludes any enduring 'substances' in the universe, we may try to conceive these principles as qualities simply (and 'quality' is a common meaning of *dharma* later on in the history of Indian philosophy, in the Brahmanical as well as Buddhist schools), or perhaps as events (kinds of event which occur in the evolution of the universe). The Buddhist lists of *dharmas* include mental as well as physical principles. The early texts (used in VIII above) do not attempt to enumerate them, but the schools later worked out their total number as one hundred or less (it varied with the school, see XIII-XIV below), of which all nature consisted.

Another prominent meaning of *dharma* in Buddhist texts is the Buddhist 'doctrine' itself, apparently in the sense of the 'principles', or 'natural science' or study of the nature of the universe. In this sense the word is used also for the doctrines of other schools and probably it was current among the *śramaṇas* in this meaning before the time of the Buddha.

The Jainas have a special use for *dharma* as meaning 'activity' (with its opposite, *adharma,* meaning 'inactivity'), regarded as a kind of substance (see IX above).

In the orthodox Brahmanical tradition *artha,* 'wealth', came to be accepted as a second end of life alongside, but inferior to, *dharma* (here meaning virtue and duty). There seems to have been a good deal of controversy among the brahmans as to the proper relationship between these two ends, and some seem to have put wealth first: the view generally regarded as orthodox perhaps came to predominate during the 2nd or 1st century B.C. Two or three centuries later the orthodox accepted 'pleasure', *kāma*, as a third legitimate end, on condition that it was subordinated to the first two and should give way in case of conflict, just as wealth should give way to virtue. These are the well known three ends of life in India, to which 'liberation', *mokṣa*, was sometimes and later added as a fourth 'end' distinct from virtue, involving renouncing the 'world' altogether.

The science of *artha* includes everything connected with the acquisition of wealth, therefore political economy but also the strategy and tactics of political power: the object of government is to increase the wealth of the country, especially of the treasury (through revenue), but also to strengthen its political and military position. The earliest extant treatise on *artha*, the *Arthaśāstra* of Kauṭalya (apparently late 4th century B.C., though the text is probably not free from interpolations of later date), is of considerable importance in the history of philosophy on account of the author's statements of his philosophical position and methodology, which moreover provide much-needed information on the contemporary state of philosophy generally. Kauṭalya was a highly successful minister of the Empire of Magadha.

According to Kauṭalya (I.2) there are four *vidyās*, or departments of learning: philosophy (*ānvīkṣikī*), the three *Vedas* (*trayī*), political economy (*vārttā*) and politics (*daṇḍanīti*). Philosophy is the highest of these, the 'light' of all the others: it is noteworthy that the author, a brahman, thus places philosophy above the *dharma* of the *Veda* in his scheme, and we find later in his work that he regards religion simply as a useful instrument of policy, to be promoted by rulers in such a way as to strengthen the government but not to be believed by them.

Philosophy is described as consisting of Sāṃkhya, Yoga and Lokāyata. Sāṃkhya and Lokāyata have been discussed above (there is, however, practically nothing in the *Arthaśāstra* to indicate precisely what forms of these doctrines Kauṭalya studied, and whether he recommended actually following either system, or a combination of the two, or simply studying them as useful intellectual exercises). Yoga here probably does not refer to the school or schools of Sāṃkhya later called by that name. The word is known to have been used in early times for the school generally called Vaiśeṣika (see XVI). Though that school as now known to us probably did not exist as early as Kauṭalya, it is possible that a precursor of it, or an earlier form of its doctrines under the name Yoga, existed then. In his 15th chapter Kauṭalya seems to use *yoga* in the sense of predication or 'judgment' (cf. its cognate *yukti* used among the early logicians). Logic was certainly cultivated by the Buddhists by the 3rd century B.C. (see XIII below), among whom the word *vādayukti* was used for their standard form of debate (a logical debate). It is likely that the brahmans did not ignore the science which developed out of debating in this period, slender as is our evidence to confirm the supposition. The Vaiśeṣika as known to us, on the other hand, is not concerned directly with debating (though its doctrines are highly relevant for arguing), but is dominated by a theory of 'categories' (*padārthas*), as kinds of object (*artha*) to which words (*padas*) may refer, distinguished and classified according to their characteristics. The inductive method of agreement and difference is the means used to establish true conclusions, and the school became a pioneer in developing a theory of knowledge. Possibly Kauṭalya was following the old Yoga school in his 15th chapter, which deals with the methodology (*tantrayukti*, perhaps literally translatable as 'congruence of the system') of his (or any) science.

Kauṭalya's position (not that of later orthodox Brahmanism) on the question of the three ends of life (*trivarga*) is that wealth is the most important, since it is the basis of the other two (i.e. one cannot pursue either virtue or pleasure without it). Pleasure should be sought in so far as it does not conflict with virtue and wealth, because one ought not to be unhappy (I.7.3-7). In this discussion Kauṭalya seems to have studied the *Lokāyata Sūtra*, but he offers different conclusions (cf. VII above): even the style of his discussion seems to reflect that of the *Lokāyata Sūtra* as known to us in its fragments.

The 15th chapter, on methodology, exemplifies a branch of study which we find taken up by various schools about this time, including philosophical schools such as those of the Buddhists but also other schools of scientific enquiry, such as medicine. The Mīmāṃsā is a parallel development within the discipline of Vedic interpretation. The different schools were to varying extents concerned with the correct and internally consistent interpretation of their ancient texts and with the proper construction of new texts (in such a way as to guarantee that they would be correctly understood), as well as with reliable procedures in scientific enquiry. Their methodology (*tantrayukti*) is thus a kind of applied logic.

Kauṭalya's methodological chapter is, unfortunately for us, very laconic in style: in fact it is a good example of the prose *sūtra* style favoured by Indian writers on technical subjects, in which part of the aim is extreme brevity (such texts were meant to be learned by heart, it was also assumed that they would be studied with a teacher who could clarify the brief statements and bring out all their implications, so that the laconic text would afterwards serve the student as notes recalling to mind a full exposition and discussion of the subject). Remote in time as we are from Kauṭalya, it is difficult for us to be sure of anything intended by him beyond his own words, since we cannot be certain that any later Indian expounders of his topics were teaching precisely his doctrine and not ideas developed later (this difficulty applies to many other ancient texts). He first enumerates thirty-two *yuktis*, i.e. methods or points of method, then gives very brief definitions and illustrations. These thirty-two were a standard list known to other schools as well: we have later expositions of them, but sometimes with variants substituted, the interpretations diverging somewhat from what we know of Kauṭalya's. They are:

topic (*adhikaraṇa*)
table of contents (*vidhāna*)
premise (?—*yoga*, predication or judgment)
meaning of a word (*padārtha*, dictionary definition)
cause (*hetvartha*)
preliminary synopsis (*uddeśa*)
detailed exposition (*nirdeśa*)
instruction (*upadeśa*)
citation of authority (*apadeśa*)
extension (*atideśa*—of a rule or law to cover some case)
reference (to another section of a work, *pradeśa*)
similarity (*upamāna*)
implication (*arthāpatti*)
doubt (*saṃśaya*; difficulty requiring discussion)
parallel procedure (*prasaṅga*)

contrary implication (*viparyaya*)
ellipsis (*vākyaśeṣa*; a word to be understood to complete the sentence)
accepted (statement of another teacher—if it is cited and not contradicted explicitly it means it is accepted; *anumata*)
elaborate explanation (*vyākhyāna* ; commentary)
derivation (*nirvacana*; etymology of a word)
illustration (*nidarśana*, of a rule)
exception (*apavarga*, to a rule)
technical term coined by the author, or the school (*svasaṃjñā*)
opponent's view (*pūrvapakṣa*)
own view (*uttarapakṣa*)
certainty (*ekānta*; decision)
'see below' (*anāgatāvekṣaṇa*—reference to a later section)
'see above' (*atikrāntāvekṣaṇa*—reference to an earlier section)
decision (*niyoga*, between two alternatives, only one being acceptable)
allowable alternative (*vikalpa*)
conjunction of possibilities (*samuccaya*)
judgment (*ūhya;* estimate, induction)

This is the order of enumeration, presumably traditional rather than logical. We could classify them in three goups. First there are devices of arrangement of a treatise: setting out material under a topic (chapter heading) whereby the student understands that everything there stated is to be applied in the context of that topic, table of contents, synopsis or summary, detailed exposition, references to other parts of the work, parallel procedure (meaning continue as before, avoiding a repetition of something), commentary and citation of authority. These lead into a second group, of conventions to be understood in interpreting a treatise: the use of technical terms (to be understood in a technical sense as defined by the author), an instruction, dealing with alternatives in the cases where one is rejected ('decision'), either is allowable, or both are possible simultaneously, exception to a rule, ellipsis, doubt (introducing a discussion), certainty (firm conclusion) and accepted citation.

The third group, partly growing out of the second, is of conventions and methods bearing on logic: the difficult term *yoga* seems here to mean a predication or premise (stating that *a* is *b*), Kauṭalya's example being 'the people are the four classes and four age-groups', this is evidently to be distinguished from the derivation of a term (word) and from its direct (dictionary) meaning (the object it refers to), the cause is simply the objective cause (the term is not yet being used for the middle term in an inference), judgment (*ūhya*) here seems wider than the estimate of probabilities for which this term is used in other discussions on methodology (here it seems to include moral judgments, a proper decision avoiding injury to either party in a transaction), extension and illustration of a rule are clear, similarity and implication are much discussed in later epistemology (as possible means of knowledge which might be distinguished from inference), contrary implication seems hardly to be a separate process from implication (the example given is of finding evidence opposite to that known to indicate some state of affairs, and concluding the reverse), finally it seems to be a universal procedure in Indian philosophical works that under any topic the proposition(s) taken up for discussion first *(pūrvapakṣa)* will be the erroneous view of another school of thought (to be analysed and shown to be unacceptable), the view the author holds to be correct being reserved for the concluding part of the discussion (*uttarapakṣa*).

XII ANCIENT INDIAN SCIENCE

Something has been said in III above about what is known of science in the Vedic period. Here it will be useful to review its history from those beginnings down into the 1st millennium A.D., with reference to the ideas it could offer to philosophers.

It is probably true to say that linguistics was the most advanced branch of science in India throughout its history. It was so advanced that even today it remains modern, and it is the methods of the ancient Indians which have formed the basis of modern linguistic science in the West. The most remarkable point here is that linguistics was from the Vedic period an independent science, using scientific method in the analysis of the data with which it was concerned: it was not a branch of philosophy or an application of philosophical or logical concepts to the study of language. (In this it differed fundamentally from Western 'grammar' stemming from the ideas of Aristotle.) Indian linguistics in fact is as old as Indian philosophy and older than Indian logic; it thus established itself on its own ground before it could be influenced by logic: it applied itself to the analysis of the sentences of natural language as they occur, not trying to force them into the pattern of the artificially formulated propositions of logic. Linguistics exerted a strong influence on other sciences because it was widely recognised to be a model of what a science should be, with careful, painstaking analysis of its data and precise formulation of the resulting description. The same influence affected philosophers and encouraged a preoccupation with precise definitions, also with economy of statement.

The highest peak of achievement in linguistics was probably reached as early as *c.* 350 B.C. with Pāṇini's description of the Sanskrit language, which seems still to be more complete, as well as more scientific, than any other description yet produced of any language. It is also highly economical of words and as far as possible uses symbols instead to indicate the phenomena of the language. The entire language is shown analysed into its constituent meaningful elements, namely roots, suffixes and inflections, with the various ways in which these combine. An important feature is the use of a symbol for zero (*vi*) in the description (where mere common sense would say there is 'no' suffix in the form of a certain word): this enables Pāṇini to operate consistently, distinguishing analysis at the level of words from that at the level of roots (a root is not a word: all words contain suffixes, in certain cases 'zero' suffix). This invention of zero to take care of 'empty' places in a system seems to have been due to the linguists: mathematicians are known to have used it only somewhat later. By the 2nd century A.D. the idea got into philosophy in a modified form, combining with the conception that things are not what they appear to be but are 'empty' (*śūnya*, 'zero'), are like places in a system and nothing in themselves (e.g. Nāgārjuna).

In mathematics itself the decimal system with place notation was developed early, though it is not yet possible to say how early (most of the extant mathematical treatises are relatively late, having superseded earlier ones). At any rate the philosopher Vasumitra *c.* 100 A.D. borrowed the idea of place notation in trying to explain a problem about 'existence' in the past and future. The old Vedic geometry (of the *Śulvasūtras*) did not develop far as a pure geometry (unlike Greek geometry), because the Indians very early invented algebra and trigonometry, which superseded it. In the early centuries A.D. trigonometry was brought into its modern form, with the study of sines and versed sines, the making of tables of sines and of other functions, and the development of spherical trigonometry (applied in astronomy). In algebra meanwhile a method of solving indeterminate equations was developed. These developments are attested in the classic work of Āryabhaṭa at the end of the 5th century A.D. After him the solutions of more complex equations were successively worked out (in the 7th century indeterminate equations of the second degree, 'Pellian' equation, diagonals and areas of cyclic quadrilaterals, study of negative numbers and terms—Brahmagupta; in the 9th century areas and circumferences of ellipses, square roots of negative quantities—Mahāvīra; culminating perhaps in the 12th century with solutions of some indeterminate equations of the third and fourth degrees, general form of the 'Pellian'—Bhāskara). Some techniques of the calculus were in use by about the 5th century, including infinitesimals and the method of exhaustion in finding areas. Brahmagupta discusses infinitesimals in connection with the question of zero, whilst the philosopher Vācaspatimiśra says that his Buddhist opponents used the idea of the infinitesimal increment in time in order to explain their philosophical doctrine of the momentariness of all principles without getting involved in the difficulties of a theory of 'atoms' of time. The study of zero and infinity was always stimulating to philosophers. [*NVTṬ* 550f. (XXV)]

Vedic astronomy was concerned primarily with the problems of the calendar and with the positions of the constellations (especially the 28 *nakṣatras* or lunar mansions) as a basis for establishing an accurate calendar. Following this the study of the movements of the planets seems to have come to dominate astronomy (e.g. in the 2nd century B.C. knowledge of the 12 year cycle of Jupiter—Gārga), eclipses also were studied and predicted (there is indirect evidence of a successful prediction of the total solar eclipse of B.C. 249 by a Buddhist monk), whilst a Buddhist text of about the 4th century B.C. mentions observations of a comet (the appearance of which was believed to be of political significance). At an unknown date the study of the movements of the planets led to attempts to calculate the lengths of grand cycles of time over which the combined motions of all the known planets should repeat, and at the commencement of which they should all start together from a common starting point (or line?). The extant calculations concerning this seem to be fairly late, but it seems likely that in the ancient period they had something to do with the enormous time scales found in philosophical speculations about the evolution of the universe. All schools (brahmans, Buddhists, Ājīvakas, Jainas) conceive of this on a scale approaching an infinity of time (the Buddha is recorded to have said that the universe is beginningless, he and others thought of it as cyclic, enormous cycles repeating). The astronomical investigations of cyclic time, as a natural extension of research on the calendar, would point to cyclic periods of millions of years required to contain the calculated complete movements of the planets, and on the rather natural assumption that these heavenly cycles were significant for life on earth too (as the annual cycle was accompanied by the seasons) they encouraged conceptions of physical, moral and social causation (evolution, transmigration, etc.) working out over immense periods. As astronomical observations became more accurate, the grand original conjunction of planets at the beginning of the present cycle receded further into the past (what is to be counted as a perfect conjunction depends on the degree of exactness demanded). The general effect of this on philosophers was to develop a broad and universalist outlook: the history of the civilisation known to us is as a speck of time in infinity, it cannot be assumed to be in any way unique or special, but must be a brief phase among countless others. The same conception applies in space: it is not assumed that ours is the only inhabited world, on the contrary it appears to be taken for granted in India that there are many other inhabited worlds among the stars.

There appears to have been a considerable improvement of astronomical instruments (particularly the gnomon, water clock and armillary sphere) in India during the early centuries A.D., resulting in more accurate observations as the basis of the work of Āryabhaṭa and later writers. Eclipses could then be accurately forecast, and the precession of the equinoxes was investigated. Attempts were made to determine various astronomical constants: the diameter of the Earth (about 9,000 miles according to Āryabhaṭa) and that of the Moon (about 2,800 miles)—these are not too far out, but that of the Sun (estimated at about 40,000 miles) could not be obtained satisfactorily (the planets also were not successfully measured, and were believed to be smaller than the Moon). The Earth had for some time been known to be spherical, but Āryabhaṭa was perhaps the first to suggest that it rotated on its axis (thus explaining the apparent revolution of the stars); he may also have held that the Earth revolved round the Sun (explaining the annual movement of the stars), but this is not certain since his terminology and explanations have not yet been definitively interpreted. In working out a theory of the epicyclic movements of the planets he calculated that they revolved round centres other than the centre of the Earth (he assumed wrongly that all the planets moved at the same speed), thus he was certainly working away from any geocentric conception of the solar system. Some of these measurements and calculations were improved by Brahmagupta, though he did not develop the idea of the Earth not being fixed. Bhāskara gives still more accurate values for the sizes of the Earth and the Moon and the distance between them, but his figures for the Sun remain much too small (distance about 3,000,000 miles).

Ancient chemistry is reflected in various books, though we have no very ancient work on chemistry itself. Thus Kauṭalya discusses mineral resources, and the ores and extraction of metals, at great length, on account of their economic importance, and further explains qualitative and quantitative analysis for the purpose of detecting fraudulent practices on the part of smiths (especially goldsmiths). The list of chemical substances known to him seems most impressive for his time, to judge from histories of Western chemistry. The extant medieval treatises on chemistry have not yet been properly evaluated, but are largely preoccupied with the study of mercury.

Physics seems to have been cultivated partly by philosophers, as part of their own study of the nature of reality (the question of the elements of which the universe consisted, various atomic theories, the study of light, heat, sound, and so on), and partly in its applications in technology (hydrostatics for irrigation works, etc., military engines, mechanical toys) and in such studies as the theory of music. The Vaiśeṣika school of philosophy was particularly concerned with problems of physics.

Progress in medicine is marked especially by the great work of Caraka (*c.* 100 A.D.). In the history of philosophy this is remarkable because it contains a section on logic, as a branch of knowledge requiring to be cultivated by doctors both for purposes of making inferences in diagnosis and for argument with colleagues and others, also for the study of ethics in the medical tradition.

XIII ABHIDHARMA AND LOGIC

Whilst the Buddha himself categorically rejected all authority except experience, his followers in the course of time tended more and more to regard his statements, as handed down among them, as authoritative. In a desire to maintain his teaching faithfully, many of them seem to have adopted an attitude which could be described as flatly contradictory to his own. In any case the early Buddhists during the first centuries after the time of the Buddha attempted to systematise his doctrines in a consistent and orderly manner. Besides the records they preserved of dialogues between the Buddha and others, in which he set forth his views discursively, varying according to the exigencies of the occasion, they had some sets of brief notes or headings (*mātṛkā*) summarising the doctrine in a more regular, but highly condensed, form intended for ease of memorising. These notes served as a basis for the elaboration of systematic texts, known as *Abhidharma,* which began by selecting relevant explanations in the dialogues to attach to the headings and continued by annotating these with new analysis, definitions and discussions. The aim was precise formulation and the working out of a system in which all the terms are defined and arranged in their mutual relations. During the first two centuries after the *parinirvāṇa* of the Buddha there appears to have come into existence an *Abhidharma* in three main sections: (1) analysis and definitions of the topics and principles propounded by the Buddha; (2) classification of principles in various ways and listings of those principles which can occur in conjunction; (3) a study of conditionality and causality, the different types of condition or causal relation found in the sequence of conditioned origination. This *Abhidharma* does not survive, because during the second century and afterwards the Buddhists divided into several schools which disagreed especially over this systematic extension of their doctrine and consequently produced their own separate versions of it. An approximate idea of it can be obtained by comparing the extant *Abhidharmas* of the Buddhist schools (see Bibliography on these).

The divisions among the Buddhists which led to the formation of the separate schools were naturally accompanied by much controversy, including public debates. Public debating was in fact an ancient custom in India, reflected in the *Upaniṣads* and in the earliest Buddhist texts. It had then been relatively undisciplined and rhetorical, as far as one can see from those texts. When, however, the Buddhists became divided over various philosophical questions they sought more rigorous methods of argument which might clarify their difficulties. This happened just at the time when in the *Abhidharma* they were elaborating entire texts containing only precisely formulated, in other words logical, discourse, with strictly controlled deductions from accepted premises. The *Abhidharmas* of the schools include texts which record what purport to be actual debates with other schools, carried on in regular form and against checks supplied by logical method. The most important of these is the *Kathāvatthu* (in Pali, of the Sthaviravāda school), a collection of more than two hundred debates supposed to have been compiled in the 3rd century B.C. but undoubtedly added to after that date (a parallel text of another school is found in the *Vijñānakāya* of the Sarvāstivāda, see Watanabe, Chapter 11). These debates are refutations in strict logical form of propositions maintained by other schools of Buddhism. They generally turn on the question of the consistency of these disputed propositions with those accepted statements which all schools admitted to have been enunciated by the Buddha.

Ancillary to the debates proper the *Kathāvatthu* shows us a variety of logical methods for dealing with new propositions, or new terms, presented for discussion. These are:

(1) Checking against all the accepted terms in the system to see how it fits in—this gives us a 'tetrad scheme' of: I, is the new term identical in meaning (though not in name) with any of the accepted terms? (this leads further into an 'examination of concepts' and a study of synonyms); II, is it different from all the accepted terms? III, is it part of any of the terms? and IV, is one of the terms part of it? (this 'scheme' is to be applied for all the accepted terms, with reference to the new one).

(2) Considering the logical 'quantity': does the proposition cover all instances of a given term or only some?

(3) Discussing the possible classification of a new term under

the classes of the system, its definition or description, the conditions under which the principle in question occurs.

(4) Any special discussions which may be relevant.

(5) Adducing statements from the accepted texts (*Tripiṭaka*) to confirm or controvert a proposition.

The method of the debate proper is based on placing two propositions side by side, one of which is the disputed one and the other related to it in such a way that one must either affirm both or deny both. The second proposition is itself either taken directly from the accepted texts or so clearly implied by them that all Buddhists must admit the implication (consequently that the proposition must be affirmed or must be denied, as the case may be). If the disputed proposition is inconsistent with the system (and therefore with the accepted texts), it will be found that the 'opponent' (representative of the other school) in the debate affirms one of the two related propositions but denies the other: the protagonist of the Sthaviravāda then asserts the relationship between them (adding further analysis where necessary to establish the relationship) and calls upon the opponent to admit the refutation. The actual form of the debate in the *Kathāvatthu* is much longer than would seem necessary to set out the refutation, and presumably represents some conventional procedure in public debating which laboriously established the positions of the two parties and reiterated the argument until no one could escape seeing the conclusion. It contains forty-two steps in argument, besides the initial statements of the two related propositions, in which the opponent first sophistically refutes the Sthaviravādin (e.g. by equivocation, which has eventually to be exposed by an ancillary method) in a twenty-one step argument, maintaining his proposition (cf. the *Arthaśāstra's pūrvapakṣa*, opponent's view), after which the Sthaviravādin gains the initiative (*uttarapakṣa*, own view) in a second twenty-one step 'refutation' and (properly, this time) refutes it.

What is logically important here, apart from the rigid formalisation of discourse, is the relationships between the two propositions round which the debate turns. In effect the opponent's proposition (statement to which he assents, *pratijñā*; whether affirmative or negative) is analysed by substituting for it one of which it is a ponential or a biconditional (i.e. which implies it), but which the opponent must deny (on grounds of the agreed texts or of experience). Where necessary the relationship will then be proved. Alternative methods of analysis of the disputed proposition include substituting a synonym for one of its terms or bringing out its implications by showing that one of its terms belongs to some class or is causally related to some other term. All these procedures bridge the gap between the disputed proposition and accepted doctrinal statements and so establish a deduction from accepted doctrine of the untenability of the disputed proposition. The form of the debate may be summarised as follows:

(1) The opponent is asked whether he assents to his (disputed) proposition, and does so (p).

(2) The opponent is asked whether he assents to another proposition (which clearly is contrary to the accepted doctrine), but he denies it ($\sim q$).

(3) The Sthaviravādin asserts that if you accept p then you must accept q ($p \supset q$).

(4) The Sthaviravādin shows why $p \supset q$, by analysing p, concluding that if $\sim q$ then $\sim p$.

Examples of the pairs of propositions (the first is the disputed one, the second that clearly related to accepted doctrine):

(a) (1) There is that which is unknown to a 'perfected one (*arhant*)'.
(2) There is ignorance in a perfected one.

(b) (1) The discourse of the Buddha is 'transcendental'.
(2) The discourse of the Buddha is audible only to transcendental ears, not to worldly ones.

(c) (1) There are two 'cessations' (leading to *nirvāṇa*).
(2) There are two cessations of unhappiness (this would duplicate one of the Four Truths, which is untenable).

(d) (1) The 'person' (soul) exists in the real, ultimate sense.
(2) The person exists in the real, ultimate sense in the same way as those (agreed principles) which are real and ultimate (i.e. as the groups matter, experience, etc., and other principles; the opponent cannot maintain the person in the same way because it lacks any characteristics to identify it and can be argued for only indirectly as neither the same as the groups nor different from them, and so forth).

(In each case the opponent assents to (1) but denies (2).)

XIV BUDDHISM: STHAVIRAVĀDA (THERAVĀDA) AND OTHER SCHOOLS

The Buddhists became divided into a number of schools over a variety of questions of doctrine and discipline. The first of these schisms (perhaps in B.C. 349) was over the nature of a 'perfected one (*arhant*)' and resulted in a majority of the community of monks maintaining a lower standard, with the possibility of relapsing back into the 'world' and of being ignorant of some matters. As they claimed to be a majority they took the name Mahāsaṅghika for their school. The minority, who insisted that a perfected one should be equal to a fully enlightened Buddha in everything except the latter's special ability to teach, consisted of the more senior monks, or 'elders' (*sthaviras*), and consequently is called the Sthaviravāda. On the whole the Sthaviravāda probably remained closer to the original teaching, at least to the letter of the teaching, but just because of this it tended to be rigid and scholastic. The Mahāsaṅghika was more flexible: its chief departure from the probable original teaching was to separate the characters of 'perfected one' and Buddha completely, with the result that in time the Buddha came to be regarded by them as a very special, even supernatural, figure, whilst his followers who, learning from him (directly or in later centuries from the teaching as handed down in the schools), became 'perfected' had not achieved anything very wonderful. This trend of separation of Buddha (and consequently of anyone aspiring to become a *buddha,* i.e. of a *bodhisattva*) from perfected one eventually produced the Mahāyāna (see XVIII below). The Sthaviravāda also raised the standard for a Buddha, requiring omniscience instead of just understanding of the Four Truths and the process of 'rebirth', but they raised the standard for a perfected one at the same time (making it practically unattainable). Both schools subsequently divided into others. Those of the Mahāsaṅghikas seem in themselves relatively unimportant, except as successive steps towards the Mahāyāna (but we know little about them, since not much of their literature survives—philosophically the Kaurukullaka, Bahuśrutīya and Prajñaptivāda seem important). Two of those which seceded from the Sthaviravāda, on the other hand, require separate mention.

The first of these was the 'Person' (*pudgala*) school, which appeared about 286 B.C. All other Buddhists maintained that the word 'person' (*pudgala*), sometimes used by the Buddha himself, contained no more meaning than a mere pronoun. It indicated separate individuals as numerically distinct, but did not refer to any positive entity. An elder named Vātsīputra, and the school named Vātsīputrīya after him, maintained instead that the 'person' is in some sense real, even though not an eternal 'soul' such as non-Buddhists believed in. Their explanation seems rather vague: that the person is not the same as the 'groups' (constituting the material and mental organism of a living being), nor is it different from them; it is not a completely independent 'soul', yet it is something more than just the groups and can be said to transmigrate (as non-Buddhists maintain a 'soul' does). The 'Person' school itself subdivided in the course of time and one of its sub-divisions, the Saṃmitīya, is best known later as representing it.

The other was the 'All Exist' school (Sarvāstivāda), which originated probably in 237 B.C. It maintained that in some sense all principles, all the *dharmas*, 'exist', including those of the past and the future. (Other Buddhists maintained that only those of the present 'exist' with perhaps in a sense some past actions which had not yet produced their full results.) The Sarvāstivāda developed a very energetic scholastic tradition and exerted considerable influence thereby, partly because it used the 'standard' Sanskrit language of India.

The remaining Sthaviravāda school adhered to an older, originally vernacular, dialect, now known as Pali (Theravāda is its Pali name). Its special doctrines appear to be that a perfected one is absolutely incorruptible and that understanding (of the truths, i.e. enlightenment) comes all at once, not gradually. It alone has survived, among all the early (pre-Mahāyāna) schools, and consequently its doctrines are most fully available to us and can serve us as an example of the work of the schools.

In their *Abhidharma* (*Abhidhamma* in Pali) the Sthaviravāda set out lists of *dharmas* (principles or qualities), as connected with types of 'thought' or with matter or *nirvāṇa*. They were further classified in many ways, as (morally) good, bad or indifferent (a 'triadic' classification—contraries admitting a third position between them), as being causes or not causes (a 'dyadic' classification—contradictories), and so on. The school found that the *Tripiṭaka* (or rather the *Sūtrapiṭaka*) mentioned about two hundred *dharmas*, which it proceeded to collect in an *Abhidharma* text (the *Dhammasaṅgaṇi*, 'Enumeration of Principles'). These, however, could be reduced to well under one hundred by eliminating mere synonyms. We can review them here under the headings (classification) of the groups:

(1) Matter (*rūpa*, physical principles)—
earth, water, heat, air (primary kinds of matter, defined as what we would call properties of matter: hardness, cohesion, heat and agitation)
sight, hearing, smell, taste, touch (secondary matter, the senses)
visible object, sound, scent, taste object (also secondary, the objects of the senses: there is no separate 'tangible', since this would be nothing but the primary elements themselves)
femininity, masculinity, life (secondary, physical 'faculties')
gesture, speech
space (=gaps in the primary matter)
lightness, suppleness, malleability, accumulation, extension, ageing, impermanence (of matter)
material-food

(2) Experience (*vedanā*)—
happiness, unhappiness, equanimity

(3) Perception (*saṃjñā*)—this 'group' contains only perception itself (but there are 6 kinds relating to the 6 senses)

(4) Forces (*saṃskāra*)—
contact (stimulus), volition, reasoning, reflection, joy
concentration, energy, confidence, self-possession, understanding
life (a homonym of the physical faculty, but here distinguished as mental)
right speech, right work, right livelihood
self-respect, fear of blame
desire, aversion, delusion (the three 'roots' of bad action)
non-desire, non-aversion, non-delusion (the three 'roots' of good action; in fact non-aversion reduces to benevolence, but both aspects are very prominent in Buddhist theory: this

point of different aspects of the same principle accounts for the great difference in number between the reduced and unreduced lists, moreover the various aspects are often so important, when considering experience from different points of view, as to justify what in the final analysis is a repetition, since the situations contemplated in the different contexts are practically different and the overall structures of principles may be much more significant than their atomic constituents; non-delusion likewise reduces to understanding; non-desire is the cause of generosity)

vanity, uncertainty

tranquillity, lightness, suppleness, malleability, efficiency, straightness (of the living body and of thought)

intending to find out something unknown (this is a 'faculty') (many more forces are noted in the *Dhammasaṅgaṇi,* but they all reduce to one of the above; however the text adds in several places, in discussing the contents of particular 'thoughts', 'and whatever other principles occur on that occasion through conditioned origination . . . ', and the school later produced a commentary which purports to complete the enumeration, adding will, intentness, attention, impartiality, compassion, gladness at others' well-being, abstention from bad conduct of the body, abstention from bad speech, abstention from wrong livelihood)

(5) Consciousness (*vijñāna*)—

thought (*citta,* a synonym for consciousness itself)

mind (a 'faculty' or a 'base', but it reduces to thought)

consciousness of sight, of hearing, of smell, of taste, of touch

consciousness of mind (i.e. of the mind=thought of the previous moment in the stream or series of consciousness; this provides for continuity among the transient principles of consciousness)

Outside the five groups we have finally 'unsynthesised base' (*asaṃskṛtadhātu,* or 'unactivated base'), containing simply extinction (*nirvāṇa*).

In the study of logic, the Sthaviravāda school supplemented its *Kathāvatthu,* or collection of debates, with a long set of exercises entitled the *Yamaka*. It sets out an enormous number of pairs (*yamaka*='pair') of questions of the form 1) is all S P? and 2) is all P S? In other words it lists a large number of propositions with their converses, enquiring whether both are true. Each proposition, or 'question' (*pṛcchā*), consists of two 'terms' (*arthas*), the copula being understood (as regularly in Sanskrit and Pali) and only the order indicating which is subject and which predicate. The answers to these questions are given throughout. The main purpose of these exercises is to prepare the student against the logical traps (which might threaten him in a debate) inherent in conversion, including those which arise from words being used in more than one sense or figuratively. An example is: (1) is all eye eye-entrance (=the sense of sight)? and (2) is all eye-entrance eye? —Answers : (1) the 'divine eye' and the 'eye of understanding' are eye but not eye-entrance, and (2) yes.

The *Paṭṭhāna* ('Basis') seems to be the latest addition to the *Abhidhamma* of the Sthaviravāda (it was perhaps completed in the 1st century B.C.). It is probably an elaboration of the last section of the original *Abhidharma* of the undivided Buddhists, on the theory of conditions and causal relations. It sets out to classify the different types of conditional relationship among all the principles recognised in the system of the *Dhammasaṅgaṇi*. The basic formula is of the form: *x* occurs conditioned by *y* through the *p*-condition. Here *x* and *y* are any of the principles, or any classes of principles, and the gigantic work proposes to check off every possible pair. The pairs are also inverted and obverted: non-*x* occurs conditioned by non-*y* . . , *x* occurs conditioned by non-*y* . . and non-*x* occurs conditioned by *y*. (Converted and contrapositive forms are unnecessary because any principle may be *x* or *y*.) There are, further, twenty-four possible conditions to substitute for *p*, moreover there are six other expressions to be substituted for 'conditioned by' in the formula. The available manuscripts and editions resort to extreme abbreviation in order to be able to encompass such a study, which the school says (in a commentary) would be infinite in extent if set out in full.

The most noteworthy contribution of this work of Buddhist theory is its twenty-four conditions (*pratyayas*). Among these only four seem to be more or less 'original' Buddhism, and even these are differently described in the other schools whose *Abhidharmas* are known. The twenty-four are:

(1) (moral) cause (*hetu*, but restricted to the six 'roots' of good and bad action)
(2) support (mental object in thought, 'idea', as condition for consciousness)
(3) dominant (e.g. certain of the 'forces', such as will, energy, capable of directing and strengthening other principles in the stream of consciousness; cf. the 'instrumental cause' found in some schools of Indian philosophy)
(4) immediate (the relation of immediately succeeding principles continuing a series, such as 'mind' immediately followed by 'consciousness of (that) mind')
(5) quite immediate (taken over from earlier Sthaviravāda *Abhidharma*, but found to be synonymous with No. 4)
(6) simultaneous origin (of principles which occur simultaneously in the same sequence—for example the four properties of primary matter, also secondary matter with primary matter)
(7) reciprocal (covers part of No. 6, since reciprocal dependence can obtain only between principles occurring simultaneously—e.g. the four primary properties, but not secondary and primary)
(8) dependence (as of secondary on primary matter, mind on the matter of the body)
(9) immediate dependence (similar to No. 4 but of wider extension—of any member of a sequence and that immediately preceding it)
(10) produced before (this includes the external sense object, matter as condition for mind through the senses)
(11) produced after (a principle which may occur later considered as a condition operating on what precedes it, expected future experience acting on the body, as an incentive)
(12) habit (repetition as strengthening mental principles)
(13) action (moral, always conjoined with volition)
(14) result (in itself not productive of a direct effect, but may be conducive to the attainment of other results in the same sequence)

(15) food (four 'foods' are mentioned in the *Tripiṭaka*; they are material-food of the body, contact (stimulus), volition of the mind and consciousness-food, the last being experience through the living body which 'feeds' consciousness)
(16) faculty (the senses and other 'faculties', especially 'life', as specific conditions)
(17) meditation (as condition for the principles occurring in it)
(18) the way (of Buddhism, likewise for the principles occurring in it)
(19) conjoined with (part of No. 6, the four immaterial groups together, a term much used in earlier *Abhidharma*)
(20) disjoined from (the relation between material and immaterial principles as conditions for one another)
(21) existing (simultaneously, mostly included in No. 6, but wider than that, including also parts of Nos. 2, 8 and 10)
(22) not existing (the cessation of an 'immediate' condition, or more generally of any 'thought' or mental principle, which operates on principles present at the same time)
(23) without (a synonym for No. 22)
(24) not without (a synonym for No. 21)

Substituting six other expressions for 'conditioned by' we have altogether seven ways of articulating the formula, as follows:

(1) *x* occurs conditioned by *y* through the *p*-condition.
(2) *x* occurs simultaneously originated with *y* . . .
(3) *x* occurs through the condition *y* . . .
(4) *x* occurs having depended on *y* . . .
(5) *x* occurs associated with *y* . . .
(6) *x* occurs conjoined with *y* . . .
(7) is *x* a condition of *y* by the *p*-condition?

Although only No. 7 is conventionally called a 'question', all the propositions are in fact taken as questions in the *Paṭṭhāna*, since of course many of them are not true. The text sets out the answers as it goes along, or at least (in view of abbreviation) notes whatever reservations there are against unqualified acceptance of the given proposition.

Besides these texts included in its *Abhidharma*, the Sthaviravāda produced other philosophical works. One, the *Paṭisambhidāmagga* ('The Way of Comprehension'), is included in the *Sūtrapiṭaka* of the school, though it is evidently completely apocryphal and the result of discussions within the school only. It supplements the analysis of topics in the *Abhidharma* (and particularly the *Vibhaṅga*), adding new topics, but it arranges its discussions in order as a kind of guide to the 'way' and is generally more practical. The central topic is 'comprehension' (*pratisaṃvid* is the Sanskrit equivalent of *paṭisambhidā*), which seems designed to establish the school's special doctrine that insight comes not gradually but in a sudden flash of enlightenment. It has four aspects, comprehension of principles (as conditions), of objectives (*arthas*, principles as effects), of language and of 'intuition' (*pratibhāna*, here meaning that kind of knowledge, or knowing, *jñāna*, which makes possible the other three aspects). The whole work is concerned with different kinds of knowledge or insight relevant to the Buddhist way, which is presented as in essence a system of knowing things. Its date may be in the 2nd century B.C.

The *Peṭakopadesa* ('Instructions about the (Three) Traditions', i.e. about interpreting the *Tripiṭaka*) is a work which the Sthaviravāda does not usually recognise as part of the *Tripiṭaka* (but in Burma it is so recognised), but rather as part, and a basic and preliminary part, of the commentaries on their Pali Canon. It is a kind of methodology, concerned with all aspects of interpretation of texts, including paraphrasing for teaching purposes, and it is therefore related in subject to Kauṭalya's methodology (see XI above). It also overlaps with logic in that it aims to determine what statements are congruent with, or can be deduced from, the accepted statements of the *Tripiṭaka*. This methodology operates at two levels: (1) the wording of statements and (2) the meaning of statements. Ultimately the aim is to reduce all the various statements of the *Tripiṭaka*, and especially its more poetic statements, to a relatively simple system of meanings (corresponding of course to the system of Buddhist doctrine worked out in the school).

At the level of the wording, according to the *Peṭakopadesa*, the interpreter should watch for such points as the following. A word may be simply a synonym for the standard name of some principle recognised in the system, it may state a characteristic (*lakṣaṇa*) of some principle or its immediate cause (*padasthāna*). One may make a citation (*apadeśa*) from another text in order to establish the congruence (*yukti*) of one's comment on some statement with the received doctrine. One should determine whether the text to be explained is about the (four) truths, the groups, bases, entrances, faculties or conditioned origination, for there is no *sūtra* (in the *Tripiṭaka*) which is not about one of these six.

At the level of the meaning, it is said that the doctrine of the *Tripiṭaka* may be summarised in one of three ways. (1) It is about the 'four errors' or their opposites (the four errors are the opinions that there is permanence in what is impermanent, happiness in unhappiness, a soul in non-soul or beauty in what is ugly). (2) It is about the three roots of bad action or the three roots of good action. (3) It is about desire (in the bad sense, *tṛṣṇā*, 'thirst') and ignorance or about calming (*śamatha*, according to the *Dhammasaṅgaṇi* this is the same as concentration) and insight (*vipaśyanā*, the same as understanding). All statements of doctrine may be subsumed under one of these three types (this is shown in detail). Furthermore type 1 (called the pair of tetrads) can be reduced to type 2 (the pair of triads) and type 2 can be reduced to type 3 (the pair of dyads). These three types are called three 'schemes' (*nayas*) of the meaning.

When we have checked the wording as indicated above (but there are altogether sixteen investigations to be applied to it) and thus reduced it to the standard terminology of the system, it can be fitted into one of the above standardised meanings. To do this we apply two 'schemes' (*nayas*). According as it has tetrad, triad or dyad form it will fit into one of three types above. Then according as it is about either the bad or the good half within each type it is ranged under that side.

Besides this remarkable method of simplifying the interpretation of the *Tripiṭaka*, the *Peṭakopadesa* is important for mentioning some significant new points of doctrine in the school. In connection with conditioned origination (p. 104) it brings in the concepts 'own-being' (*svabhāva*) and 'other-being' (*parabhāva*), apparently not used earlier in Buddhism and afterwards singled out for special criticism by Nāgārjuna as representing the misinterpretation of the Buddha's teaching by the early schools. In the *Peṭakopadesa* the 'cause' (*hetu*) of a principle is its 'own-being', which is internal to the series or sequence in question. Its 'condition' (*pratyaya*) on the other hand is an 'other-being', external to the series. Then in giving definitions the *Peṭakopadesa* uses (128f.) a threefold scheme stating the 'characteristic', 'appearance' (*pratyupasthāna*, way in which it manifests itself) and 'immediate cause' of a principle. The date of the *Peṭakopadesa* may be the 1st century B.C.

To complete this brief survey of the work of the Sthaviravāda Buddhists we must note some further ideas which appear in the commentaries which their school prepared on the *Tripiṭaka*. These commentaries may be taken to represent the teaching of the school as it had crystallised by the 1st century A.D. (See Adikaram, *Early History of Buddhism in Ceylon*, for this chronology.) The most important new idea is the definition of 'principle' (*dharma*, condition, regularity): 'principles are what have their own own-being' (in Pali: *attano pana sabhāvan dhārentī ti dhammā*, Commentary on the *Dhammasaṅgaṇi*, p. 39). In other words to be recognised as a separate principle a thing must have a distinct being of its own. This is qualified by saying that principles naturally (*yathāsvabhāvatas*) have their being through conditions (*pratyayas*), a qualification which might either head off Nāgārjuna's criticism or enable him to allege inconsistency in the Sthaviravāda system. A 'principle' is further described as an 'existent' (*bhāva*, p. 40). This *Dhammasaṅgaṇi* commentary then seeks to complete and finalise the work of its text by enumerating and defining all the principles to be recognised as real, reducing all synonymous terms. To the threefold scheme of definition of the *Peṭakopadesa* it adds a fourth aspect of each principle, its 'function' (*rasa* in a technical sense). Thus the principle 'earth' has the characteristic of 'hardness', the function of 'supporting' and the appearance of 'accepting (a weight)'. 'Water' has the characteristic of 'fluidity', the function of 'making increase' (because it makes things swell up) and the appearance of 'cohesion'. 'Heat' has the characteristic of 'hotness', the function of 'maturing' and the appearance of 'making soft'. 'Air' has the characteristic of 'inflating', the function of 'movement' and the appearance of 'making move'. As for the immediate causes of these four elements, they are all said to be immediate causes of one another (for they cannot occur independently according to this school and are regarded as properties which enter into the constitution of all matter) (Commentary on the *Dhammasaṅgaṇi*, p. 332). To take an example from the 'forces', 'compassion' is said to have the characteristic of 'promoting the removal of the unhappiness of others', the function of 'not enduring the unhappiness of others', the appearance of 'harmlessness' and as immediate cause 'seeing the state of helplessness of those overwhelmed by unhappiness' (ibid. p. 193).

Developing the critique of concepts, the commentators distinguish a 'concept' (*prajñapti*) based on an ultimately real principle from one based on something unreal such as a 'person' (e.g. Commentary on *Puggalapaññatti*, p. 172).

Though generally building on the traditional doctrine they had received from their teachers, the Sthaviravādins did to some extent make new observations of the world about them in order to supplement it. Thus in discussing the functioning of the senses it was observed that sound travels more slowly than light, as when one watches a man cutting down a tree and sees the movement of chopping before hearing the sound (*Atthasālinī*, p. 313).

A description is attempted of the mechanism of the stream of consciousness or 'thought-series' (*cittavīthi*) (*Dhammasaṅgaṇi* Cy. 269 ff., developed from *Paṭisambhidāmagga* I pp. 79-83). For example if the series is in a neutral state, as when a person is sleeping, it may be disturbed as follows by some outside event producing a sensory impression. This results in a 'support' and then in thoughts registering the 'impression', 'investigation' and 'delimitation' of the support. A further series of mental events may then occur, leading perhaps to the 'identification' of the disturbing support. If the support is of no interest the series may then revert to its neutral state, otherwise there may be further results. Each mental event requires a minimum of one 'moment' (*kṣaṇa*) in which to occur, the moment being taken as a kind of atomic instant in time. The minimum case of a neutral series disturbed as above but reverting at once on account of the support being of no interest is reckoned to take seventeen moments, including a neutral moment at either end. The doctrine of 'moments', which we meet first in discussions of mental events (the term is found already in the *Paṭṭhāna*, but apparently not yet as a definite measure of time), afterwards spread among the Buddhist schools as a general theory about the momentariness and transient nature of all principles.

The other early schools of Buddhism worked along roughly parallel, or to some extent diverging, lines. Each produced its list of the principles, thus the Sarvāstivāda eventually fixed their total at 75, with considerable variations from the Sthaviravāda list and some different classifications, the Bahuśrutīya (a branch of the Mahāsaṃghikas) theirs at 84, generally closer to the Sthaviravāda account. The Sarvāstivāda theory of conditions and causes differs widely from the Sthaviravāda. Thus it has six kinds of 'cause' (*hetu*): conjoined with, simultaneously existing, similar ('unchanged' continuity), universal, result and instrumental (including sense objects). Distinguished from these it has four 'conditions': (moral) cause, quite immediate, support and dominant.

On those Mahāsaṃghika schools which appear to have been philosophically important, it is reported that the Kaurukullaka held the *Abhidharma* to be the real doctrine (not the *Sūtra*). They held that there is no real happiness except 'extinction' (Nirvāṇa, which is cessation of unhappiness). The Bahuśrutīya, which seceded from them, agreed that all experience is really unhappiness. They held that the five groups are real, but are unhappiness, which also is real. They are also impermanent. Perceiving that they are impermanent is knowledge of emptiness. The cessation of the groups is their 'non-soul-ness' (lack of 'self' or of substance). The thought (even) of emptiness ceases in final extinction. (Vasumitra says the five words impermanence, unhappiness, emptiness, non-soul and extinction were regarded by them as the Buddha's 'transcendent' teaching, the rest being 'of the world'.) Visible objects, tasteables, scents and tangibles are matter and are real, but the four elements (or properties), sound and the five senses are concepts. The mental principles (forces) are kinds of thought. They have the four types of condition cause, support, immediate and dominant, which thus seem to be original Buddhism. Past and future principles do not exist (the characteristic doctrine of the 'All Exist' school is thus not original). There is no 'intermediate existence' (of consciousness between two lives, here they agree with Sthaviravāda against the Sautrāntika). But there is the principle 'unmanifest' (*avijñapti*, unseen but morally potent aspect of an action, rejected by Sthaviravāda). Against the Mahāsaṃghika and Kaurukullaka they held that thought is not by nature pure. The Prajñaptivāda (according to Vasumitra and Paramārtha) distinguished real principles from concepts. Thus the 12 entrances and 18 bases are not real but conceptual, the 5 groups and unhappiness are real, but not the same.

XV JAIMINI AND VĀRṢAGAṆYA

The *Mīmāṃsā Sūtra* mentioned above (X) as ascribed to Jaimini, an ancient sage, may have been composed in approximately its present form anywhere between the 2nd century B.C. and the 2nd century A.D. It seems likely that originally it contained more than its present twelve chapters, having a concluding portion corresponding to the present *Brahman Sūtra* (*Vedānta Sūtra*), which appears to have been a separate text *c.* 200 A.D. (when it was revised). As handed down in twelve chapters, however, it deals strictly with the 'Pūrva' (Prior) Mīmāṃsā, i.e. the ritual enjoined by the *Veda* and the metaphysics of Vedic authority. The *Sūtra* opens with a definition of *dharma,* stating that *dharma* constitutes its subject-matter. This *dharma* is the good (*artha,* sic!—object, advantage) which is indicated by the Vedic injunctions. It can be known only from the *Veda,* not by any other means such as sensation (*pratyakṣa*): other means (of knowledge) relate only to the here and now, not to the future (or the next world). There is an original (*autpattika*) relation (i.e. a necessary and eternal relation, according to the interpretation of the school) between words and their meanings, consequently words (this is taken to mean specifically those of the *Veda*) are absolutely authoritative. The school further interprets the text to the effect that words, and the text of the *Veda,* are eternal, have always existed, whether or not they were known to men and even before there were any men to know them. Speech was not created by men (or by a God). The Vedic text thus contains original and absolute knowledge of the most important matters (the highest good) relating to the universe: all that is necessary to attain this is to ascertain the correct interpretation of it and to act accordingly. Explaining the eternal nature of words, the *Sūtra* states (I.1.15) that a word is one (and eternal), though apparently repeated ('performed', we might say) on many occasions by different people, just as there is only one Sun, though it is seen by many people in various places. It continues that the amount of noise (*nāda*) may vary, but not the speech-sound (*varṇa,* phoneme) proper.

The *Veda* is the means of knowing the imperceptible good, it does not deviate from this (*avyatireka*, this is interpreted to mean that it is infallible) and it is a means of knowledge of it because it is independent (*anapekṣatvāt*, i.e. requires nothing else to support or confirm it, in fact there is nothing else available to us which bears on these imperceptible things except the eternal words inseparably connected with their meanings) (I.1.5). This is the basis of the Mīmāṃsā position: whatever we may think of the nature and reliability of a supposedly revealed sacred text, this is in a way an unassailable position, on which the Vedic metaphysics is built. Its doctrine concerns things concerning which no other knowledge exists, things beyond sensation, inference or any other means of knowledge or verification. It cannot therefore be contradicted by any other source of knowledge: everything else concerns this world only, and worldly affairs, this relates to another world which without it would simply be unknown to us. It is an ideal system of metaphysics: it can be rejected as a whole, by those who do not accept the *Veda* as self-authoritative, but otherwise it is beyond the reach of criticism, except on grounds of internal consistency.

In connection with the problem of what are the primary actions enjoined by the *Veda* and what things are merely secondary or subordinate (*śeṣa*) to these, the *Sūtra* (III.3.14) enunciates a series of means of knowing (*pramāṇas*) how to proceed. There are six of these and their relative strengths have to be determined. In effect they constitute a set of rules of interpretation of the Vedic text (the word *pramāṇa* used for them is the same as that used generally for 'means of knowledge', but these are the Vedic means relating to the sacred text, not the worldly means relating to this world). They are, in order of strength, (1) the *Veda* itself (*śruti*, i.e. the explicit statements of the text wherever these are clear), (2) implication (*liṅga*, of the text, as that the injunction 'drink!' implies picking up the vessel and other necessary actions; afterwards the term *liṅga* was used in the sense of a 'middle term' in an inference, which is quite a different idea), (3) sentence (*vākya*, meaning its syntax and grammar and the possible lexical meanings of its words, consideration of which may lead us to the proper interpretation when the text seems at first doubtful), (4) context (*prakaraṇa*, neighbouring statements which indicate how the text is to be understood), (5) position (*sthāna*, the order of the words in an enumeration may indicate the order of performance of the actions referred to), (6) designation (*samākhyāna*, the mere name of something may imply how it is to be treated, for example which priest is to recite a given prayer). Some later writers attempted to systematise these and numerous other principles of interpretation gleaned from the *Mīmāṃsā Sūtra* as sets of *vākyadharmas*, 'qualities of sentences' (qualities which help to distinguish their meanings).

The Mīmāṃsā investigation naturally leads to a consideration of the conditions for a sentence. The Vedic text, especially its prose parts (which were the most important to the ritualists since they prescribe the ritual), being handed down through oral tradition was not clearly punctuated: sometimes it seemed possible to divide it up in different ways, thus producing different sentences and different meanings. The *Sūtra* therefore gives rules for determining the proper divisions (II.1. 46-9): (1) the principle of syntactic connection: if there is 'expectancy' (*ākāṅkṣā*) between certain words, in that after the utterance of some of them there is still expectation of more in order to complete the sense, then all the expected words must be regarded as belonging to the same sentence (*vākya*); (2) the principle of syntactic split: if the pieces (groups of words) in a passage can be understood separately, on the other hand, they should be taken as separate sentences (thus the sentence is the minimum independent piece); (3) the principle of elliptical extension: in certain cases it may be supposed that where a statement appears to be incomplete the necessary completing words are to be understood from another, parallel, context which is complete; such a completion may be taken only from the immediate context—if other, unconnected, words intervene the extension is impermissible. The first of these three principles formed the basis of various later attempts at more precise definitions of the sentence.

Sūtra I.3.33 is interpreted by the school to state that words denote classes (*ākṛti*, 'type', is the term appearing in the *Sūtra*) rather than individual objects, or at least that they denote primarily classes and the individual members of the classes only indirectly. The reason given in the *Sūtra* is that the meanings relate to actions (the Vedic texts are all supposed to refer to actions, the *Veda* being in principle a set of injunctions; therefore presumably the meanings of words always relate to 'types' or norms as general principles and not to any particular thing or occasion).

It is noteworthy that the *Sūtra* in stating the reason for anything (as in I.3.33 just referred to) uses as a kind of shorthand formulation the ablative case. Afterwards among logicians this became the conventional formulation for an inference. The impression given is that 'Jaimini' immediately preceded the period of this more restricted logical usage, an impression strengthened by other loose anticipations of logical terminology as standardised for all schools from about the 1st century B.C. or 1st century A.D. onwards (the use of *liṅga* in a non-logical sense has been noted above; the term *anumāna*, standard for 'inference', is used in I.3.3 for the 'inference' of a lost Vedic text from a statement in a secondary authority).

The Sāṃkhya system of Vārṣagaṇya appears to have originated in about the 2nd century B.C. (the sources for it include the *Śvetāśvatara Upaniṣad* and Aśvaghoṣa's *Buddhacarita* XII, see Johnston, *Early Sāṁkhya*, pp. 8-10, 78, 82ff., etc.). In it the 24 physical 'realities' (cf. X above) are classified as either 'primary' (*prakṛti*, 'original', 'natural') or 'secondary' (*vikāra*, 'derived', 'transformed'), eight of the former and sixteen of the latter. This idea may be compared with the Buddhist distinction of primary and secondary matter (see XIV above). The realities are the same as in the system believed to be Pañcaśikha's, except that the 'great self' is replaced by 'self-consciousness' (*ahaṃkāra*, 'egoism'). Perhaps the intention here was to distinguish more clearly between this physical reality and the soul (*puruṣa*, 'man'). The eight primary physical realities are the unmanifest, consciousness, self-consciousness (egoism) and the five elements (including space). The derivatives are mind, the senses and faculties and the sense objects.

Knowledge of the system, which leads to a state of 'goodness' (*sattva*), is opposed to a fivefold ignorance (*avidyā*) which causes the attachment of the soul to physical reality. The five kinds of ignorance are called 'darkness' (*tamas*), 'delusion' (*moha*), 'great delusion' (*mahāmoha*) and the twofold 'darkness' (*tāmisra*). Here the first darkness is lassitude, delusion is death and birth, great delusion is passion (*kāma*, or pleasure) and the twofold darkness is anger and despair. Thus we are offered a way to freedom (of 'man') which resembles in important respects that taught by the Buddha.

The system is atheistic: the psychical side of reality consists simply of the souls and there is no supreme being, though the souls appear to include the gods mentioned in Vedic tradition (the Mīmāṃsā likewise was atheistic though accepting the gods of the sacrifice as described in the *Veda*). Thus it is said that the 'ignorant' Prajāpati (creator-god in the *Veda*) produced the material universe, whereas the enlightened Kapila (founder of Sāṃkhya) taught the way to freedom. In other words the creator-god was an ignorant soul who perpetrated evil, promoting unhappiness, whilst an enlightened man upheld goodness in contrast to this (*Buddhacarita* XII. 21).

Vārṣagaṇya, or his school, is quoted (*Abhidharma Kośa* V: see Stcherbatsky, *Central Conception of Buddhism*, p. 89, for a translation of the relevant passage from the Tibetan version) for the celebrated doctrine that 'there is neither production of something new nor extinction of something existent: what exists is always existent, what does not exist will never become existent'. This was developed among the Sāṃkhyas into the theory that effects are already present in their causes (*satkāryavāda*), in other words that effects are the same as their causes. In a sense this doctrine may be said to go back to Uddālaka (there must always have been 'being'). The idea that existence implies always existing, being eternal, was very influential in ancient Indian philosophy, and we find that in order to avoid the possibility of having to accept that there was anything eternal the Buddhists rejected the conception that principles really 'existed' (see VIII above). This Sāṃkhya doctrine helps to explain the Buddhist position.

XVI VAIŚEṢIKA

The origin of the Vaiśeṣika school is very obscure, since the only ancient text extant is the *Vaiśeṣika Sūtra* ascribed to Kaṇāda, which presents the system already fully elaborated and has no very evident affinities to any known earlier philosophical doctrines. Possibly the school had no earlier history but was brought into being by a single philosopher in the form we find in this *Sūtra*. The silence of the Buddhist poet Aśvaghoṣa (1st century A.D.) about the system has been supposed to indicate that it could not have been in existence much before his time, since he was interested in philosophy and discusses several other schools. However, the mere absence of evidence from an ancient period from which relatively little has survived is not a very strong argument. There is thus a possibility that the 'Yoga' philosophy referred to (but not explained) by Kauṭalya (see XI above) was a forerunner of the Vaiśeṣika of Kaṇāda, since 'Yoga' is known as an old name for the Vaiśeṣika school. On account of certain affinities of terminology it may be supposed that the *Vaiśeṣika Sūtra* is not too remote in date from the *Mīmāṃsā Sūtra*, though this does not take us very far. Perhaps also we can say that it is later than the references to philosophical discussions about categories, inference, etc., in Patañjali's *Mahābhāṣya* (2nd century B.C.), though not much later. Those fragmentary discussions might show us a phase of development between the 'Yoga' known to Kauṭalya (perhaps a methodology of predication and categories) and the Vaiśeṣika of Kaṇāda, within a single school of philosophers.

As if in deliberate opposition to the *Mīmāṃsā Sūtra*, the *Vaiśeṣika Sūtra* begins by proposing to explain *dharma*. It appears, however, to understand *dharma* in a rather different sense (when the school became more orthodox later on, the tendency was to reconcile the Vaiśeṣika to the Vedic tradition as far as possible: here we seek to interpret the text in a more straightforward way, without straining the meanings, which are in fact very much clearer than those of the *Mīmāṃsā Sūtra*). The meaning of *dharma* in this context, in view of what follows, appears to be 'quality' (by extension from 'virtue', perhaps with the added sense of 'good' quality). *Dharma* is here defined as that which brings about 'exaltation' (*abhyudaya*) and the 'supreme good' (*niḥśreyasa*, 'than which nothing is better'). 'Exaltation' is interpreted to mean heaven and the 'supreme good' to mean release from transmigration. The *Sūtra* adds that any authority (*prāmāṇya*) attaching to tradition (*āmnāya*, supposed by the later school to mean specifically the *Veda*) results from its being an expression of that (*dharma*). In other words, then, the *Veda* has no independent authority and the real authority is this *dharma*, the nature of which is now going to be explained. The supreme good is next said to result from the knowledge (*jñāna*) of reality (*tattva*) through agreement (*sādharmya*, similar quality) and difference (*vaidharmya*, different quality) among the categories, the knowledge resulting from the discrimination (*viśeṣa*) of qualities (*dharma*; this last clause has also been translated 'resulting from a special quality', in order further to strain it into a more Vedic meaning of *dharma*, but that does not seem appropriate here). (This *sūtra* I.1.4 is not found in the text from Kerala edited by Anantalal Thakur.) As in the case of the Sāṃkhya and Buddhism, it is made clear here that it is the knowledge of reality which enables one to attain whatever good one seeks, and it seems to be specified that it is the 'qualities' (*dharmas*) of reality which make the attainment of the supreme good possible, when they are discriminated. The investigation is to proceed through the inductive methods of agreement and difference among the qualities of things. The 'categories' (*padārthas*, 'objects of words', classes of object to which words refer) are here specified as substance (*dravya*), quality (*guṇa*, here 'quality' in the restricted sense of features such as colour found in the substances, whereas the more general *dharmas* which may be found in entire categories include 'existence', being causes or effects, being eternal or non-eternal, etc.), action (*karman*), universal (*sāmānya*), particular (*viśeṣa*) and combination (*samavāya*).

The *Sūtra* goes on to list the substances, qualities, etc., and to discuss their agreements and differences. Before studying these, however, it may be useful to look at some later parts of the text which further clarify the methodology and the theory of knowledge of Kaṇāda. Two means of knowledge are noted (X.1.3), sensation (*pratyakṣa*) and inference (*laiṅgika*, i.e. through a 'characteristic', *liṅga*, serving as middle term to establish the presence of something else which it characterises, and in the absence of which the characteristic cannot appear). These two means of knowing belong to a quality (*guṇa*) in the Vaiśeṣika system, namely 'consciousness' (*buddhi*, which is a quality of the substance 'soul', *ātman*). Sensation is a sufficient means to establish the reality of some objects (e.g. substances such as 'earth' and qualities such as 'colour'), but there are others which cannot be sensed (e.g. 'soul') but, according to Vaiśeṣika doctrine, whose reality can be established by inference. Inference is based on certain relations (*sambandhas*), namely effect (*kārya*), cause (*kāraṇa*), conjunction (*saṃyoga*), contradiction (*virodha*) and combination (*samavāya*) (IX.2.1f). Elsewhere (III.1.9) 'co-combination' (*ekārthasamavāya*, i.e. 'combination (of two things) in the same object') is added as another relation used in inference. These relations provide us with characteristics (*liṅgas* or *apadeśas*, 'citations') through which inferences can be made. *Liṅga* can thus be translated 'middle term', with the understanding that 'term' here is used in a rather loose sense referring to objects argued about as well as (its strict sense) the words used in a formal argument. The Vaiśeṣika is a system of induction, not a formal logic of deduction such as grew in the *Abhidharma* debates of the Buddhists. The basis of inference is stated as 'this of this' (*asya idam*), the genitive or possessive 'of' indicating relation (IX.2.1). As a stock example Kaṇāda gives the *liṅga*, characteristic, of cattle (the Indian variety) as 'horns, a hump, a tail with hairs at the end and a dewlap'. Apparently all these features are necessary together. If we sense this 'characteristic' in some animal, then by the knowledge of the relation that it constitutes the characteristic 'of' cattle we are able to infer that the animal before us belongs to that class (II.1.8). By applying our knowledge of this relation as learned through such examples, we are able, according to Kaṇāda, to ascertain less obvious facts about reality. Thus it can be established that 'air' is a substance, and an independent substance (separate from the other known substances), because it has its own 'characteristic': it has touch (can be felt) but is invisible (II.1.9ff.)—and there is no other substance which has just this 'characteristic', yet it must be some substance because it has quality (touch) and action but is found separately from other substances. In this case therefore the inductive method establishes the existence of something which according to Kaṇāda cannot be directly sensed, we are able to push our knowledge of reality beyond the limits of sensation.

Evidently mistakes are possible in attempting such inductions, and Kaṇāda has something to say about false characteristics (*anapadeśa*, non-characteristic), a doctrine out of which was developed the later theory of logical fallacies (III.1.3ff.). Kaṇāda gives two kinds of false characteristic (if we ignore what are probably misinterpretations): 'not being' (*asant*) and 'doubtful' (*sandigdha*) (III.1.15). The not-being is something not related at all to the thing supposed to be characterised, non-existent in it, for example 'horns' would be a false characteristic of horses. The doubtful is something related to the thing in question, but not adequate to establish the presence of just that thing, for example 'horns' (alone) as characteristic of cattle (other kinds of animal have horns, so we remain in doubt unless we can see the complete 'characteristic' of cattle as mentioned above). Such false characteristics clearly are mistakes in the method of agreement and difference, which requires us to establish precisely the distinctive (characteristic) features among the various classes of object studied.

The notion of causality is very important in the *Vaiśeṣika Sūtra* and there are some further statements and definitions connected with it which form part of the methodological basis of the system. The nature of the causal relation is defined as follows (with a view to its application in induction):

(1) From the non-existence of the cause we can infer the non-existence of the effect. (2) But from the non-existence of the effect we cannot infer the non-existence of the cause (I.2.1f.). The relation is explained further as of different kinds and is analysed under the category 'combination' and the quality 'conjunction' (*saṃyoga*). Combination is defined (VII.2.26) as that by which one has the notion (or infers) 'this is in this' (*ihedam*, or 'this is here' or 'it is this in this case') from (their being) cause and effect (i.e. this effect in this cause). 'Combination' is in fact a rather wide notion covering the relation between a whole and its parts, between qualities and their substances, etc. (the Lokāyata had used it earlier for the combination of the four elements to form everything). Contrasting with combination, which covers such cases of complete fusion as chemical com-

pounds, 'conjunction' covers the case of physical collision or mixture, resulting from action, in which no intrinsic change takes place (it may be followed by 'disjunction', *vibhāga,* also a quality and also produced by action). Combination and conjunction may operate independently as causes or they may operate together, so that we get a dependent cause; there can also be double combination (co-combination, two combinations combined). Thus the *Sūtra* speaks of 'combinative causes' (*samavāyikāraṇa*), such as a substance as combinative cause of its qualities, or atoms as combinative causes of substances. A quality cannot be a combinative cause (it cannot possess another quality, for instance) but it may serve as a dependent (*sāpekṣa*) cause through conjunction with another quality, though there must also be an action to produce the conjunction (action is an independent, *anapekṣa,* cause of conjunction).

One final item in the methodology of induction in the *Sūtra* is the method of 'exhaustion' (*pariśeṣa*), i.e. when all other possibilities seem to be exhausted the remaining one may be accepted as the correct conclusion (II.1.27).

In the actual construction of its system the *Sūtra* applies the methodology of agreement and difference and other parts of the theory of induction we have just studied. Beginning with the categories (I.1.8ff.) it states that the first three of these, substance, quality and action, agree in 'being' (*sant*), in being impermanent (*anitya*; in the case of substances, only their constituent atoms are held to be eternal or permanent), in possessing substance (as their combinative cause) and in being either effects or causes and either universals or particulars. They are different in that (1) substances possess actions and qualities and are combinative causes (and can be causes of other substances, whilst further they do not destroy one another in the causal process); (2) qualities are dependent on (*āśrayin*) substances, do not possess (other) qualities, do not cause conjunction or disjunction and may be destroyed in the causal process; (3) actions have one substance (at a time), do not possess qualities, are independent causes of conjunction and disjunction, do not cause other actions but do produce inertia (*vega,* 'impulse', in I.1.20 presumably = *saṃskāra,* 'inertia', a quality, in V.1.17f., the latter being the standard term in the system afterwards), which in turn produces a further action, which in turn produces a further inertia, and so on until the movement is checked by an obstacle or by gravity (the latter takes over when the action is not strong enough to produce further inertia, and causes falling) and they are destroyed by their effects (thus actions produce only the three qualities conjunction, disjunction and inertia).

The categories universal and particular agree in being dependent on (the quality) consciousness (I.2.3)—which presumably distinguishes them from the first three categories—but (may presumably be distinguished in that) 'existence' (*bhāva*) is only a universal, because it is the cause of repetition (*anuvṛtti*, repeated occurrence in time, extension, permanence), whilst there are on the other hand ultimate particulars (*antya viśeṣas*, which cannot be universals); everything in between, such as 'substanceness', 'qualityness' and 'actionness', may be either universal or particular (depending on whether they are considered as members of higher classes or as classes of lower members). 'Existence' (a universal) is that by which one has the notion (or infers) 'being' (*sant*) with reference to substances, qualities and actions: it is a different object (category) from these three because it cannot be 'either universal or particular' (but only universal), also it is not a quality or action because it exists in both these (these have existence, but a quality cannot exist in another quality nor an action in another action).

The final category, combination, has been defined above in relation to causality. As in the case of 'existence' it is a different category from substance and quality (etc.). It is a reality (*tattva*) because of existence (*bhāva*). These last two statements are too laconic and therefore most obscure: disregarding the school (i.e. the much later school alone known to us, which is notorious for reading all sorts of extraordinary interpretations into the *Sūtra*) we may conjecture that (1) combination can be distinguished from substance, quality and action in that it is relations between these and not one of them (or one substance) alone and (2) combination can be distinguished from universal and particular in that it is a reality objectively, independent of consciousness. (This explanation is pure conjecture.)

There are nine substances: earth, water, heat, air, space, time, position, soul and mind. These of course agree in having the nature of 'substance' as defined above; they are distinguished from one another by the different qualities they can have. The first four agree in having the quality 'touch', but only the first three have 'colour', the first two 'taste', and earth alone has 'smell' according to Kaṇāda (II.1.1ff.) (Other substances may appear to have smell only from an admixture of earth). Water has as characteristic that its touch is cold, in addition it has the qualities 'fluidity' and 'viscosity' (the latter is the adhesive quality which enables water to clean things). Heat has as characteristic that its touch is hot (evidently water and heat can be mixed and their characteristics confused). The characteristic of air is that its touch is invisible.

Space (*ākāśa*) lacks all these qualities but is supposed to have the quality 'sound', because this was believed not to be possessed by any other substance and to require the assumption of some special substance as a medium to carry it (hence some modern interpreters have preferred to translate it 'ether'). (Modern physics of course contradicts the Vaiśeṣika by demonstrating that sound is carried only by solid, liquid or gaseous matter, and thus up to a point supports the Mīmāṃsakas, who rejected the Vaiśeṣika theory and held that sound passes through the air.) In order to prove his notion of space having sound, Kaṇāda tries to apply the method of exhaustion, showing that sound does not belong to any of his other eight substances, space alone remaining as a possible home for it.

Various explanations of physical phenomena are given by the *Sūtra.* Thus the melting of metals when heated is described as conjunction with the substance heat. In the absence of conjunction with anything which would interfere with their movement, earth and water fall, because they have the quality 'gravity' (*gurutva,* or 'weight'). When heat is conjoined with water (e.g. the Sun's rays falling on it) there may occur also conjunction of that water with air, resulting in the action of 'rising' (overcoming gravity) (V.2.5).

The Vaiśeṣika is well known as having an atomic theory, but the references to atoms in the *Sūtra* are remarkably obscure and in some very important cases read into the text by commentators on the flimsiest assumptions concerning the implications of the actual words. It is inferred by commentators from, rather than stated in, IV.1 that there must be atoms to account for the persistence of superficially impermanent matter, these atoms being eternal and uncreated (but the text there does not mention atoms at all). On the other hand VII.1.8ff. discusses atoms (*aṇu* = 'minute', 'atomic') and if *parimaṇḍala*, the 'perfectly spherical', in VII.1.20 means the atom (it does later) the *Sūtra* says the atom is permanent. At the beginning of VII.1 we find that qualities are impermanent in the impermanent substances earth, water, etc., but permanent in what is permanent, which latter may mean the atoms of those same substances (but the reference may be to some other substances, which are eternal, as we shall see below). Between Kaṇāda and Praśastapāda (6th century) the Vaiśeṣikas worked out a detailed atomic theory, the material substances having impermanent (gross) and permanent (atomic) aspects, with a molecular theory of how the atoms combine to produce gross matter. According to Kaṇāda (V.2.13) the first actions of atoms are caused by an 'unseen' (*adṛṣṭa*). Presumably some invisible force starts the atoms in motion, or rather started them at the beginning of evolution. Later Vaiśeṣika writers have elaborated this hint into a doctrine that it is the presence of souls in the universe, with their moral qualities, which set up this force or tension, causing the universe to evolve and provide all the varied possibilities of experience which the souls deserve. When these deserts are exhausted the universe disintegrates into its separate atoms and the cycle of evolution ends. It does not seem possible to find out what Kaṇāda had in mind with reference to his 'unseen cause' (or perhaps causes). He invokes it (them) to account for several otherwise unexplained phenomena: magnetism (V.1.15), osmosis in trees (V.2.7), the (initial) upward movement of heat and sideways movement of air (V.2.13), the movement of a gem used in divination (V.1.15), the first action of mind (V.2.13), possibly earthquakes or at least otherwise unaccountable movements of earth (V.2.2) and various actions of living beings (V.2.17). In the absence of the unseen force there is liberation (*mokṣa*), which is the absence of conjunction and of any appearance (anything visible) (V.2.18).

On the other substances, Kaṇāda says that space (physical space, *ākāśa*) has sound as its uniform characteristic, and for this reason and because of 'existence' it is a reality. It is a substance, just as air is (because it does not have any other substance, i.e. as its combinative cause), and likewise it is eternal (for the same reason of having no cause). The statement that it is a reality is interpreted by the school to mean that it is one reality, there is only one space. There is however a following statement that space has 'one individuality', conformably to the uniformity of its characteristic (II.1.24-31). Space is inactive (V.2.21). It is infinite (VII.1.22).

The characteristics of time (*kāla*) are succession, simultaneity, long (time), quick. It is a substance, is eternal and a reality for analogous reasons to space (and air). It is spoken of with reference to causes because it exists in impermanent things but not in permanent (eternal) things (the latter have no causes) (II.2.6.9). It is inactive (V.2.21). It is explained (presumably defined or demarcated) by a cause (by causal processes in it) (V.2.26).

The characteristic of position (*diś*, mathematical space) is that it is that by which one has the notion (or infers) 'this is from here' (*ita idam*, i.e. a direction/distance from this place or origin). It is a substance, eternal and a reality, like the preceding substances, but is manifold because of the variety of its effects (unlike space). 'East', 'South', etc. are known from their conjunctions (at various times) with the Sun (II.2.10ff.). It is explained (defined or demarcated) by its qualities (which are farness, nearness, etc.) (V.2.25 and VII.2.21).

The existence of souls is known only by inference: by the study of sensation we are to infer the existence of something else besides the sense organs and their objects (III.1.2). From one's own experience, of the activity and inactivity of one's own soul, one can infer that others have souls too (since they show similar activity originating in the soul) (III.1.19). The characteristics of the soul, through which its presence can be inferred, are breathing, blinking, opening the eyes, life, the movement of the mind (the mind itself is another substance in the system, but its 'movement' from object to object is supposed to require the action of the soul), changes in the other senses, happiness, unhappiness, desire, aversion and effort (*prayatna*) (III.2.4). That the soul is a substance and is eternal is to be inferred in the same way as in the case of air, space, etc. (III.2.5). The soul is also infinite in space (VII. 1.22). Nevertheless there is a plurality of souls (III.2.20) because they depend on different bodies. Such statements as 'Devadatta goes' are due to 'transfer' (*upacāra*), i.e. metaphorical, since only his body goes (the soul being infinite cannot move: the body is simply moving round inside it) (III.2.12). The existence of the soul is not established by authority (*āgama*, scripture) but by induction (III.2.18).

Mind is atomic (*aṇu*), i.e. infinitesimal (VII.1.23), and is a substance and eternal (by inference, as in the case of air, etc., III.2.2). Its characteristic, through which it is inferred, is the existence or non-existence of knowledge (*jñāna*, or cognition) when the soul, a sense organ and a sense object are in contact (III.2.1). In other words there must be some further entity involved, since although the sense, the object and the soul may be in contact there still may be no knowledge arising if the mind is not present. Mind is necessary to account for the fact of attention, its absence explaining inattention. (The conception of mind as atomic explains this, since it may move from sense to sense and even not be present in more than one at a time, and it may be absent from all of them; the soul being infinite is always present, but is unaware of the senses and their objects unless the mind is in the right position.)

The qualities are initially listed as 17 in number, but others are mentioned later in the *Sūtra*, bringing the total up to 24. These two totals seem to represent two stages in the historical development of the system. The 17 are: colour, taste, smell, touch, number (*saṃkhyā*), magnitude (*parimāṇa*), individuality (*pṛthaktva*), conjunction, disjunction, farness (*paratva*), nearness (*aparatva*), consciousness (*buddhi*), happiness, unhappiness, desire (*icchā*), aversion (*dveṣa*) and effort (perhaps one might translate *prayatna* here instead as 'volition') (I.1.6). The absence of sound from this list is extraordinary and might lead one to think that at one time it was held to be a substance by the Vaiśeṣikas (as by the Mīmāṃsakas). We have seen above that elsewhere in the *Sūtra* it appears as the characteristic of space, and the school later takes it as a quality of space. Inertia (*saṃskāra*) also is essential to the system as expounded by the (complete) *Vaiśeṣika Sūtra* and has been referred to above. The other additional qualities are gravity (*gurutva*, or weight), fluidity (*dravatva*), viscosity (*snigdhatva*), all mentioned above, and 'good quality' (*dharma*, or simply 'goodness') and 'bad quality' (*adharma*, 'badness'), which are additional qualities of the soul (VI.2.14). In relation to these last two the *Sūtra* (in Book VI) develops an ethical theory, connected also with 'exaltation' and liberation.

The 'mathematical' qualities, number, magnitude and individuality, are treated like other qualities in substances. Thus magnitude plus colour in a substance makes its sensation possible (IV.1.6, if *mahant*, 'great', here is a synonym for magnitude). Number, magnitude and individuality are directly seen in substances having colour (IV.1.11). Cause and effect are not numerically one (VII.2.7), having one individuality.

Conjunction is produced by action or results secondarily from another conjunction, likewise disjunction (VII.2.9f.).

In connection with the quality consciousness the *Sūtra* discusses sensation and inference (i.e. the theory of knowledge) and also the categories universal, particular and combination (Books VIII and IX and the last statements of Book VII, i.e. between the accounts of nearness and happiness).

The actions are dealt with before the qualities, in Book V. There are five of them (initial statement in I.1.7): lifting (*utkṣepaṇa*), dropping (*avakṣepaṇa*), contracting (*ākuñcana*), expanding (*prasāraṇa*) and movement (*gamana*, meaning horizontal movement). Some of them are associated with particular substances: lifting with heat, movement with air. Dropping is caused by the quality gravity. To the points noted above about the nature of action (distinguishing it from other categories) it may be added that some further details are given in the Fifth Book. An action is communicated from one body to another by conjunction. There is reaction (*abhighāta*) between hard bodies causing action to be communicated, but mediated by conjunction (since actions do not directly produce one another, as stated above). The action of living beings is caused by the effort (volition) of and conjunction with the soul.

Although the other extant Vaiśeṣika works are much later than the *Sūtra*, there is evidence in other sources of a variety of developments in the early period. The most noteworthy of these sources is the medical work of Caraka (*c.* 100 A.D.), which is familiar with characteristic parts of the system, such as the six categories and the groups of qualities, 'ending with effort' (*prayatnānta*). However, Caraka knows many more 'qualities' than the standard 24, which perhaps were drawn from different schools within the Vaiśeṣika. It appears indeed that the definitive list of 24 is rather arbitrary, and since it is not presented as fixed in the *Sūtra* this limitation may not have been the original intention, which may have been merely to investigate some of the more important facts of nature without prejudice as to further studies (the Vaiśeṣika would then be a 'science' rather than a 'system', open rather than closed). The *Sūtra* has in its initial list qualities which may be grouped as related to the senses (colour, etc.), as mathematical (from number to nearness) and as psychological (from consciousness to effort). Another 'group' is represented only by scattered qualities mentioned later in the text (physical qualities: gravity, fluidity and viscosity; inertia probably belongs with conjunction among the 'mathematical' qualities). Caraka instead enumerates a group of 20 qualities beginning with gravity and including fluidity and viscosity but of which the other 17 are new (lightness, dryness, firmness, hardness, softness, etc.). Under 'farness, etc.', corresponding to the mathematical qualities, Caraka has a list containing the 7 from number to nearness, inertia and two new qualities: connection (*yukti*, perhaps grouping) and repetition. Caraka has the five psychological qualities, plus consciousness. If we add the five related to the senses, Caraka seems to have a list of 41 qualities, which may have been borrowed from a branch of the Vaiśeṣika (see Caraka I, 1.44ff., I.25. 35-6, I.26.10-1 and 29-35; Cf. I.22, etc.).

We shall see below that the Vaiśeṣika doctrine of inference was elaborated much further before the 2nd century A.D., and that the branch of the school which specialised in this study then became recognised as a separate school under the name Nyāya.

XVII FURTHER DEVELOPMENTS IN LOGIC AND EPISTEMOLOGY

In the period of the development of the Vaiśeṣika system the various other schools of Indian philosophy worked along partly similar lines, within their special theories. Something has been said above about the Buddhist schools (XIV, also XIII). We now have to examine some significant developments among the Jainas, Ājīvakas and Lokāyatikas from about the 1st century B.C. onwards.

The earliest Jaina texts do not give us much philosophy (IX above). For this we have to turn to a series of texts which are substantially later, though included by the Śvetāmbara school in its Canon, especially the *Sthānāṅga* (1st century B.C. or later), the *Bhagavatī* (=*Vyākhyāprajñapti*; somewhat later) and the *Uttarādhyayana* (later still). Probably about the same period as the *Uttarādhyayana* is the *Daśavaikālika*. The *Niryukti* on this by Bhadrabāhu (there were several Bhadrabāhus in Jaina history) is a commentary containing some interesting logical doctrines. Its date may be about 100 A.D. or later. (All these dates are guesses.)

The *Sthānāṅga* is perhaps the Jaina work nearest in style to the Buddhist *Abhidharma* literature and may therefore be contemporary with the latest *Abhidharma* texts examined above (XIV). It presents a theory of knowledge. Knowledge can be obtained in two ways, direct knowledge or sensation (*pratyakṣa*) and indirect knowledge or 'beyond sensation' (*parokṣa*, 'beyond the senses'). These may be compared with the sensation and inference of the Vaiśeṣikas. On the other hand there is a fourfold classification of the sources of knowledge: sensation, inference, similarity (*upamāna*) and authority (*āgama*, tradition or scripture, also the authority of recognised teachers). These are practically the same as those of the later Vaiśeṣika school called Nyāya (see XIX and XXI) and it has not been determined who first set out this list. These four sources, or rather means, of knowledge are called 'causes' (*hetus*, *sūtra* 338) or 'authorities' (*pramāṇas*, the usual later word for means of knowledge). (It may be noted that the Buddhist text **Upāyahṛdaya*—see XIX below—appears to use identical terminology, pp. 13-4; cf. also Caraka, *Vimāna* 8.33.)

The *Bhagavatī* elaborates the specifically Jaina doctrine of 'schemes' (*nayas*, see IX above). It gives seven of these (instead of the original two—but later Jaina writers say that the number is infinite). A thing may be considered from different points of view as (1) particular or individual (*naigama*), (2) a class or collection (*saṃgraha*), (3) the object of everyday usage (*vyavahāra*) or unphilosophical convention, (4) in its present modification (*ṛjusūtra*), (5) its name (*śabda*, the word for it), (6) the synonyms for its name (*samabhirūḍha*) and their precise meanings and (7) characterised by various characteristics (*evaṃbhūta*).

The *Uttarādhyayana* (Chapter 28) sets out a theory of categories which may be compared with that of the Vaiśeṣika, though it derives from earlier Jaina doctrine (the Jaina tradition in fact claims that the Vaiśeṣika was founded by a Jaina teacher named Rohagupta, who broke away and established a separate school in A.D. 18). There are only three categories (the word category, *padārtha*, does not actually appear in the text, however; later Jaina writers speak simply of *artha*, 'object' or 'meaning', in this connection: see e.g. Siddhasena Divākara in his *Sanmatitarkaprakaraṇa*): substance (*dravya*), quality (*guṇa*) and modification (*paryāya*)—which evidently are to be compared with the older Jaina theory of two schemes (*nayas*), substance and modification. Substances possess qualities and both substances and qualities have modifications. There are six substances, which are the old five 'substances which exist' (*astikāyas*), namely matter, soul, space, activity (*dharma*) and inactivity (see IX above), plus time. The universe consists of these. Activity, inactivity and space are one only, whereas time, matter and soul are infinite in number (the question whether time is one or many was much argued about in the later schools of Indian philosophy, the Vaiśeṣika school maintaining that it is one although their *Sūtra* does not seem to be clear on the point). The characteristics of activity and inactivity are movement and rest respectively. Those of space and time are to contain everything and duration (*vartanā*). That of matter is sound, darkness, radiance, light, shade, sunshine, colour, taste, smell and touch. That of soul is knowledge, happiness, unhappiness, conduct, asceticism, insight, energy, etc.

The qualities are not separately discussed, but are presumably the characteristics of substances given above. Modification on the other hand is explained as oneness, individuality, number, appearance, conjunction and disjunction. It thus appears that qualities characterise groups of things, classes, whereas modifications characterise individual things, make them appear as one distinct object. Later Jaina writers are not agreed on this, and some of them treat qualities and modifications as synonymous.

The *Uttarādhyayana* concludes (Chapter 36) with an elaborate cosmology, including a reference to atoms and their compounds.

Bhadrabāhu's *Niryukti* on the *Daśavavikālika* sets out a form of argument or proof to be used in debating. This is closer to the form used by the Nyāya school than to that of the *Kathāvatthu* (XIII above), and is given the same name (*vākya*, 'sentence'), but it consists of ten steps whereas the Nyāya has only five (both schools call the step *avayava*, 'member'). There is some evidence that the Nyāya arrived at their five steps by excluding some others which seemed superfluous, in other words that Bhadrabāhu's form of argument is an earlier one (the *Kathāvatthu* form had many more steps than this and was also very different in content; it would appear that the argument or proof was gradually reduced to its logical essentials). Bhadrabāhu's form is:

1. proposition (statement to be proved), *pratijñā*,
2. delimitation of the proposition, *pratijñāvibhakti*,
3. 'cause' (reason or middle term proving the proposition), *hetu*,
4. delimitation of the 'cause', *hetuvibhakti*,
5. counter thesis, *vipakṣa*,
6. exclusion of the counter thesis, *vipakṣapratiṣedha*,
7. example (which exemplifies the major premise), *dṛṣṭānta*,
8. doubt (questioning the validity of the example), *āśaṅkā*,
9. exclusion of the doubt, *āśaṅkāpratiṣedha*,
10. conclusion, *nigamana*.

Underlying this demonstration there is an argument of the 'syllogism' type: the third step in effect provides the minor premise, that the subject of the proposition to be proved is characterised by the middle term; the seventh step indicates the major premise, that the middle term is in turn characterised by the predicate of the proposition to be proved, though it does so by exemplifying the relation (is thus 'inductive').

There is not much evidence for the development of Ājīvaka philosophy. A Tamil source, the *Maṇimēkalai*, of about the 6th century, gives incidentally an account of the fully developed Ājīvaka atomic theory. The date when this was worked out can only be guessed at present. It does not seem to have been part of the original theory of Kakuda (see VII above), though he provided the basis for it by postulating atomic (uncuttable) elements, but may have been elaborated in the school at any time after him. It seems likely that the Ājīvakas pioneered the theory of atoms and their combinations, and that the Jainas, Vaiśeṣikas and Buddhists borrowed and adapted the conception from them, with successive additions as it developed further. The direction of the development has been indicated above. The *Maṇimēkalai* specifies that the atoms are of four kinds (presumably the four physical elements), plus souls, happiness and unhappiness (this would seem to be the same as saying that there are seven kinds of atom). The atoms are invisible, but when they combine the four physical kinds can be perceived by the soul. These combinations are of various kinds: thus diamond is a very close combination of atoms, bamboo a loose one. The ratios of combination are fixed according to the 'name' (presumably of the element earth, etc.). Another (later) Tamil text, the *Civañāṉacittiyār,* elucidates this a little by saying that 'earth' consists of molecules made of four earth atoms, three water atoms, two heat atoms and one air atom. Presumably the other three 'names' (the combined or visible elements, which perhaps were thought of as existing in name only, since the atoms are not in fact changed when combined—cf. Kakuda's doctrine) have other ratios, with different atoms predominating (or possibly simply successively dropping the first group). (The Buddhists have a similar theory that the elements are not found in a 'pure' state but only as molecules of this kind—Sthaviravāda school, see XIV above, the other schools seem to have agreed—though the Buddhists seem to be speaking of properties of matter and certainly not of eternal atoms.) The *Maṇimēkalai* notes the properties or characteristics of the atoms: earth is hard and has gravity or downward tendency, water is cold and also has gravity, heat burns and has rising tendency, air has horizontal movement (cf.

Kaṇāda, XVI). Another later Tamil text, the *Nīlakēci*, adds that earth has all the sense qualities except sound (this also agrees with Kaṇāda), sound apparently being a quality of air only (contrary to Kaṇāda). The *Civañāṉacittiyār* explains that the horizontal movement of the air atom holds the molecule together by checking the downward or upward tendencies of the others, this also holds the soul in combination with the body. On 'name'=organisation see p. 19.

The Lokāyata during this period is of great importance for developing a critique of the theories of inference expounded by other schools. From this time on the school is frequently called the Cārvākas, or followers of Cārvāka. Cārvāka is supposed to have been a pupil of Bṛhaspati who spread his teaching in the world. He appears in the Epic (*Mahābhārata*) and reproaches Yudhiṣṭhira for having killed his kinsmen in the war of succession (this would place him in about the 10th century B.C.). Whether there was such a person in history or not, it seems that some later Lokāyata text was circulated under his name. This text has not been preserved but references in the works of other schools tell us a little of the 'Cārvāka' doctrine. In part this is simply a restatement of the views maintained in the *Lokāyata Sūtra*, but there are new developments in response to the arguments of other schools. The *Sarvadarśanasaṃgraha* presents the Lokāyata doctrine under the name of Cārvāka, 'Bṛhaspati's follower', with pleasure (*kāma*) as the aim of life, and concludes with the statement that in kindness to all living beings we should resort to Cārvāka's teaching.

This Cārvāka doctrine had developed a theory of knowledge as the basis of its position and of its criticism of the Brahmanical (Vaiśeṣika, Mīmāṃsā, etc.), Buddhist and other schools. There is only one means of knowledge: sensation. No other means can be accepted. Inference by definition is knowledge through some characteristic, or middle term, known to be present in the subject of the inference and also known to be invariably related to the predicate to be inferred (if we observe the characteristic we are supposed to be able to infer the existence of the predicate although we cannot sense it). But how is it to be known that the characteristic is invariably related to the predicate? This invariable concomitance cannot be known by sensation because it is not possible to sense all cases of the relation, for example cases in the past and future cannot be sensed now. Thus even in the stock illustration of inference, where the characteristic is 'smoke' and the predicate is 'fire', although we may see many cases of smoke related to fire, this does not enable us to claim that we 'know' that smoke is always related to fire, since there are so many cases which we have not been able to inspect (we cannot 'know' through sensation that there are not cases of smoke unrelated to fire). But equally the invariable concomitance cannot be known by any other means. It cannot be known by inference itself, for this would involve setting up some second inference to prove the first, and that would require a further inference to prove that, and so on in an endless regression which would never establish any conclusion. Authority also is rejected, since we have no reason to believe another's statement just because it is a statement of some person. 'Similarity' (which means identification of a predicate through comparing it with something familiar which resembles it but which is distinguished in stated ways) cannot help since it is only intended to relate a name to some object and can tell us nothing about any invariable concomitance. In fact an invariable concomitance cannot be known, so that there is no possibility of knowing anything through inference. If even the existence of sensible objects such as fire cannot be established in such cases (where it is not directly sensed), there is absolutely no way of establishing the existence of unseen entities, which are admittedly never sensed and are maintained purely on the basis of supposed inferences. If other schools argue that at least it can be inferred that some cause exists or existed for the way things now are, although it cannot be sensed, Cārvāka contends that on the contrary we can only say that things are what they are by their own-being (following the old Lokāyata)—it is their nature to be so and there is nothing to be inferred beyond that.

More details of what is probably the Cārvāka critique of inference are found in Jayanta's *Nyāyamañjarī* (pp. 119f.). Those who use invariable concomitance as a basis for inference may try to establish it by way of 'universals' (*sāmānyas*). These universals, however, are not realities (*vāstavas*), they do not exist at all. Moreover it is not possible to sense all cases of smoke and fire and thus to eliminate any doubt that there could be a contrary case, of smoke without fire. If it were possible and all cases were sensed, then any inference would be redundant since its conclusion would be known already by sensation. It is not conclusive to observe a large number of cases (*bhūyodarśana*) and say that there is invariable concomitance between the middle term ('cause' or characteristic) and the predicate. The properties of things vary according to place, time, circumstance, etc., so that one cannot establish a regular (*niyama*, regularity, rule; necessary) invariable concomitance (*avinābhāva*, 'not existing without'). Thus the method of agreement does not establish a regularity (necessity) as a basis for inference. Likewise the method of difference, attempting to establish, for instance, that wherever there is no fire there is no smoke, is not feasible (who could examine all places in the universe where there is no fire?).

A famous illustration of the unreliability, and moreover the deceitfulness, of inference as used by metaphysicians is the 'footprints of a wolf' (*vṛkapada*), cited for example by Candrakīrti (*Madhyamakāvatāra* p. 210) and by Haribhadra (*Ṣaḍdarśanasamuccaya* 81). A Cārvāka philosopher with his lady faked the footprints of a wolf in the dust on a road, learned men afterwards inferred from seeing them that a wolf had come to the village and through this he showed her that inference is not to be trusted, for example the supposed inference that there is another world.

According to Jayanta there were two schools of Cārvākas, the Dhūrta Cārvākas ('Rogue Cārvākas') and Suśikṣita Cārvākas ('Cultivated Cārvākas'). These perhaps correspond to two different commentaries on the *Lokāyata Sūtra* referred to by Kamalaśīla. In fact their antecedents can be seen as early as the Pali *Dīgha Nikāya* (Vol. I p. 34) in a discussion of various forms of the 'annihilationist' doctrine concerning the 'self' or soul. In this doctrine there is no survival of a soul after death, but during life there is a 'self' (*ātman*) or even more 'selves' than one. One view is that this 'self' is purely physical, a compound of the four elements. Others are that there is in addition some kind of spiritual 'self', made of 'divine' matter, or made of mind (immaterial), though this too is annihilated at death. The first view would seem to be closest to that of Ajita and Bṛhaspati (that consciousness is simply a property of the body as compound of the four elements). One later school, presumably the Rogue Cārvākas, maintained this position strictly, that there is no such entity as a soul, even temporarily, but only the four elements compounded as the body. The

Cultivated Cārvākas on the other hand, according to Jayanta (*Nyāyamañjarī* p. 467), maintained that there is a real entity (*tattva,* reality) which knows (*pramātṛ,* the knowing subject), which persists as long as the body lives and is destroyed at death, there being no transmigration or future life. This resembles the other kind of view.

The Rogue Cārvākas, according to the *Nyāyamañjarī* (p. 64), in due course produced a comprehensive critique of the Nyāya scheme of categories (see XXI below), namely means of knowledge, objects of knowledge, etc., maintaining that it is not possible to construct such a scheme. The most comprehensive critique of all, covering all the principles of all systems, is that of Jayarāśi, the *Tattvopaplavasiṃha,* the only Lokāyata work known to be extant, which apparently was written in about the 8th century A.D. According to Jayarāśi even the four elements propounded by Bṛhaspati cannot be philosophically established as 'realities' *tattvas,* do not stand critical examination, being accepted only at the level of popular thinking, still less can any other, more metaphysical, 'realities' be established—Bṛhaspati's purpose was not to set up the four elements as 'realities', but only by reflecting the popular conception to show people how to think critically. Jayarāśi's total scepticism regarding philosophy seems to represent an extreme Rogue Cārvāka view.

A Cārvāka writer named Purandara (whose date is not known except that he lived before the 8th century A.D.), on the other hand, proposed to accept inference to a limited extent, with respect to this-worldly matters only and absolutely excluding any possibility of 'inferring' anything about anything beyond the world of experience (Kamalaśīla, introducing *Tattvasaṃgraha* No. 1482). This perhaps is a 'Cultivated' view. Purandara is also quoted by a Jaina writer (Vādideva, *Syādvādaratnākara* II.131) as holding that it is difficult to attain certainty about any object through inference, which is secondary (*gauṇa*), i.e. indirect. It is not proper to extend inference to any object beyond the senses (*parokṣa*), because there is no knowledge of invariable concomitance (*avyabhicāra*) in such a case (this may be possible in this-worldly inference, where it is controlled by the possibility of sensation, but cannot be valid for the entities inferred in metaphysical systems, where there can be no evidence of invariable concomitance among them). Gaṅgeśa in the *Tattvacintāmaṇi,* introducing the criticisms which had been made of inference, suggests that the critique amounts to saying that inference is a matter of probability (*sambhāvana*) only, based on a large number of observations. Sensation makes the conclusion probable, though never certain, but inference as such adds nothing to this knowledge from sensation and is therefore not a separate means of knowledge. It does not seem clear whether Purandara or any other Cārvāka writer actually developed a doctrine of probability, though such a doctrine would be implicit in Purandara's known views.

XVIII MAHĀYĀNA BUDDHISM

The Mahāyāna movement in Buddhism appears to have originated in South India, more precisely in the Āndhra country, in the 1st century A.D. (or perhaps at the end of the 1st century B.C.). It developed out of one of the schools into which the Mahāsaṅghika school (see XIV above) had by that time become divided, namely the Pūrva Śaila school. As noted above, the tendency of the Mahāsaṅghikas was to downgrade the 'perfect one' (*arhant*), the successful follower of the Buddha, leaving the Buddha only as the ideal, even supernatural, figure. This tendency was carried so far, in the course of time, that eventually the aim of becoming an *arhant* began to appear worthless. Instead, the possibility of becoming a *buddha* began to be taken quite seriously as an aim for any really earnest Buddhist. The Buddha was never looked upon as unique: there had been others in past ages, according to legend, and there should be more in the remote future, to restore Buddhism in the world after it had disappeared. Moreover this is not the only 'world': it was believed that there were countless other worlds among the stars. Consequently the need for *buddhas* in the universe could hardly be satisfied even if many Buddhists attempted this extremely difficult feat. The way in which the Buddha had become a *buddha* was described in the ancient Buddhist texts. Amongst others, the *Jātaka* collection purported to describe many of his former lives, showing how he had gradually perfected in himself the virtues and powers needed to perform the feat of attaining enlightenment and establishing Buddhism in the world. This description was generally accepted by all the ancient schools. The basic idea of the Mahāyāna was to take this description and turn it into a prescription: just as the future Buddha had become a *bodhisattva*, a being seeking enlightenment (i.e. to attain enlightenment as a *buddha*), so all real Buddhists ought to do the same thing, become *bodhisattvas* with the declared aim of becoming *buddhas* after many lives in which they would perfect themselves for this ideal. This meant that they would abstain from attaining complete detachment and *nirvāṇa*, as *arhants*, which would cut short their activity in the world and thus cut short their benevolent actions helping other beings, above all would eliminate the possibility of the supremely benevolent act of being a *buddha* establishing the teaching. The way of the *arhant* came to be regarded as the easy way out. One should remain in the world out of compassion for living beings, inspired by the thought of enlightenment (*bodhicitta*), i.e. of becoming a *buddha*. Progress on the way of the *bodhisattva* was partly through moral practice, partly through philosophical understanding. It consisted primarily in fulfilling six 'perfections' (*pāramitās*): generosity, virtue, tolerance, energy, meditation and understanding. Understanding (*prajñā*) was generally looked upon as the most important of these, and in the new *sūtras* (all supposed to have been spoken by the Buddha himself) which the Mahāyānists composed a new philosophical trend was developed, which was intended to supersede the original teaching, or at least to give it an interpretation conformable to Mahāyāna ideas, and especially to supersede the *Abhidharma* systems of the ancient schools. The actual perfections, etc., were not new.

After some early Mahāyāna *sūtras* expressing the *bodhisattva* ideal, moral progress on the way to becoming a *buddha* and some of the new philosophical ideas, a much more extensive *sūtra* was elaborated (it actually exists in several different recensions) under the title 'Perfection of Understanding' (*Prajñāpāramitā*), i.e. the sixth of the perfections of the *bodhisattva*, which sets out the new ideas very fully (though not very systematically). We may follow the 'Eight Thousand' (*Aṣṭasāhasrikā*) recension of this *sūtra*, as probably the oldest available.

The earliest Mahāyāna *sūtras* had already stressed the original Buddhist view that there are no 'beings' (souls, 'persons', or any synonym), but whereas original Buddhism looked upon the principles (*dharmas*) as real, though transient (contrasting them with 'souls'), the new movement began to circulate the idea that there are no principles either. More precisely, the new *sūtras* said that all principles are 'empty' (*śūnya*). Now, in original Buddhism and in the ancient schools the idea is that all principles are empty of any soul, of any enduring entity or substance. The Mahāyāna proceeds to press this to the position that principles are totally 'empty', have ultimately no reality of any kind. They are no more real than the supposed souls or persons of the ancient controversies.

The 'Perfection of Understanding' *Sūtra* elaborates this Mahāyānist trend as follows:

(1) What principle is designated by '*bodhisattva*'? —None! But anyone who does not despair at this thought is surely a *bodhisattva*! He should not 'flatter himself' with the thought of enlightenment (i.e. of becoming a *buddha*), because that thought is non-thought. The nature of thought is perfectly translucent (clear).

(2) Does this thought which is 'non-thought' exist? This cannot be said, but it can be said that non-thoughtness is non-changing, non-imagining.

(3) All principles are without 'own-being' (contrary to the position by this time of many of the early schools, which defined principles as having distinct own-beings).

(4) All principles are 'not produced' (*ajāta*).

(5) Beings, and also principles, are not what they seem. They are based on artifice or trickery (*māyā*), like a puppet show or a painting or a clay model. Therefore no being attains omniscience (enlightenment is now understood to imply omniscience) or extinction (*nirvāṇa*).

(6) Principles are completely 'separate' (from any characteristics or own-beings), therefore neither 'It is' nor 'It is not' applies to them.

(7) The impermanence of principles should not be misunderstood as the 'destruction' (annihilation) of principles (as a real destruction of previously existing principles).

What is entirely new, as contrasted with earlier Buddhism, is the speaking of principles (*dharmas*) in the same way as 'beings' (*sattvas*, equivalent to persons or souls). The non-origination of all principles means that they are not (really) principles: there are now said to be no principles which occur or cease. When one has the perfection of understanding one does not perceive 'principles' (i.e. the *bodhisattva* who attains that perfection no longer sees principles: this relates the philosophical outlook to the progress on the way of the *bodhisattva*, and explains why the *arhants* of the ancient schools still believed in principles). The *sūtras* speak of the 'thusness' (*tathatā*) of all principles (instead of their origination, etc.—the reference is to Mahāyāna *sūtras*, of course). This thusness is one thusness and not a duality. It is not made, not originating, etc. It is even a thusness of nothing at all. (Yet conditioned origination is not here denied, but only said to be 'profound'.)

These paradoxes (1, etc.) have frequently been misunderstood and misinterpreted. The student of Buddhism will see here just a figure of speech. The Buddha when speaking 'philosophically' had said there is no person 'who' acts, etc., but only the event (pp. 51, 58 above). But in everyday language addressed to non-philosophers he spoke of persons doing things. The Mahāyāna *Sūtras* seem deliberately to exploit these two levels of speech by mixing them together, producing paradoxes which the student must resolve by giving the correct answers. Thus a *bodhisattva* is a person, not a principle. A conversation which starts thus at the 'concealing' level must immediately switch to the ultimate if the correct answers are given. This was later called 'empty conversation' (*Vimalakīrtinirdeśa* p. 219). But having eliminated this figurative language the question of the nature of the 'principles' remains.

XIX DEBATE AND LOGIC (CARAKA AND OTHERS)

Between the system of debating and logic found in Buddhist texts of the 3rd century B.C. onwards (*Kathāvatthu*, etc., see XIII above) and the next major sources for the development of these techniques there is something of a gap. The *Vaiśeṣika Sūtra* expounds rather a methodology of induction, but introduces the idea of inference through a characteristic or middle term (*liṅga*), not found in the earlier Buddhist texts but of central importance in all later systems of argument. The Jaina *Daśavaikālika Niryukti* (XVII above) gives a form of proof or demonstration, called simply a 'sentence' (*vākya*), which applies a middle term (here called *hetu*) in order to prove a given proposition or statement (*pratijñā*). The date of this text, however, is completely uncertain, though its long 'sentence' in ten steps (*avayavas*, 'members') may appear primitive relative to the form in only five steps regularly used later. The Vaiśeṣika school in about the 1st century A.D. threw off a branch, later called Nyāya, which specialised in the methods of debate, but its available texts begin only from the end of the 2nd century A.D. Representing methods of debating and demonstration at about A.D. 100, we have two other texts extant, of other schools but closely related in their general ideas (of debating as a kind of science or discipline common to most philosophers, rather than as a special doctrine of a school) to the Nyāya. These are the medical work of Caraka (already referred to at the end of XVI) and a Buddhist text (of one of the early schools, the Bahuśrutīya?) preserved only in a Chinese translation, of unknown authorship (the *Fang pien sin louen*, retranslated into Sanskrit by Tucci under the title **Upāyahṛdaya*, which apparently means something like 'Essentials of Method'—in debate).

The *Carakasaṃhitā* (III.8.27ff.) introduces the debate under the name *vāda* ('speech', 'discussion'; some of Caraka's ground here is covered by the term 'rhetoric'; already in the earliest Buddhist texts *vāda* is used for a debate or argument, as well as for the statement of a philosophical position, subsequently it is used for a school of philosophy). A *vāda* proper is in Caraka a constructive discussion guided by the laws of logic, as between members of the same school wishing to advance their philosophy. It is contrasted with two other kinds of debating, namely *jalpa*, 'dispute' between opposed schools, where the object is not to advance knowledge but to defeat the opponent (hence a debater may disregard logic if he can get away with it), and *vitaṇḍā*, 'eristic' or purely destructive sophistry where the sole object is to demolish the opponent regardless of the means used and without maintaining any position of one's own. (The difference between these two would appear to be one of degree only, moreover the terms tend to be applied differently by different schools, *vitaṇḍā* being a derogatory term for other people's methods of argument, especially when they involve severe criticism of one's own position: both the Lokāyata and the Buddhist Madhyamaka—XX below—were called *vitaṇḍā* schools by those they criticised, in attempts to discredit them.)

At public debates there was a chairman, who ought to be neutral, responsible for conducting the proceedings according to fixed conventions and for determining when a debater was defeated. There was also an audience, likely to contain partisans of the protagonists. Caraka warns his students (18ff.) to be careful before entering a debate to ascertain what kind of assembly it is likely to be, whether friendly, hostile or neutral. One should refuse to take part if the assembly is hostile. One should also consider the character of the opponent, his abilities and his weaknesses, before deciding whether to meet him and how to tackle him. Purely psychological attacks are recommended in some cases (this would seem to constitute the *jalpa* element), such as perplexing the opponent with tremendous quotations from *sūtras* or demoralising him through satire and jokes.

As in the early Buddhist debates, the thesis maintained by a protagonist is called a 'statement' (*pratijñā*). The argument or proof to establish it is called a *sthāpanā*, 'establishing' (this term also had been used by the Buddhists, but for the antecedent in a conditional—potential—argument, though this may be a statement being contested). The statement is established through a middle term (*hetu*) and the proof consists of five steps. The statement is the first step, and its predicate is repeated as the fifth or 'conclusion' (*nigamana*) with the addition of the word 'therefore'. The second step gives the middle term and the fourth, the 'application' (*upanaya*), states that the subject of the statement is qualified by the middle term (the early Buddhists used the terms *upanayana* and *nigamana* for two subsections in their scheme of argument: again the continuity of debating is shown but the conventions have been greatly modified). The central, third step is called the 'example' (*dṛṣṭānta*), and its function is to show that the middle term is qualified by the predicate of the statement. We can say that the 'example' supplies the 'major premise' for a deduction, linking the middle and major terms, whilst the 'application' provides the 'minor premise', linking the minor and middle terms. Thus the last three steps amount to a deduction of the statement from two premises. However, the proof is not simply a deduction: the 'example' brings in an inductive element, the induction of the major premise from examples. The other party to the debate will try to establish a contradictory statement through a different middle term and example, Caraka therefore sets out a 'counter-establishing' (*pratiṣṭhāpanā*), in exactly the same form. The resulting pair of establishings, each of five steps (but five identical steps, hence the pair does not resemble the ten steps of the *Daśavaikālika Niryukti*), may be compared with the old Buddhist (*Kathāvatthu*) pair of refutations where first the opponent appears to establish his statement but secondly the Sthaviravādin establishes its contradictory. The arrangement also corresponds to the procedure noted already by Kauṭalya of stating an opponent's view (*pūrvapakṣa*) first, followed by one's own view (*uttarapakṣa*). If we symbolise the terms in the demonstration to make its form clearer, using S for the subject, P for the predicate, M for the middle term, and M_1 for an example (of M being P), Caraka's five steps are as follows:

1. (To prove) S is P,
2. (We give as middle term) Because of M,
3. (Now) M_1 is M and it is also P,
4. And as M_1 so also S is M (and)
5. Therefore P.

The example M_1 is of course meant to point out that any examples of M, such as M_1, M_2, M_3 . . . M_n, which could be adduced would be evidently P, in other words that all M is P (the 'major premise'). If the opponent could adduce an example of M not being P the argument would at once be refuted and its protagonist declared defeated. (The middle term, step 2, is given in the ablative case, 'because of', as is done already in the *Vaiśeṣika Sūtra* in giving 'characteristics'.)

Caraka gives (31) the following illustration of this kind of argument; first the 'establishing':

1. 'Man' (*puruṣa*) is permanent (statement)
2. Because of not being created (*akṛtakatvāt*) (middle term)
3. Space is uncreated and it is permanent (example)
4. And as space so also man is uncreated (and) (application)
5. Therefore permanent (conclusion)

The 'counter-establishing' follows (32):

1. Man is impermanent
2. Because of being a sense-object
3. A pot is a sense-object and it is impermanent
4. And as a pot so also man is a sense-object
5. Therefore impermanent.

Caraka adds that (33) the middle term may be derived from sensation, inference, tradition (*aitihya*) or similarity (*aupamya*). Thus 'smoke' to establish the presence of fire is derived from sensation, 'bad digestion' to establish illness is derived from inference, 'uncreated' to establish permanence is derived from tradition, 'like the Moon' to establish beauty is derived from similarity.

The example (34) is supposed to adduce facts known to everyone and accepted equally by the learned and by popular opinion, as for instance that fire is hot. Literally 'example' (*dṛṣṭānta*) means a 'seen conclusion', a 'sense datum'. This contrasts with a 'proved conclusion' (*siddhānta*) demonstrated by inference (37).

Caraka's form of proof, though with many modifications, remained the basis of debate and argument in India down to modern times. The Nyāya school have even retained the same five steps, with minor shifts of detail from one to another. At the same time the theory behind the form was gradually made more rigorous.

Caraka enumerates (54) five faults which must be avoided in a proof: 'deficiency' (*nyūna*) is missing out any part of the argument; 'redundancy' (*adhika*) is repeating anything or including something irrelevant; 'meaninglessness' (*anarthaka*) is meaningless words; 'disorder' (*apārthaka*) is lack of proper connection in the formulation; 'contradiction' (*viruddha*) is saying something which contradicts either the example or a 'proved conclusion' to which one is supposed to be committed (i.e. part of the doctrine one is publicly defending).

A separate topic which is essential to the discussion of proof and much analysed by later writers is that of middle terms which are false, or literally 'non-middle-terms' (*ahetus*). This corresponds to the false characteristics of the *Vaiśeṣika Sūtra*, though Caraka (57) has three kinds: 'begging the question' (*prakaraṇasama*, 'similar to the topic', i.e. to the question not yet proved) is when the middle term itself is not established (is not evident or has not been proved, so that the opponent can immediately reject it); 'doubtful' (*saṃśayasama*, 'similar to doubt') is a middle term whose extension is too wide, so that it does not prove precisely the predicate required (this is the same as the doubtful characteristic in the *Vaiśeṣika Sūtra*); 'with a doubtful example' (*varṇyasama*, 'similar to what is to be described', i.e. doubtful because the example shown is doubtful) is when the example of the middle term adduced in the proof is not accepted as something which has the predicate (it is enough if the opponent does not accept that M_1 is P, because the example is supposed to be a fact known to everyone and impossible to dispute).

'Equivocation' (*chala*) is defined as deliberately misinterpreting an opponent's words. It is of two kinds, verbal equivocation (between homonyms) and 'universal' equivocation (between universals or classes in the Vaiśeṣika sense), the latter being when the meaning of the words is taken to extend through a higher class instead of being limited to what was intended.

The topic of 'defeat situations' (*nigrahasthāna*) is obviously important in the laws of public debating, where the chairman has to rule on whether a debater is defeated. Caraka (58ff.) lists them, including perpetrating any of the faults or non-middle-terms mentioned above, abandoning one's own 'statement', failing to rebut an opponent's charge that the debater has committed a fault, irrelevant middle term, irrelevant matter, untimely speech (saying something at the wrong time), etc., and finally not answering at all even when the opponent has repeated his last statement three times.

Caraka defines a number of minor topics, several of which are found later among the sixteen 'categories' of the *Nyāya Sūtra,* as are most of the above topics. They can be omitted here.

Caraka discusses (I.11.17ff.) the 'means of knowledge' or 'tests' (*parīkṣās*), accepting four of these. (1) Sensation (*pratyakṣa*), defined as a consciousness which is clear and immediate and which arises through the conjunction of the soul, the mind, the sense organ and a sense object (I.11.20; cf. the Vaiśeṣika theory, which appears identical). (2) Inference (*anumāna*) is subordinate to sensation and is of three kinds with reference to the time dimension: simultaneous (from smoke to fire), of the past (from pregnancy to sexual intercourse) or of the future (from seed to fruit). (3) Authority (*āptopadeśa,* 'instruction from a reliable person'). (4) Judgment (*yukti*) or estimation of probabilities (*sambhava,* cf. III.8.49). This last seems to be peculiar to Caraka and represents another use of the rather obscure term *yukti.* It is explained here as weighing a number of conditions operating together (hence *yukti* might mean this 'combination' or 'grouping'), in order to arrive at a conclusion, for instance when forecasting the harvest. A commentator on Caraka remarks that this is what is popularly called *ūha,* 'judgment', 'conjecture' (Cakrapāṇi on I.11.25).

The **Upāyahṛdaya* covers much the same ground, beginning with debate and setting out the topics required for it. It does not actually describe the formulation of a proof, except indirectly through other topics, though clearly it assumes one very similar to Caraka's. As with Caraka, the example should be something accepted by everyone. There is a similar, but longer, list of faults, divided into those of the words and those of the meaning. There are eight kinds of false middle term. First the two kinds of equivocation (the same as in Caraka). Then the three kinds given by Caraka as 'non-middle-terms' (the doubtful, begging the question and with a doubtful example). There is the apparent difference when it is argued that because two things differ in one way they must have contradictory predicates in all other ways (this is a very common source of confusion in argument), for instance the soul is different from the body, therefore it is permanent (eternal)—because the body is impermanent. Then there is the imaginary middle term, perhaps corresponding to the 'not being' of the *Vaiśeṣika Sūtra.* Finally there is the contradictory, conflicting either with the example or with known facts about the world.

The defeat situations described are mostly similar to Caraka's. Apparently new additions are: changing one's 'statement', incomprehensibility, inability to repeat what the opponent has said and making an excuse to break off the debate.

A topic which appears to be entirely new is that of sophistical refutations (*jātis*). A sophistical refutation is an attempt to refute a valid proof by means of a sophistical (i.e. fallacious) argument. The topic became a standard one for works on debating and logic from this time on, since it was a necessary item in the equipment of a debater to be able to defend himself against various kinds of deceptive argument which might be used to outwit him even when his own position was logically sound. The **Upāyahṛdaya* proposes to analyse all sophistical refutations (it describes twenty of them) by means of reference to the methods of agreement and difference in the methodology of induction. Agreement means belonging to the same class (*jāti*, perhaps the use of the word *jāti* for a sophistical refutation derives from this meaning, through the idea of a confusion of classes or of the setting up of a bogus class as the basis for a sophistical argument). If two things agree in one respect it may be falsely argued that they must agree in others. On the other hand if two things differ in one property or predicate, and are therefore supposed to belong to totally different classes, it may be equally falsely argued that all their other properties or predicates must be different or contradictory. Thus for instance if sound is different from sight (object) in some respect, such as that they are sensed by different senses, it could be sophistically argued that if a sight (object) is impermanent then sound, being different, must be permanent (eternal). The twenty sophistical arguments set out by the **Upāyahṛdaya* all appear to be based on false middle terms. The author, being a Buddhist and rejecting the reality of an eternal soul, supposes that an opponent tries to prove the opposite statement, 'the soul is permanent', by assigning a middle term, usually 'because of being unobserved', adducing examples (e.g. space). According to the form of the argument the sophistry can be exposed by adducing a counter-example or in some other way.

The **Upāyahṛdaya* accepts four means of knowledge: sensation, inference, authority and similarity (cf. the *Sthānāṅga*, XVII above). Similarity here means using similes (p. 14), particularly those given in the *Tripiṭaka.* However, it had long been recognised that argument by analogy is not logically cogent and we find that all known Buddhist writers after this reject such a means of knowledge (the Nyāya, accepting 'similarity', redefine it to make it identification from a description). There was a certain overlap at this stage of the theory between means of knowledge and kinds of middle term (derived from various sources). Caraka gives them differently, with judgment (*yukti*) as a means but instead similarity as a source of middle terms. The **Upāyahṛdaya* has them the same (pp. 6 and 13f.), which seems more logical. It considers sensation to be the best and also the basis for the other three. Inference is of three kinds: arguing from the past to the present, from a sample to a whole class, from something observable to something unobservable on the basis of their belonging to the same class of events.

The *Nyāya Sūtra* as we now have it seems to have been compiled or revised at the end of the 2nd century A.D. or even later, since it contains a defence against the criticisms of the Madhyamaka school. The *Sūtra* may also be composite, a combination of two previously existing books, one on the means of knowledge (*pramāṇa*) and the other on the debate. These were produced by a school or schools of the Vaiśeṣika, but the combined school of the *Sūtra* came later to be known as Nyāya from the 'method' (*nyāya*) of the proof in five steps followed in it. The historical relationships between the various schools which concerned themselves with the doctrine of the debate, and the formulation of proofs, are not known. Thus it is possible that the Vaiśeṣikas were the pioneers and that Bhadrabāhu, Caraka, the **Upāyahṛdaya*, etc., were all borrowers. It is also possible that the Buddhists or some other school led the way. In any case we should note here that although the extant *Nyāya Sūtra* is later it is fairly certain that the Vaiśeṣika school had developed these studies in the period now under discussion. Though the *Sūtra* in its finished form belongs below (XXI) we can note here its general position relative to the texts we have just examined.

Books II to IV of the present *Sūtra* deal with the means of knowledge (*pramāṇa*) and the objects of knowledge. They form a supplement to and in important respects a modification of the doctrine of the *Vaiśeṣika Sūtra.* Thus the new means of knowledge authority and similarity are added (authority will pave the way for the assimilation of the school to the Vedic tradition).

Books I and V of the *Sūtra* form on the other hand a complete work, independent of the other Books, on the subject of debate (*vāda*). The ground covered is almost exactly the same as that of Caraka's section on debating or of the **Upāyahṛdaya*. Book I deals with the debate, proof and the steps in a proof, false middle terms and equivocation. Book V deals with sophistical refutations and defeat situations.

The five steps in a proof are practically the same as in Caraka (but as no actual illustration is given, but only bare definitions, the exact form is not clear; it may not be as supposed by the commentators on the *Sūtra* , who introduce new distinctions and meet criticisms of the old formulation). The example step, however, is renamed 'illustration' (*udāharaṇa*), apparently just a synonym.

There are five kinds of false middle term, which were perhaps originally the same as in the **Upāyahṛdaya* except for omitting the two kinds of equivocation (given as a separate topic, as by Caraka) and the imaginary middle term. However, we find an obscure *sādhyasama* in place of the one with a doubtful example (*varṇyasama* is the term used in Caraka), which as interpreted by the commentators is much the same as begging the question. Then in place of the apparent difference we have 'untimely speech' (*kālātīta*, a defeat situation in Caraka and the **Upāyahṛdaya*), strangely interpreted by the commentators as meaning that the middle term does not coincide in time with the major term. [The other three are the doubtful (*savyabhicāra*, the middle term whose extension is too wide), contradictory (*viruddha*) and begging the question (*prakaraṇasama*).]

There are 22 defeat situations, generally the same as in Caraka and the **Upāyahṛdaya*, especially the latter, but incorporating the old set of 'faults' in a proof, which are no longer dealt with as a separate topic.

The sophistical refutations differ rather widely from those of the **Upāyahṛdaya*. There are 24 of them, of which eight or perhaps nine agree with the **Upāyahṛdaya's*, four derive from false middle terms and two from equivocation and the rest seem to be new. The first two, however, are the 'appearance of agreement' (*sādharmyasama*) and the 'appearance of difference' (*vaidharmyasama*), given as the underlying sophistries of all such refutations in the **Upāyahṛdaya.* Six more are based on the relationship between the major term and the example (among these, the expression *varṇyasama* appears, originally a kind of false middle term; there is also a *sādhyasama* among them, suggesting that this expression among the false middle terms in the *Sūtra* may have once had a meaning similar to *varṇyasama*). Then the *prasaṅgasama* (*prasaṅga* = 'necessary consequence', i.e. that something further is implied as necessary) claims that the example should first be established by means of a middle term (it was perhaps inspired by the Lokāyatikas or the Madhyamakas). There are at least two others which seem to have been suggested by the Madhyamaka methods of refutation (e.g. the *arthāpattisama,* that every statement implies its contradictory), thus the long set was probably completed only in the final version of the *Sūtra* and does not belong here. Concluding this discussion, the *Sūtra* raises another point, obscurely treated in the **Upāyahṛdaya,* called in later writings the *ṣaṭpakṣin,* 'six sided (argument)'—actually there are two sides and each speaks three times. The problem is whether a sophistical refutation can be refuted by another sophistical refutation. The answer is that if this is done the opponent will do the same (this gives four 'sides' so far, including the original statement, the opponent having the last word). It might then seem possible to attack the opponent for having admitted by his last rejoinder that his first rejoinder was not valid (a defeat situation, admitting the charge), but this will not do because the opponent can still do the same (the sixth 'side'). Thus the protagonist cannot defend himself successfully by replying in kind with sophistical refutations, but must use sound arguments, i.e. point out the opponent's sophistry.

The *Mahāvibhāṣā* has some relevant discussions, e.g. that the Mahāsaṃghikas held that knowledge knows itself (as well as other principles), as a lamp illuminates itself. This is refuted by the Vaibhāṣika author (Vasumitra) on the ground that the lamp is not living (T. 1545 pp. 42a-43a).

XX MADHYAMAKA

The Madhyamaka school of Buddhism was effectively established by Nāgārjuna in the middle of the 2nd century A.D., though his teacher Rāhulabhadra is sometimes regarded (e.g. Tāranātha Chapter XIV) as the original founder. Nāgārjuna's books constitute the philosophical basis for the school. Mahāyānist Buddhists commonly regard Nāgārjuna as the great philosophical protagonist of the Mahāyāna, yet in those books generally accepted as his he nowhere mentions the Mahāyāna, nor does he ever refer to any Mahāyāna *sūtra.* Notwithstanding this silence he is looked upon as the systematiser of the *Prajñāpāramitā Sūtras,* as clearly explaining the apparent paradoxes and poetic expressions of those amusing dialogues among the initiates into 'emptiness'. As a matter of fact Nāgārjuna refers only to texts of the ancient *Tripiṭaka* as recognised by all the early schools. He criticises the interpretations of some of these which we find in the early schools, saying that such interpreters do not understand the teaching of the Buddha, but he accepts the texts themselves and does not propose to add new ones, as the Mahāyānists did. He claims to be reestablishing the proper interpretation of the Buddha's words. There is no clear evidence that he was a Mahāyānist by conviction except later Mahāyānist claims. The impression his works give is rather that he aimed to prevent any such division into factions, by producing an agreed doctrine based on texts which all Buddhists accepted. This doctrine was simply the original teaching of the Buddha, essentially the four truths and conditioned origination, freed from the metaphysical systematisation which had been superimposed on it by the schools.

The works generally agreed to be Nāgārjuna's are the *Mūlamadhyamakakārikā* (often referred to as just the *Kārikās*), *Vigrahavyāvartanī, Śūnyatāsaptati, Yuktiṣaṣṭikā* and *Vaidalyaprakaraṇa.* Less generally enumerated among his works are the *Suhṛllekha, Ratnāvalī* and some *stotras* in praise of the Buddha. The last three are popular and poetic in character, though the last two express Madhyamaka philosophy. They suggest Mahāyānist ideas and the *Ratnāvalī* actually names Mahāyāna (IV.66ff.). The *Kārikās* constitute the basic text and the other four philosophical works merely add a few supplementary discussions. The more popular works may be apocryphal and in any case have a different standpoint. There were several other Nāgārjunas in the history of Buddhism, also Nāgas, Nāgabodhis and other similar names. By 'Nāgārjuna' in our discussions we mean the author of the *Mūlamadhyamakakārikā* and probably of the four other philosophical works listed above.

The name Madhyamaka, 'Intermediate', suggests the intention of reestablishing the original teaching of the Buddha, often explained as 'intermediate' (*madhyama*, etc.) in the earliest texts, especially as intermediate between various extremes. The main contention of the *Kārikās* is that it was not the intention of the Buddha to set out lists of principles which in some sense 'existed', and still less to maintain that such principles had 'own-beings'. That would be an extreme view (the 'existence' extreme) and is inconsistent with conditioned origination. Buddhism should not be a metaphysical system or speculative doctrine (*dṛṣṭi*), but a purely empirical study: the investigation of the four truths and conditioned origination.

The concepts used by philosophers are speculative and do not apply (*na upa-pad*) to the actual world of experience. It can be shown by rigorous analysis that such concepts as 'time', 'space', 'movement', 'cause', 'agent', 'occurrence', 'characteristic', etc., are self-contradictory when their implications are examined: no rational account can be given of any of them.

Nāgārjuna claims not to hold any speculative opinion himself. Buddhism is not a speculative system and the *Tripiṭaka*, properly interpreted, does not offer any position among such conceptual systems, on which one could take a stand against other positions. Consequently the critiques of philosophical concepts which Nāgārjuna offers must start out from the positions to be criticised themselves, showing that they imply absurdities. The method then is to deduce from any speculative position a 'necessary consequence' (*prasaṅga*) which shows that it is untenable. (In the *Vigrahavyāvartanī*, 29, Nāgārjuna explains more fully that he makes no 'statement', *pratijñā*; the teaching of 'emptiness', that principles are empty of any 'own-being', is not itself a 'statement', it is only not making any such statement, not holding any opinion.)

Nāgārjuna took over from the earliest Buddhist texts the dialectics of the tetralemma (*catuṣkoṭi*) (see VIII above) concerning the idea that there was a soul or person or 'being' or 'thus-gone' (*tathāgata*, whether a *buddha* or any other 'living being' supposed to transmigrate in the world or to go beyond it) which continued through the sequence of conditions and the series of events in the apparent continuity of consciousness. It cannot rationally be maintained that the 'thus-gone' (1) exists after death, or (2) does not exist after death (is destroyed at death), or (3) both exists and does not exist, or (4) neither exists nor does not exist after death (*Mahānidāna Sūtra*: Pali D No. 15, Chinese T 14, T 26 No. 97, T 52; *Kārikās* Chapters 27, 22, 25 etc.). The same tetralemma form is used about whether the 'universe' is 'eternal' or 'infinite' or not. Nāgārjuna points out (Chapter 27) that these arguments reduce to a dilemma (a supposed entity, such as the 'soul', is either the same as some other entity or is different from it—for example the 'thus-gone' at different points in its supposed history, or the 'soul' and the 'body'). Anything eternal, he explains, could not be 'born' and 'transmigrate'; if on the other hand it were not eternal (but was destroyed at some point in its history, being subsequently non-existent) the sequence of conditions would not apply to it (i.e. an entity which continued indefinitely could not be subject to change by conditions, nor could an entity which ceased to exist). The theory of 'both' (eternal and not eternal, exists and does not exist) does not explain the difficulty, merely encountering both types of objection simultaneously. The 'neither' position would make sense only if the two terms denied had first been explained ('eternal' and 'non-eternal' in relation to the changing sequence).

The dilemma proper was perhaps suggested as much by the *Abhidharma* logic (where a controversial concept is checked against all the terms of the system to decide whether it is identical with or different from any of them) as by the original dilemma of the soul and the body. Nāgārjuna demonstrates it in connection with the concepts of 'desire' and a 'desirer' (Chapter 6), which of course is original Buddhism to the extent that no agent (desirer) can be established (there is just the event, the occurrence of desire) but in which Nāgārjuna objects to the concept 'desire' (a *dharma* or principle accepted in the early schools) as well. If either the desirer or the desire existed first, without the other, the position is nonsensical: a desirer without desire, in whom nevertheless desire occurs afterwards; or a desire coming from nowhere, in no desirer. Then let it be supposed that they come into existence simultaneously? This also is nonsensical because to occur at the same time the desirer and the desire would have to be independent of one another, depending on other (preceding) conditions. Further, if they are simultaneous they cannot be identical, for if a thing occurs 'with' something that other thing must be different; nor can they be different, because that would imply that they could exist without each other. Thus Nāgārjuna throws out such principles as 'desire', at least when supposed to be independent entities, in just the same way as he rejects the idea of a personal agent to whom such principles occur. In Chapter 8 he criticises the concepts of 'agent' and 'action': agent and action are mutually dependent, therefore their independent existence cannot be demonstrated. The dilemma applies to all relations, such as possession, cause and effect, part and whole, etc. (8, also the end of Chapter 10). It is further examined in Chapter 10 on 'fire' and 'fuel', which cannot be different from each other (cannot exist independently), nor can they be identical (if one is supposed to be the agent operating on the other). The further possibilities are explored that the fire possesses the fuel, or is in the fuel, or that the fuel is in it. These are only special cases of 'difference', which is implied by them, so that all five positions are rejected (this fivefold analysis is another standard Buddhist formulation, used of the 'soul' in relation to the 'groups' in the earliest texts, see VIII above). The argument is in effect summed up in *Kārikā* 18.10: Whatever is conditioned by something is not identical with that, nor is it different from it; therefore nothing is either annihilated or eternal.—This relates the whole problem to conditioned origination: if all principles are conditioned by one another there are no independent 'entities', either temporary (annihilated) or permanent.

When speaking of various principles, particularly those listed in the *Abhidharma*, Nāgārjuna generally uses the term *bhāva* for them instead of the usual term *dharma*. Thus he seems to be attacking the Sthaviravāda commentators (XIV above). The word *bhāva* would mean 'being' or 'existent principle', stressing presumably the idea of a real existence which Nāgārjuna objects to. Such existent principles, or entities, would be inconsistent with conditioned origination. At this point we may take up one of the fundamental arguments in the *Kārikās*, that of Chapter 15 on the question of 'own-being', a doctrine of the early schools (for example of the commentaries of the Sthaviravāda) which Nāgārjuna contended was inconsistent with the teaching of the Buddha. If an 'own-being', he says, were related to causes and conditions it would be artificial (*kṛtaka*, something 'made', not something original in itself). This would contradict the conception of its being an 'own-being', which ex hypothesi should be independent of anything else (*nirapekṣa*).

Nāgārjuna continues this discussion as follows. If there is no 'own-being' then there can be no 'other-being' either, since this could be understood only in contrast to 'own-being'. (See XIV above on the Sthaviravāda doctrine of 'own-being' and 'other-being' in the *Peṭakopadesa*.) In the absence of either own-being (*svabhāva*) or other-being (*parabhāva*) how can there be any 'being' (*bhāva*, existent principle, i.e. as existing naturally either in itself or in relation to something else)? If 'being' (*bhāva*, existent) is thus denied, then 'non-being' (*abhāva*, non-existent) also cannot be affirmed, for 'non-being' is only the 'otherwise-being' (*anyathābhāva*, otherwise-existent) of 'being' (existent). Those who see 'own-being' and 'other-being', 'being' (existent) and 'non-being' (non-existent), do not see the reality (*tattva*) of the doctrine of the Buddha. In the *Kātyāyanāvavāda Sūtra* (this has been quoted above in VIII, it appears in *Saṃyutta Nikāya* II 17 and its Sanskrit and Chinese parallels: Nāgārjuna seems to show a preference for the *Saṃyutta* among the original Buddhist texts) the Master, explaining existent and non-existent, has rejected both 'It exists' and 'It does not exist'. . . These correspond to eternalism and annihilationism, eternalism deriving from the idea that what existed by its own-being could not (ever) be said not to exist and annihilationism deriving from the idea that something exists no more after having formerly existed.

This makes it clear that Nāgārjuna takes the words 'exist' (the verb, *as*, to be or to exist) and 'existent' (the noun *bhāva*) as implying eternal existence, i.e. of an eternal soul or an eternal substance. If we speak of philosophical concepts in this way we are hypostatising them as eternal entities in nature. The transitory 'principles' spoken of in conditioned origination should not be described in these terms (instead it must be said that they are all 'empty'—Chapter 24).

It is an important methodological principle with Nāgārjuna that contradictory statements imply one another. They are interdependent: thus we could understand 'neither exists nor does not exist' if we could explain 'exists and does not exist'; if there could be an 'own-being' then there could be an 'other-being'; if we could understand 'principles exist' then we could understand 'principles do not exist'. It certainly does not follow that because we reject one extreme view we must accept its contradictory. On the contrary we must reject both, and they stand or fall together: they are interdependent speculative constructions and in fact they do not apply to the world of conditioned origination. We reject every speculative opinion precisely because we reject its opposite also. Thus it follows (7.33) that if the 'synthesised' (*saṃskṛta*) principles do not 'exist' then an 'unsynthesised' (*asaṃskṛta*) principle (i.e. *nirvāṇa*, extinction) does not 'exist' either.

The first chapter of the *Kārikās* deals with the 'conditions' (*pratyayas*) and is directed against the interpretations of the doctrine of conditions which had grown up among the early schools. There are no existent principles (*bhāvas*, beings) anywhere, Nāgārjuna begins, which occur (*ut-pad*, but perhaps this stands here for *sam-ut-pad*, 'originate', the choice of words being a little cramped because the *Kārikās* are metrical) out of themselves, or out of an other, or out of both, or without any cause . . . There is no own-being of an existent principle (being) in the various kinds of condition proposed in the schools (the 'cause', the 'support', the 'immediate', the 'dominant' are listed here—they correspond to the Sarvāstivāda and Bahuśrutīya theory noted p. 96 above). In the absence of any own-being there can be no other-being either. . . Let those things be called 'conditions', conditioned by which other things occur, but how can they be 'conditions' before the latter have occurred? Neither a non-existing object nor an existing one is congruent with (*yujyate*) having a condition: of what non-existing thing can there be a condition? And what use is a condition for a thing which (already) exists? . . . If existent principles have no own-being then they have no existence (*sattā*, 'existing-ness'). Thus 'this being, that is' (the old formula for a condition, it is given in the *Saṃyutta Nikāya* II 65, Sarvāstivāda Sanskrit version Tripāṭhī 145, 147, 157, Chinese Taishō 99 section 12 No. 13) has no application (*na upa-pad*) (I.10). The result does not exist in any of the conditions taken singly, nor in all of them together. How could there be something 'from the conditions' which was not in them? (I. 11). Or, if something which did not exist in them started 'from the conditions', why should the result not start equally well from what were not conditions? . . .We conclude that there exist no conditions and no non-conditions, since no results of them exist.

Does this mean that Nāgārjuna rejected the doctrine of conditioned origination (especially as he seems to set aside the old formula which is used in the *Tripiṭaka* itself)? No. It is precisely because he accepts it, he says, that he rejects the idea that there is anything eternal, or that anything 'exists', that anything has an 'own-being' (and also the opposites of these speculative theories). This has been argued above. In the twenty-fourth chapter he takes up the matter again against a Buddhist, evidently of the early schools, who suggests that Nāgārjuna has rejected the four truths (and with them conditioned origination). The opponent is supposed to say that if everything is empty then there is neither origination nor cessation, from which it necessarily follows that the four truths do not exist. . . Nāgārjuna replies that the opponent does not know what emptiness means. The *buddhas* teach the doctrine on the basis of two levels of truth, the 'concealing' and the 'ultimate'. (Cf. the fact that in the earliest texts the Buddha is sometimes represented as using the ordinary everyday language and speaking of 'persons' acting in various ways, whilst on other occasions when the discussion can be said to be at the rigorous philosophical level he insists that such personifications must be dropped and we must say only that there is such and such an event through such and such a condition; cf. also in the *Abhidharma* the listing of the principles supposed to be real and ultimate, excluding the 'person' and other fictions of everyday language; Nāgārjuna uses terms current in the early schools for these two levels of discourse: *saṃvṛti*, 'concealing', for everyday language and *paramārtha*, 'ultimate', for philosophical language; he simply rejects the misleading language of 'own-being'.) Those who do not discern the difference between these two truths (levels) do not discern the profound reality (*tattva*) of the doctrine of the Buddha. The ultimate truth cannot be taught without depending on conventional usage (we have to use language more or less as we find it); extinction (*nirvāṇa*) cannot be attained without depending on the ultimate truth. Like a snake grasped in the wrong way or a science wrongly applied, emptiness misunderstood destroys those of weak intelligence . . . For whom emptiness is 'congruent' (*yujyate*, is logical, agrees with his other conceptions) everything (in the Buddhist doctrine) is congruent; for whom the empty is not congruent everything is not congruent . . . If because of the (supposed) 'own-being' you envisage an 'existing (real) existence' (*sadbhāva*, 'existing being') of existent principles (*bhāvas* , beings), then you must see these existent principles as without causes and conditions. You must reject cause and effect; agent, instrument and action; origination and cessation; and any result (of conditions). It is conditioned origination which we call 'emptiness'. It is a 'concept based on' (*upādāya prajñapti*, 'concept attached to') something, and precisely it is the 'intermediate way' (avoiding the extremes 'It is' and 'It is not'). Since no principle (*dharma*) occurs (*vidyate*) which is not originated by conditions, no principle occurs which is not empty. If everything were not empty then there would be neither origination nor cessation, from which it would necessarily follow that according to you the four truths would not exist. . . (so it is correct to speak of *dharmas*, not *bhāvas*).

Thus principles are not 'existent' or 'non-existent': it can be said that they 'occur' (*vidyate* or *ut-pad*), that they originate and cease, only provided that this is understood of 'empty' principles, not of 'existent principles'. It is also necessary to note that 'emptiness' is not itself the 'own-being' of principles (Chapter 13)—this would be the worst possible speculative opinion.

It has already been noted (7.33) that *nirvāṇa* does not 'exist' any more than the synthesised principles. In Chapter 25 this is discussed further. *Nirvāṇa* is not existent, not non-existent, not both existent and non-existent, not neither existent nor non-existent. (But principles also are none of these, is *nirvāṇa* then the same as principles?) There is no distinction (*viśeṣaṇa*) at all between extinction (*nirvāṇa*) and transmigration (*saṃsāra*, the conditioned world). There is no distinction at all between transmigration and extinction. The limit of extinction would be the limit of transmigration (but neither has a limit)... The speculative opinions about (the 'thus-gone') beyond cessation, about finite and infinite, eternal and non-eternal, are of the same kind as those concerning extinction. Since everything is empty what is finite or infinite or both or neither, what is identity or difference, what is eternality, non-eternality, both, neither? Happiness consists in the calming of these differentiations (*prapañca*).

We have still to examine some of Nāgārjuna's critiques of philosophical concepts, showing that they are not valid, at least as customarily applied. He uses what may be called a 'temporal' analysis to dispose of any concept involving the idea of a process in time, as well as the concept of 'time' itself. In effect it is a trilemma showing that it is impossible to give a coherent explanation of the concepts in relation to 'past', 'present' or 'future' time. In his second chapter Nāgārjuna investigates the concept of 'motion'. First he formulates the trilemma as follows: (1) that which is 'gone' (*gata*, i.e. past) is not 'being gone' (*gamyate*, i.e. present as being moved, the 'motion' which we seek to identify, to catch in the act of 'happening' in order to define it); (2) that which is 'not gone' (*agata*, i.e. future) is not 'being gone'; (3) a 'being gone' (*gamyamāna*, i.e. present—here the participle is used, not the present tense, distinguishing the concept as subject of the proposition from the predicate intended to define it) independent of 'gone' (past) and 'not gone' (future) is not 'being gone' (*gamyate*, present tense). In other words we cannot understand the motion as 'being' what has already happened and ceased, or as being what has not yet started; as for a 'being gone' to be understood as happening at present, we could understand 'present' only as being something in between the 'past' and the 'future', not independently of these two—and since we have not been able to understand 'being gone' as related to 'gone' or 'not gone', the possibility of understanding a present motion dependent on past and future is not open to us.

An opponent is then imagined to seek to define a present 'motion' independent of 'being gone', in order to evade the trilemma and understand 'being gone' by reference to this present 'motion' only and independently of 'gone' and 'not gone'. Nāgārjuna replies that there cannot be a 'being gone' distinct from 'motion', which could be defined by pointing out the relation between them. The attempt to improve the definition merely multiplies the entities for which definitions must be sought: we have two 'motions' (*gamanas*, 2.5) instead of one and are no nearer any solution, rather we might have to look for two agents supposed to perform the two motions (this incidentally brings up the question of an 'agent' who or which moves, the absurdity of which offers another method of exploding the concept of 'motion'). Various other methods are available to criticise the concept: for instance the absurdity of the concept 'being stationary' is demonstrated, whence it follows that the contradictory of this (which must be understood by contrast as other than stationary) is equally absurd.

The critique of 'time' is given in Chapter 19. Suppose we try to conceive a 'present' or a 'future' time in relation to 'past' time, this relation cannot occur unless the 'present' or 'future' occurs simultaneously with the 'past', therefore in the past. Occurrence in the past of course destroys the concepts of 'present' or 'future', yet there is no way of demonstrating their occurrence independently of a 'past'. Therefore 'time' does not occur (*na vidyate*). Evidently the concept of a 'past' time can be exploded in exactly the same way, but the triple analysis is equally destructive of other triads of concepts, such as 'low', 'intermediate' and 'high'. In principle it can be applied to any pair of contradictories also, such as 'unity' and 'multiplicity', whence we see that it is nothing but an extension of the principle of the interdependence of contradictories (such as 'own-being' and 'other-being'). The same chapter shows also the impossibility of conceiving either a 'time' which is changing or a 'time' which is constant.

The triple method of analysis applies also to the concept of 'occurrence' (*utpāda*) if hypostatised: neither that which 'has occurred', nor that which 'has not occurred', nor that which 'is occurring', occurs, by what we might call the first 'theorem' of the second chapter (on 'motion') (7.14). If, further, there were an 'occurrence' of that which 'is occurring', we would then be led to posit the 'occurrence' of that 'occurrence' and so on *ad infinitum* ('occurrence' of the 'occurrence' of the 'occurrence' of the . . . of the 'occurrence') (7.18f.)—the infinite regression (*anavasthā*) being another useful device in Nāgārjuna's dialectics.

Nāgārjuna's fifth chapter is directed against attempts to speak of a 'characteristic' (*lakṣaṇa*) of an existent principle (*bhāva*) which would then be 'characterised' (*lakṣya*) by it (cf. the 'desire' and the 'desirer' in 6). An existent principle does not occur before its 'characteristic' (otherwise it could occur without it, which would be self-contradictory). If, however, we suppose a 'commencement' (*pravṛtti*, 'engagement') of the characteristic we introduce an additional concept of which we are unable to give a satisfactory account. Yet in the absence of the commencement of the 'characteristic', the 'characterised' has no application (to reality). Thus the 'characterised' and the 'characteristic' do not occur.

The fourth chapter argues that matter is not perceived without the 'cause of matter', nor is the cause perceived without matter; matter without a cause would necessarily be causeless, and there is no object anywhere which is causeless, likewise the cause of matter without matter would be a cause without an effect, which cannot be. Whether matter exists or not, its 'cause' does not apply (this probably should be referred to the first chapter, a cause being a kind of condition), but nor does 'matter' apply in the absence of its cause, therefore one cannot imagine any 'imaginings' (*vikalpas*) relating to matter. It does not apply, that the effect should be similar to the cause, nor that it should be dissimilar. The same method (of argument serves to dispose of) the other four 'groups' (*skandhas*) and of all principles as 'being'. When one argues on the basis of emptiness, any attempt (by the opponent) to avoid the critique fails because it becomes 'similar to what is to be proved' (*samaṃ sādhyena*, presumably this is the *sādhyasama* of the logicians, mentioned in XIX above, which in this period is somewhat obscure; here the commentator Candrakīrti, *c.* 600 A.D., explains that 'the existence of matter' is 'what is to be proved' and that the existence of the other groups is what is 'similar', thus these other concepts are like that which has already been refuted and can therefore be refuted in a similar way, they cannot be used to establish the existence of matter; this seems to be a variety of 'begging the question', in that a parallel or example, here another 'group', taken to prove as major premise that all groups exist, is as much in need of being proved itself as the subject of the argument, 'matter exists'). In general in any explanation an objection can be rejected as *samaṃ sādhyena* (begging the question) if one argues through emptiness.

The *Vigrahavyāvartanī* largely, and the *Vaidalyaprakaraṇa* exclusively, are devoted to the criticism of the doctrines of the Vaiśeṣika (and Nyāya, in fact of the subject matter of the *Nyāya Sūtra* mostly). Thus the four means of knowledge are attacked at *Vigrahavyāvartanī* 30ff., on the ground that such means (*pramāṇas*) require some means themselves in order to be known and established, and these in turn will require further means, resulting in an infinite regression. The work goes on to attack the objects of knowledge (*prameyas*), supposed to be known by the means, and finds that they can be established neither in relation to the means nor without relation to the means. The *Vaidalyaprakaraṇa* criticises these concepts further (using for example the 'which comes first?' argument) (1-19) and also criticises all the rest of the sixteen 'categories' (*padārthas*) of the *Nyāya Sūtra* (as did the Rogue Cārvākas, perhaps at about the same time, but the Cārvāka critique does not seem to have been preserved). The form of a proof is criticised (32-48) among these and the theory of debate (*vāda*, etc., 51-6), of false middle terms (57-66), of sophistical refutations (68-9) and of defeat situations (70-2). The doctrine of the five steps (members) of a proof, for example, is attacked by means of the part and whole argument (dilemma). The extant version of the *Nyāya Sūtra* attempts replies to some of these attacks and is therefore presumably later than Nāgārjuna.

Nāgārjuna's pupil Āryadeva continued his master's work but unlike him placed the *bodhisattva* in the foreground. He criticises some of the same philosophical concepts, but avoids repeating the same arguments (the same concepts can be attacked in different ways). He goes much further in attacking particular schools, especially the Sāṃkhya, Vaiśeṣika, Jaina, Lokāyata and theistic schools (Vaiṣṇava and Śaiva).

Nāgārjuna reaffirms the Buddha's empiricism and rejection of speculation, of concepts which do not apply to experience.

XXI AKṢAPĀDA AND NYĀYA

The *Nyāya Sūtra* has been referred to several times already and it, or more probably its component parts, existed in some form by A.D. 100 or earlier, being known (e.g. to Āryadeva in his *Śataśāstra*) as belonging to the Vaiśeṣika school. Since the text we now have, handed down in the 'Nyāya' school, tries to meet and avert many of the criticisms of philosophical concepts made by Nāgārjuna, however, it must be dated about A.D. 200. (The critique of time is taken up at II.1.39-43; that nothing has 'own-being', all 'existent principles' being related to each other, at IV. 1.37ff. in the context of a discussion on 'characteristics'; IV.1.47 seems to contain an actual quotation from Nāgārjuna's *Kārikās,* 1.7 with two words interchanged, on principles conceived as 'existent', etc., not being able to be produced from causes; the *Sūtra* generally opposes to the critiques a kind of commonsense view that we see events taking place, remember the past, etc., also that the critical philosophy is self-defeating.) The commentator Vātsyāyana (probably late 3rd century A.D.) calls the founder of the study of *nyāya* Akṣapāda, though we cannot say whether he was the author of the text we now have or of some more original form of it. From the 3rd century on the Nyāya constituted a separate school from the Vaiśeṣika, based on this *Sūtra* text.

Most of the topics of the *Nyāya Sūtra* have been reviewed above (XIX), on the assumption that they were covered in some Vaiśeṣika text of that period. Many of the definitions may have been revised to bring about their present form, however, even if the terms (the 'categories', etc.) remained the same; Vātsyāyana carried the process further by straining the *Sūtra* into meanings which seemed preferable to him. Among the means of knowledge, 'similarity' (*upamāna*) is now defined (II.1.44ff.) in such a way as to make it identification of an object, through the great similarity of that object to something already known, e.g. a gayal (*gavaya*) to domestic cattle (the *Sūtra* gives too little explanation; the idea is that one is familiar with domestic cattle but not with the wild gayal, one can identify the latter on seeing it for the first time if one has been told that it is an animal similar to the familiar one but living wild in the forest). Authority is here called 'speech' (*śabda,* II.1.49ff.), i.e. verbal testimony, but only of a reliable person. The *Sūtra* discusses four other proposed means of knowledge but rejects them. 'Implication' (*arthāpatti*) is when one statement follows immediately from another: the Nyāya school includes it in inference (the Mīmāṃsā accepted it as independent; Caraka calls it *arthaprāpti* and illustrates it 'he should not eat in the daytime' implies 'he should eat at night'). 'Non-existence' (*abhāva*) is when one picks out an object as not having a certain characteristic; the Nyāya again includes it in inference (some Mīmāṃsakas accepted it as independent). 'Tradition' (*aitihya*) refers to Epic or historical tradition, upheld as a separate means of knowledge by historians but included in 'speech' (authority) by the Nyāya (Caraka had mentioned it as a source of middle terms but not as a means of knowledge). 'Inclusion' (*sambhava*) is the mathematical relation of a smaller number included in a larger one: it seems to mean proportion, through which one can work out an amount as a given fraction of another; the Nyāya regards this as a kind of inference (the historians again make it a separate means).

Book I of the *Nyāya Sūtra* begins by listing the sixteen 'categories' (*padārthas*) or topics necessary for study (the means and objects of knowledge, which are the first two, are briefly defined in the first book, as well as more elaborately discussed in II-IV, consequently this can originally have been a table of contents for an old treatise on debate consisting of I and V only). These are:

1. means of knowledge (*pramāṇa*)
2. objects of knowledge (*prameya*)
3. doubt (*saṃśaya*)
4. relevance (*prayojana*)
5. example (*dṛṣṭānta*)
6. proved conclusion (*siddhānta*)
7. steps (*avayavas,* members of a proof)
8. judgment (*tarka*)
9. decision (*nirṇaya*)
10. debate (*vāda,* according to the rules)
11. dispute (*jalpa,* using sophistry)
12. eristic (*vitaṇḍā,* without establishing a counter-statement)

13. false middle terms (*hetvābhāsas*)
14. equivocation (*chala*)
15. sophistical refutations (*jāti*)
16. defeat situations (*nigrahasthānas*)

Nearly all these are covered in Caraka. 'Doubt' is due to common qualities, uncertainty about sensation, etc. (obviously a debater must watch such points). 'Relevance' relates to one's ultimate object. 'Judgment' is defined in the *Sūtra* (I.1.40) as an estimate (*ūha,* also translatable 'judgment', 'conjecture'; cf. Caraka's term *yukti* and Kauṭalya's *tantrayukti ūhya*—XI above) about reality based on the operation (*upapatti,* application) of causes, when the reality of the object is unknown (this topic was much discussed later and different definitions offered: the Naiyāyikas seem never to have been very happy about such a vague term; however, the original idea seems fairly clearly to have been a judgment, or estimate of probabilities, when no absolutely conclusive evidence appeared to be available, as when estimating a future event from present causes). 'Decision' resembles 'decision' (*niyoga*) in Kauṭalya, after considering two opposed statements. The *Sūtra* adds a third kind of 'equivocation' to Caraka's two, namely equivocation by 'transfer' (*upacāra*) of meaning (using words in secondary senses, i.e. metaphor, etc.).

The form of proof has been noted in XIX above as not clear. It is misrepresented by the commentator Vātsyāyana to fit his new ideas (we get: 3. Things such as M_1, etc., are M (and) P, 4. And likewise S is M, 5. Therefore, because it is M, S is P; in addition Vātsyāyana requires 'different' as well as agreeing examples to be stated, requiring steps 3a. and 4a. to be set out accordingly). The 'statement' is defined as stating 'what is to be proved' (*sādhya*), which unfortunately is ambiguous and can lead to confusion, since *sādhya* is sometimes applied simply to the predicate (only; i.e. it may mean 'P' instead of 'S is P'). The middle term is defined as proving what is to be proved through agreement with the example or difference from it (this no doubt suggested Vātsyāyana's insistence on both).

The five kinds of false middle term were compared above with those of Caraka and the **Upāyahṛdaya.* Two are not very clear. The untimely speech (*kālātīta*) is explained by the commentary as meaning that (empirically) the middle term does not agree in time with the predicate to be proved, Vātsyāyana rejecting an alternative explanation that it is when the steps in the proof are given in the wrong order (the reason for rejecting this is that it is a defeat situation in the *Sūtra*, hence need not be a false middle term as well). The *ṣādhyasama*, 'similar to what is to be proved', is explained by the commentary as a middle term not demonstrated as (not self-evidently) a predicate of the subject (of the statement to be proved). This is contrasted by the commentary with 'begging the question' (*prakaraṇasama*), which is stated to be when the middle term coincides with the predicate to be proved (is the same as it). This is not particularly convincing as the original meaning of the terms (which may very well have been the other way round). The *sādhyasama* should perhaps be understood as originally the same as in Nāgārjuna's *Kārikās* (see end of XX), though that itself needs further clarification.

Probably of about the same date as the extant *Nyāya Sūtra* is another Buddhist text on logic, of unknown authorship and preserved only in Chinese (like the **Upāyahṛdaya*), though incompletely, the **Tarkaśāstra* (according to Tucci) or *Jou che louen*. Tucci is of opinion that the *Nyāya Sūtra* (II.2.3) alludes to an argument in the **Tarkaśāstra*, which would make it earlier unless the same argument had been made earlier in some other work. This **Tarkaśāstra* is remarkable for first (as far as we know) propounding a more logical doctrine of the middle term, with as a corollary of it a more logical doctrine of false middle terms. For a proof to be valid, according to the **Tarkaśāstra*, the middle term must have three characteristics: (1) it must be a quality of the subject (of the statement to be proved), (2) it must exist in the agreeing examples, (3) it must be absent from the different examples (p. 13). To illustrate this we are given the following, as valid: speech is not eternal (statement), because of being artificial (middle term), as pots are artificial and not eternal (agreeing example), so also is speech (application), therefore speech is not eternal (conclusion). (The argument is directed against the Mīmāṃsā doctrine of eternal speech.) The argument is then repeated with the following substituted for the third and fourth steps: as space is eternal and not artificial (different example—N. B. cf. 'conversion by contraposition'), but speech is not so (application) (p. 12). [Tucci's translation is not clear: perhaps the 'major premise', 'what (or whatever) is artificial is not eternal' is actually stated as part of step three in the first part of the argument, with similarly 'what is eternal is not artificial' in step three of the second part, the form of this step being then 'What (whatever?) is M is P, as M_1 is M and P' for the agreeing example and 'What is not P is not M, as not-M_1 is not P and not M' for the different example (of course 'P' here is 'not eternal', 'not P' therefore is 'not not eternal', i.e. 'eternal').] If the middle term has these three characteristics the proof will be valid, if it lacks any of them the proof cannot be accepted. In other words both kinds of example are necessary for the proof to be conclusive.

There are three kinds of false middle term according to the **Tarkaśāstra* (p. 40, unfortunately the detailed exposition of this is in the missing part of the text): unreal, doubtful, contradictory. The unreal (or non-proving, **asiddha?*) is a middle term absent from the predicate to be proved, such as 'horns' when we are trying to establish the presence of a horse. The doubtful is a middle term whose extension is too wide, such as 'horns' to establish the presence of cattle, since goats, deer, etc., also have horns. The contradictory establishes the opposite of the predicate, as 'dawn' when the predicate is 'night'. A middle term which does not have the three characteristics is doubtful (p. 13). Lacking the detailed exposition of this topic we are not sure precisely how the false middle terms are related to the rule of the three characteristics, but it seems clear that the reduction of the false middle terms to three (as against the larger numbers given in the **Upāyahṛdaya* and *Nyāya Sūtra*) reflects a restriction of the doctrine to the essentials indicated by the rule for a valid argument. The extension of the middle term will be shown by examining the examples of both kinds: if it is present in both it is too wide and the middle term uncertain; if it is present in the different instead of the agreeing examples it will be contradictory. The significance of the first kind of false middle term is not quite clear: it is possible that what was intended here was the infringement of the first characteristic, since later writers who adopt a doctrine resembling this make that the meaning, but that is not clear from Tucci's text. The **Tarkaśāstra* seems to have arrived at its doctrine through a study of the methods of the *Vaiśeṣika Sūtra* and its two kinds of false characteristic (in the context of the method of agreement and difference).

The **Tarkaśāstra* exemplifies false statements (to be proved) as well as false middle terms, giving four kinds (self-contradictory, etc.). It has a new systematisation of the sophistical refutations (sixteen of them: ten not properly established, three which are false statements, three which are contradictory) and explains in detail why each sophistical refutation is sophistical, applying its rule of the three characteristics of the middle term. It gives twenty-two defeat situations, which appear to be identical with those of the *Nyāya Sūtra*.

There is a Chinese tradition that the **Tarkaśāstra* was brought to China from Central Asia by a monk named Dharmagupta, which might have intended originally the Dharmaguptaka School (see p. 221 below).

XXII IDEALISM: THE LATER MAHĀYĀNA SŪTRAS

The transition to an idealist outlook among some Mahāyānists begins from certain propositions in the Perfection of Understanding and in Nāgārjuna. The former had spoken of the thought which is non-thought, but added that the nature of thought is 'translucent' (clear, *prabhāsvara*), the latter had said that there is no difference between transmigration and extinction.

In the *Śrīmālā Sūtra*, written probably soon after Nāgārjuna, it is said that the idea that the forces are impermanent may lead to the annihilationist opinion, whilst the idea that extinction is permanent may lead to the eternalist opinion. For this reason it is said that ultimately transmigration is extinction. In other words the ultimate nature of principles is that they are extinct (quoted *Ratnagotravibhāga* p. 34.).

The same *Sūtra* speaks of an ultimate unchanging reality, an 'absolute' reality, which is identified with the nature of the Buddha and also with the doctrine of the Buddha, the 'substance of the doctrine' (*dharmakāya*) of the Buddha. This is not born, does not transmigrate. It is permanent, fixed, safe, eternal. It is empty and pure. The knowledge of it is the knowledge of emptiness. It is called the 'embryo' of the thus-gone, which is present in all principles, in all beings (the possibility of their enlightenment); also the embryo of the transcendental and of the ultimate purity of principles (ibid. pp. 12, 46, 73, 76). (It is no longer a set of concepts; cf. 56f. above.)

Sthiramati (3rd century A.D., not to be confused with at least one later writer of the same name) tried to systematise the doctrine of this *Sūtra* and several others of the period in his *Ratnagotravibhāga* (*Uttaratantra*). These *sūtras* teach an ultimate reality having several aspects. This is not a duality (*advaya*), therefore there is no possibility of real action or real 'defilement' (of streams of consciousness involved in transmigration). It has the nature of thought, pure and translucent. Enlightenment is seeing this translucent thought-nature. This thought-nature is hidden by the 'traces' (*vāsanā*) of defilement, although these have no (real) nature. It is this defilement, unreal though it is, which prevents all beings from being *buddhas* or Buddha-nature all the time. We thus have a single reality with two main aspects, extinction (*nirvāṇa*) or buddhahood and transmigration (*saṃsāra*). All beings share in it, therefore have the knowledge of a thus-gone, but do not understand it. This is because of their incorrect thinking ('unmethodical attention'), through which their actions and defilements originate. The defilements are unreal imaginings. Ultimate reality is without imagining. Therefore there is in fact nothing to be removed, nothing to be obtained (in attaining enlightenment), simply reality has to be seen (I.154, p. 76). The Buddha-nature is in all beings, so they have only to look into their own thoughts (IV.24-6).

With this we have reached an idealist position: the ultimate reality has the nature of thought and everything else is the product of imagining. It is hardly reconcilable with Nāgārjuna's emptiness and with his rejection of anything eternal, though some Buddhists, adopting the new view, tried to restrict Nāgārjuna's critique to the eternalist doctrines of opponents only.

As the new trend gathered momentum a large body of new *sūtras* was produced (mostly in the 3rd century A.D.). We have in fact a third phase of Buddhism. The *Gaṇḍavyūha Sūtra,* part of the *Avataṃsaka,* is a kind of religious novel on the progress of the *bodhisattva.* It describes the universe as being of such a nature that everything in it interpenetrates with everything else. Everything is in everything, without any mutual obstruction. Any atom contains the entire universe. The past and future are contained in the present moment. Transmigration and extinction are identical, with separateness of principles only on the surface and perfect harmony and unity within. All this is described poetically in this work.

For a clear and categorical statement of the new doctrine we have to turn to the *Sandhinirmocana Sūtra,* which is not poetic but is a collection of dialogues. Its title means 'freeing the connections', where the 'connections' are the real intentions of the Buddha when he uttered various *sūtras,* what he really had in mind on different occasions. The idea is that certain statements in the earlier *sūtras* are not to be taken literally but only in their deeper implications. Thus the Buddha taught the four truths to the founders of the early schools and emptiness to the founders of the Madhyamaka, but neither of these doctrines is to be taken literally. Here in this *Sūtra,* which is to be taken literally (*nītārtha,* explicit meaning, definitive), we have the ultimate, final teaching, summed up as 'all principles are without own-being, have not occurred, have not ceased, are calm from the beginning and extinct by nature'. Even this is liable to be misunderstood as implying the non-existence of principles.

In order to make everything clear we are here told that principles have three characteristics: (1) their perfected (*pariniṣpanna*) characteristic as ultimate reality, the ultimate absence of any own-being in them, this is also called 'thusness'; (2) their dependent (*paratantra*) characteristic, which is their conditioned origination, their relative nature, and the 'range' of imagining (the field in which imagining is possible, in which one can imagine they are real, have own-beings, etc.); (3) their imaginary (*parikalpita*) characteristic, which is the purely conventional and therefore imaginary assigning of names to principles, alleging they have various own-beings, distinctions, etc., i.e. inventing concepts and then thinking there are realities corresponding to them, it is the assigning of names in the range of imagining (VII. §6, VI. §6, §5, VII. §25, VI. §4, §25).

Now, the total denial of any characteristics at all to principles, on the ground of no own-being, is a misinterpretation of the doctrine of the Buddha. Though they have no own-being, they do have these three characteristics. There must really be a perfected character underlying principles and also a dependent character in them, otherwise we would not have the experience of their imaginary character: we seem to see these imaginings in the world, so there must be something underlying them, not just a total non-existence of any reality at all. The ultimate reality is the 'pure support' (of consciousness) (VII. §6). The images of thought (of consciousness) are not different from thought itself, they are 'only makings of consciousness' (*vijñaptimātra*) (VIII. §7). In other words nothing exists but consciousness, everything that appears is in consciousness, a product of consciousness.

In what we call transmigration, consciousness grows through the various differentiations (*prapañca*) which it imagines (using names and so on), and to the objects of which it becomes attached. The 'traces' (mentioned before) are traces of these differentiations in consciousness, remaining in the stream. Consciousness in transmigration is called either 'attachment consciousness' or (better known) 'home consciousness' (*ālayavijñāna*), the latter because it seeks a 'home' in the (imaginary) body of a living being, it seeks 'security' in life, united with a body. It is said here that this doctrine of an attachment or home consciousness has not been revealed in other *sūtras* because foolish people might take it for a 'soul' (V).

We may note that the Madhyamaka school completely rejected the idea that this *Sūtra* is really definitive: for them only the Perfection of Understanding is so, and these idealist *sūtras* are provisional, not to be taken literally, like the oldest *sūtras* (see e.g. Candrakīrti, *Madhyamakāvatāra* p. 131).

Lastly among these new *sūtras* we may look at the *Laṅkāvatāra*. The basic statement here, very similar to the *Sandhinirmocana* position, is that there is 'thought only' (*cittamātra*), there is nothing in the universe except thought (pp. 62, 79, 111, 154, 176, 184, 186, 199). Existents such as 'matter' are only imaginings in thought. This is in fact stated more categorically and emphatically than in the *Sandhinirmocana*. Thought in differentiation has two aspects: (1) home consciousness and (2) 'mind' (*manas*) and the consciousnesses of the six senses (pp. 220f.). This gives us 'eight consciousnesses' (p. 126), though the home consciousness is more basic, less ephemeral, than the others (it imagines the others) (pp. 221, 44ff.). All principles, beginning with these kinds of consciousness, are described as waves in the ocean of thought, or of the home consciousness. Out of the home consciousness the various kinds of consciousness arise through the imagining of subject and object, of a something which is conscious and a something of which it is conscious (pp. 37f., 46, 48). This imagining continues because of the traces which have accumulated in the home consciousness during beginningless time (p. 38). When imagining ceases, that is extinction (pp. 61f., 98f., 126).

This home consciousness is nothing but the Buddha-nature, the 'embryo of the thus-gone' (Chapter VI of the *Sūtra*). It has potentialities for bad (=imagining) and for good (=calm). When the truth is understood all imagining ceases and it becomes pure. There is no soul in it. Without it there could be no 'occurrence' of principles. At the same time this 'embryo' is emptiness (p. 78), is extinction, must not be confused with the Brahmanical 'soul' or absolute (the *Sūtra* sees a difficulty here and tries to draw back from a position which might coincide with a Brahmanical eternalist doctrine).

XXIII ASAṄGA

Asaṅga (*c.* 290-360 A.D.) was the systematiser of the idealist school of Buddhism, known as the Vijñānavāda ('Consciousness School') or Yogācāra. There has been a good deal of controversy about the works to be attributed to him. Several of them are sometimes ascribed to 'Maitreya' in traditional sources, though there is complete disagreement between the traditions of Tibet and China as to which these are: 'Maitreya' in fact seems to refer to the *bodhisattva* who will be the next *buddha* in this world, now resident in heaven until the time comes for his last rebirth, and who was supposed to have revealed the definitive teaching to Asaṅga; thus we may take it that these works were by Asaṅga but sometimes thought to have been inspired by Maitreya. Among the major works, a commentary on the *Sandhinirmocana Sūtra* and the *Abhidharmasamuccaya, Madhyāntavibhaṅga, Dharmadharmatāvibhaṅga, Mahāyānasaṃgraha* and *Yogācāra-bhūmiśāstra* are probably authentic compositions of Asaṅga. There is considerable doubt about the *Mahāyānasūtrālaṅkāra*, which may be by an unknown earlier writer.

The *Abhidharmasamuccaya* summarises the whole ancient system of Abhidharma from the new standpoint: the Madhyamaka critique of the system is set aside, but other modifications are applied to the outlook of the early schools. In Vijñānavāda there are exactly 100 principles (*dharmas,* cf. XIV above), one of which is the 'home consciousness' (which is identical with 'thought' and with 'consciousness of mind'). As in the *Sandhinirmocana,* the home consciousness is impregnated with the 'traces' (of differentiations in consciousness) and possesses all the 'seeds' (latent ideas in consciousness, through which it is productive in transmigration) (pp. 11f.). The three characteristics of all principles, as in the *Sandhinirmocana,* are noted. At the end of the text there are some notes on debating, logic and epistemology. Asaṅga here recognises three means of knowledge, sensation, inference and reliable authority. These added to the five steps of a proof taken over from earlier doctrine give the eight parts of what Asaṅga here regards as a complete proof: the five steps have to be checked by reference to the three means of knowledge and the conclusion accepted only if it is not contradicted by these. Such an idea was presumably taken from Vātsyāyana's commentary on the *Nyāya Sūtra,* which instead holds that the first four steps of the proof themselves represent the four means of knowledge recognised by the Nyāya (the statement=authority, the middle term=inference, the example=sensation, the application=similarity).

The *Madhyāntavibhaṅga,* 'Discrimination of the Mean and the Extremes', is Asaṅga's fundamental philosophical work. We may note immediately that as throughout the history of Buddhism the idea of an intermediate position (or non-position) between extremes is taken to be the basic idea in Buddhism. The problem was that the early schools, the Madhyamaka and the Vijñānavāda differed as to the interpretation of this intermediate doctrine. Asaṅga here differs so far from earlier interpretations as to hold that the early Sarvāstivāda and the Madhyamaka themselves represent precisely the two extremes the Buddha wished to avoid (respectively eternalism and annihilationism). Adopting the idealist position, he opens with the categorical statement that 'the imaginer of the unreal' (*abhūtaparikalpa*), i.e. consciousness, exists (*asti*). According to the commentary by Vasubandhu, Asaṅga's brother, this statement contradicts the (Madhyamaka) opinion that all principles have no own-being and do not exist: the imaginer (consciousness) does exist, with its own-being. It also contradicts the opposite (Sarvāstivāda) opinion that all the principles exist, by referring to these as 'the unreal' (*abhūta*). Asaṅga continues that no duality (really) occurs (exists) in consciousness, which is the 'imaginer', but emptiness occurs (exists) and the imaginer occurs (exists) in emptiness. Emptiness is synonymous with 'thusness' (cf. XVIII above, end), it is the ultimate reality and the 'base of principles' (*dharmadhātu,* an old term for the conditioned nature of principles, e.g. at *Saṃyutta* II 56, Taishō 99 section 14 No. 3, which Mahāyānists used as a synonym for their ultimate reality) (I.14). Emptiness can, however, be defiled, though not in reality but only by the imaginer. If it were not so defiled, all living beings would have been freed already.

The *Dharmadharmatāvibhaṅga* supplements this discussion with an account of the 'Discrimination of Principles (*dharmas*) and

Principleness (*dharmatā*, 'conditionedness' or 'regularity')'. 'Principleness' here means the ultimate reality, the real nature of the (supposed) principles, extinction (*nirvāṇa*), the 'unsynthesised'. 'Principles' means 'illusion' (*bhrānti*), transmigration, the 'synthesised'. Every principle is on the one hand a mere 'dependent' principle (the dependent characteristic of the *Sandhinirmocana*), as principle (*dharma*), and on the other hand (when fully understood, ultimately, the perfected characteristic) it is principleness (*dharmatā*), which is 'thusness'. (The third characteristic, the imaginary and totally unreal, is not considered here.) The correct understanding of principles thus leads to the knowledge of extinction (*nirvāṇa*).

The *Mahāyānasaṃgraha*, 'Compendium of the Mahāyāna', among other things deals fully with the home consciousness. It provides a home for all the seeds (of future events, the latent ideas), for the defiled principles, for living beings. It is the resort (*āśraya*) of the knowable (*jñeya*), i.e. the basis of the possibility of being conscious. It is also called 'attachment consciousness' (*ādānavijñāna*, this is taken from the *Sandhinirmocana*) because of its attachment to the senses. It is also called 'thought' (*citta*). Because it accepts the 'seeds', resulting from the 'traces' of all the defiled principles, the home consciousness is the productive cause of these principles: this is its 'own characteristic' (*svalakṣaṇa*). The seeds are neither identical with nor different from the home consciousness, but it is said to have the seeds because it has the power to produce. The home consciousness and the defiled principles are 'reciprocal causes' of one another. Asaṅga goes on to relate this theory to the old doctrine of conditioned origination derived from *Dīgha Nikāya* No. 15 and its parallels. In effect we have here an elaboration of the old Buddhist theory of consciousness providing continuity in a series of momentary events, but differing from it in that consciousness is ultimately something enduring, it 'exists', whereas in the old theory consciousness was even more ephemeral than other principles, though its successive moments, each reflecting the preceding one forward and itself being reflected by the next, then ceasing, provide continuity. The three characteristics also are elaborately discussed in this work.

The *Yogācārabhūmiśāstra* (an immense work, several times longer than all the others combined) is set out within the framework of the

Buddhist way, from the Mahāyāna point of view, from the old doctrine up to the 'stages' (*bhūmi* in the title means 'floor') of the way of the *bodhisattva*, followed by a series of commentaries on the main exposition. Within this framework there is included an elaborate expansion of Abhidharma theory, with special reference to the functioning of consciousness and the 'home consciousness'. The work begins with an account of the consciousnesses of the senses, followed by the mind and meditation, etc. The *Yogācārabhūmiśāstra* appears to be a later work than the *Abhidharmasamuccaya*, reworking the Abhidharma more thoroughly according to the new ideas and expounding the whole doctrine of the *Sandhinirmocana*, and is perhaps Asaṅga's final and most definitive, as well as most comprehensive statement of the idealist philosophy. We find in it a further discussion on logic and epistemology, apparently a revision of the *Abhidharmasamuccaya* account. Under the (same) three means of knowledge we are given the following definitions: sensation is that which is direct, without judgment (*anabhyūhitānabhyūhya* 'not judged nor to be judged', 'not estimated nor to be estimated', presumably free from any kind of reasoning or mental process) and without illusion (error); inference is knowledge of an object through imagining and depending on various relations, namely characteristic, own-being, action, predicate (*dharma* in the sense of quality or attribute) and causality. In place of the eight steps of a proof given in the *Abhidharmasamuccaya* we have a new form of proof, still in eight steps but representing a complete revolution in the old method: in effect two of the old five steps are discarded as logically redundant and the other five steps are epistemological and empirical in content (cf. the last three steps of the *Abhidharmasamuccaya* method):

(1) statement
(2) middle term
(3) example (*udāharaṇa*)
(4) agreement (*sārūpya*, of examples)
(5) difference (*vairūpya*)
(6) sensation
(7) inference
(8) reliable authority (*āptāgama*, reliable tradition)

Thus the first three steps alone constitute a logical proof (the 'statement' is the same as the conclusion and is followed by the minor and major premises), the old 'application' (which is the same as the minor premise, predicating the middle term of the minor term or subject) and 'conclusion' being discarded. Steps four and five are investigations of possible examples, agreeing and different, which may bear on the proof, and the remaining steps are to ensure that the conclusion (statement) is not contradicted by the three means of knowledge (as in the *Abhidharmasamuccaya*). Under agreement and difference the various relations on which the inference depends, as noted above (characteristic—*liṅga*, own-being—*svabhāva*, action—*karman*, predicate—*dharma* and causality—*hetuphala*), are brought in.

In giving credit to Asaṅga for this change in the form of a proof and the reduction of the old logical proof from five to three steps, we must note that his brother Vasubandhu, already mentioned as a collaborator, also wrote on logic and offered a form of proof simply in three steps (without Asaṅga's steps four to eight), which subsequently was taken up by other Buddhist logicians as the basis of their doctrine. The two brothers may in fact have worked together on the problem of a strict proof, giving variant solutions, of which Vasubandhu's was preferred by later writers, and we cannot say whose idea it first was to eliminate two of the old steps as redundant (later writers generally refer to Vasubandhu for this, not to Asaṅga). Vasubandhu in his *Vādavidhi* treats the means of knowledge under the heading of proof, accepting only two, sensation and inference (we do not know the **Tarkaśāstra's* position on this point, since the relevant part of the text is not available). He introduces these by saying that proof is used for instructing or convincing another person, whereas for instructing oneself the means of knowledge are to be used. Sensation is consciousness on account of an object. Inference is the cognition (*darśana*) of a necessarily related (*nāntarīyaka*) object for someone who knows this (necessary relation).

XXIV DIṄNĀGA

Throughout the history of Indian philosophy, epistemology takes an increasingly important place in all the major schools. By the time of Asaṅga (in most cases much earlier) every school had taken up the question of the means of knowledge, sensation, etc., had clearly defined its position in relation to these and had offered proofs or demonstrations of the correctness of its own doctrines through the application of those means which it accepted and according to the way in which it defined those means. The Mīmāṃsā relied on the *Veda* for its metaphysical system, but from at least the 3rd century A.D. (the *Vṛtti* of Bodhāyana or Upavarṣa on the *Mīmāṃsā Sūtra*) it recognised six of the means of knowledge discussed in the *Nyāya Sūtra*: sensation, inference, authority, similarity, implication and non-existence. It held that knowledge from sensation, etc., is inherently correct, provided it is established that there is no defect in the senses or other media, or in the object itself (such as that it is too subtle to be sensed). Knowledge gained from the *Veda* is thus impossible to fault, nothing can disprove its statements, therefore they must be accepted as true. The doctrine of the inherent correctness of cognitions is thus central to Mīmāṃsā metaphysics: it is an epistemological position which leads to the acceptance of their own system along with what appears to be a version of the more or less standard account of the means of knowledge. Among the definitions of the means, we have authority (*śāstra* 'scripture') as the knowledge of an object not sensed, through words; similarity is the knowledge of an object through the recollection of another object not at present sensed; implication is the knowledge of an object not sensed, on the ground of the impossibility of something seen or heard unless that knowledge is assumed; non–existence (*abhāva*) brings about the knowledge 'It does not exist' when an object is not sensed or known by any other means. The Vedānta, which apparently became a school independent of the Mīmāṃsā with the separation of the last four chapters of the *Sūtras* as a *Brahman Sūtra* and its revision *c.* A.D. 200 (it has a polemic against Mahāyāna Buddhism), at first rejected all means except the *Veda* itself (which seems to have been the position of the *Mīmāṃsā Sūtra* at least for the knowledge of important truths of philosophy and religion). Later the school accepted the same six means as the *Mīmāṃsā Vṛtti*, though the *Brahman Sūtra* criticises all but the *Veda*, except in so far as the Vedic text may be directly 'seen' (by seers) or may be 'inferred' from the statement of reputable ancient sages.

The Sāṃkhya, apparently in the 3rd century A.D. (between Āryadeva and Vasubandhu), produced a work called the *Ṣaṣṭitantra* ('Sixty-System'), which for a time occupied the position of basic text of the Sāṃkhya philosophy, like the *sūtras* of the Vaiśeṣika and other schools. The name of its author appears to have been lost (along with the text itself, which is now known only from quotations and a later summary), being apparently of the school of Vārṣagaṇya (some later writers ascribe the text to Vārṣagaṇya himself or to Pañcaśikha or Kapila). The work was superseded by Īśvarakṛṣṇa's elegant summary (*Sāṃkhyakārikā*, *c.* A.D. 460). The importance of the *Ṣaṣṭitantra* lies in its theory of knowledge (though it is not known how far this may have been pioneered by earlier Sāṃkhya philosophers). Though it accepts authority (testimony of a reliable person) as a means, it proceeds to construct its metaphysical system by means of inference, just as the *Vaiśeṣika Sūtra* does. Inference is deliberately put before sensation and defined first, as more important, as the establishment of the other term in a relation from the sensation of one term. Seven such relations are then laid down as the bases of inference. Among these is that of primary to secondary realities (see XV above, Vārṣagaṇya's doctrine), which already gives the epistemology a Sāṃkhya slant. Three means of knowledge are thus recognised, inference, sensation and authority. The form of a proof has five steps similar to those of the Nyāya, but besides the direct (*vīta*) proof an indirect (*āvīta*) proof is proposed, being the method of exhaustion (*pariśeṣa*) of hypotheses other than the statement accepted. The first and most important topic of the sixty from which this work takes its name is the ultimate or original physical reality (here called *pradhāna*, 'principal', but the same as the old 'unmanifest'). Five direct and five indirect proofs are offered for its existence. (The *Yoga Sūtra* of Patañjali II, probably 4th century, offers a system of meditation very close to that of early Buddhism and practically no philosophy.)

The Sautrāntika philosopher Vasubandhu is presumably to be distinguished from Asaṅga's brother as Vasubandhu II, probably 5th century, though he is sometimes regarded as the same person at an earlier stage of his career. In principle the Sautrāntikas, as their name implies, restrict themselves to the teaching of the *Sūtrapiṭaka*, regarding this as authentic statements of the Buddha whereas the *Abhidharma* was composed only later by his followers. The criticism of the doctrinal additions of the *Abhidharma* seems to have begun within the Sarvāstivāda school, in the 1st century A.D., with the work of Dharmatrāta (I) and Buddhadeva. They drastically reduced the list of principles (*dharmas*), especially denying ultimate reality to most of the mental principles as not different from 'thought' itself. A separate Sautrāntika school seems to have been established by Śrīlāta in the 3rd century. Vasubandhu's *Abhidharmakośa* and *Bhāṣya* is a detailed critique of the Sarvāstivāda Abhidharma system, noting the views of many of the early schools, and as a critical exposition it has served as an encyclopaedia of the subject widely used as a textbook, being adopted by Mahāyānists of both the Madhyamaka and Vijñānavāda trends for this purpose. Yaśomitra (probably 8th century) defended Vasubandhu from the counter criticisms of Sarvāstivāda writers in a very important commentary on his work.

Vasubandhu presents the subject as the discrimination of principles, with the definition that a principle is that which has (maintains) its own-characteristic (*svalakṣaṇa*, p. 2). The first chapter being set out under the eighteen 'bases' (6 kinds of sense–object, 6 senses including the mind and 6 kinds of consciousness, cf. p. 50 above) deals particularly with problems of sensation, perception and consciousness, all of which bear directly on epistemology, distinguishing for example the sense-object or datum (*viṣaya*) as instrumental cause (p. 96 above) from the support (*ālambana*) of mental principles (p. 90 above), which is perceived by consciousness. He accepts three means of knowledge: sensation, inference and reliable tradition (p. 76).

His pupil Diṅnāga (late 5th century?) put epistemology, the study of the means of knowledge (*pramāṇas*), in the first place: instead of taking up the *Sūtra* and *Abhidharma*, with debating and epistemology as an appendix to the latter, as the basis of Buddhist philosophy (and this was the approach of such old schools as the Sthaviravāda as well as of Asaṅga), we are to begin with epistemology in order to ascertain how we can have any knowledge at all. According to Diṅnāga there are only two means of knowledge, sensation and inference, and the supposed authority of the *Tripiṭaka*, or of the Buddha himself, is nothing beyond these: the Buddha merely exemplifies the two means of knowledge (as Diṅnāga says in the opening verse of the *Pramāṇasamuccaya*). This is really very much in harmony with the attitude of the Buddha himself, as recorded in the earliest texts, since he disclaimed any authority and rejected any other authority, urging his followers to investigate everything empirically for themselves (cf. VIII above).

At least fourteen philosophical works are known to have been written by Diṅnāga, but only nine seem to survive, and of these not one intact in the original Sanskrit, but only in obscure Tibetan and Chinese translations and fragments of the Sanskrit which appear as quotations in later Indian philosophical works. (The Sautrāntika school in India was wiped out by the Muslim Turkish invaders at the beginning of the 13th century and afterwards: had the fanatics known anything of Buddhist philosophy they would certainly have wished to suppress it as subversive of religion, but the ignorant adventurers actually claimed that they were destroying idolatry, since the monasteries and universities they razed, and whose residents they massacred, were adorned with statues of the Buddha). Diṅnāga's brief commentary *Marmapradīpa Vṛtti* on the essentials of Vasubandhu's *Abhidharmakośa Bhāṣya* is available in Tibetan. His *Hastavālaprakaraṇa* ('Trunk and Tail Treatise') considers the nature of the objects supposed to exist in everyday life, concluding that they are only concepts (the title illustrates the oddness of parts of a whole). What we suppose we see is always analysable into smaller parts: the ultimate 'atoms', sometimes held to constitute real particles of which objects are constituted, cannot be seen, nor in fact can they be conceived, since however small they are supposed to be they must still be imagined as having parts, for example an 'atom' must have an east side and a west side. Thus all the objects we think we see in the world are nothing but concepts. The *Ālambanaparīkṣā* ('Critique of the Support') carries this argument slightly further: the 'support' cannot be atoms, nor can it be an aggregate (of parts, a 'whole', since this is only a conventional thing, a concept), nor can it be an 'aggregate of atoms', since this will not explain why objects made of exactly similar atoms may appear quite different (e.g. a jar and a dish both made of clay). Explanation by differences in 'number' or 'arrangement' (figure) of atoms is no solution, since these are still only concepts. The 'object' is therefore only an appearance in consciousness, it is internal to the stream of consciousness, not an external reality. Among the apparently lost works of Diṅnāga were a series of critiques of the Brahmanical schools of philosophy, the Sāṃkhya, Vaiśeṣika and Nyāya. A 'Critique of the Universal' (*Sāmānyaparīkṣā*), i.e. of the supposed objectively real universal of Vaiśeṣika and Nyāya, is extant in Chinese.

Diṅnāga had also written a commentary on Vasubandhu's *Vādavidhāna* on logic, and his major and mature works, in which he develops entirely independent ideas, are all in the field of logic and epistemology. He became dissatisfied with Vasubandhu II's logical doctrine and proceeded to rework the entire theory in order to make it really rigorous and consistent. At first he followed Vasubandhu and the long tradition of study of the debate in treating the means of knowledge as merely a subsidiary topic under that of the proof, then he made the revolutionary change which inaugurated his new critical philosophy, by making the means of knowledge the main subject of enquiry and treating the proof as merely an incidental part of the doctrine of inference.

Diṅnāga's first independent work on logic is the short but momentous *Hetucakraḍamaru*, 'Drum of the Wheel of Middle Terms'. The 'drum' is presumably the noise of the unstoppable 'wheel' as it rolls on, a challenge to strike fear into the hearts of opponents. This 'wheel' is in fact a table showing how middle terms in proofs are either valid or invalid: it makes clear the 'characteristics' of middle terms, the rules for validity, and exposes the true nature of sophistical refutations. The text (preserved in the Tibetan *Tripiṭaka*) is illustrated by a diagram, i.e. the table, showing the concomitance between the middle and major terms as indicated by agreeing and different examples:

Table of middle terms
[minor term 'speech' (*śabda*) throughout]

	Present in different examples	Absent from different examples	Present in some but not in other different examples
Present in agreeing examples	M knowable (*prameya*) P eternal (*nitya*) E a. space (*ākāśa*) d. pot (*ghaṭa*) ? 1 (*aniścita* or *anaikāntika*)	M artificial (*kṛtaka*) P non-eternal (*anitya*) E a. pot d. space Valid 2	M non-eternal (*anitya*) P produced by effort (*prayatnottha*) E a. pot d. lightning (*vidyut*), space 3 ?
Absent from agreeing examples	M artificial (*kṛta*) P eternal (*śāśvata*) E a. space d. pot Contradictory 4 (*viruddha*)	M audible (*śrāvaṇa*) P eternal E a. space d. pot ? 5	M produced by effort (*yatnaja*) P eternal E a. space d. pot, lightning Contradictory 6
Present in some but not in other agreeing examples	M non-eternal P not produced by effort (*ayatna*) E a. lightning, space d. pot ? 7	M produced by effort P non–eternal E a. pot, lightning d. space Valid 8	M incorporeal (*amūrta*)* (*not having extended body, alternative: intangible (*asparśa*)) P eternal E a. space, atom (*paramāṇu*) d. action (*karman*), pot 9 ?

The *Nyāyamukha* insists on the necessity of both kinds of example for a valid proof.

Discussion on sophistical refutations there further elucidates the 'table'.

Pramāṇasamuccaya: the *dṛṣṭānta* shows that the middle term is followed by the major term and that wherever the major term is absent the middle term is absent.—The method may presumably be compared with Mill's joint method of agreement and difference; in fact it is noted that the two simple methods can be used only under special conditions. The method of concomitant variation (**tadvikāra-vikāritva*) is regarded by Diṅnāga as a particular case of agreement. There is also a brief reference to the method of exhaustion (used already by Kaṇāda): it too is not an independent method.

The horizontal ranks of the table show the middle term (M) present in the agreeing examples (E a.), absent from the agreeing examples and present in some, but not other, agreeing examples; these intersect with the vertical columns showing the middle term present in, absent from and present in some different examples (E d.), showing all the nine possible cases. Actual illustrations are inserted of hypothetical arguments to prove various predicates (P) or major terms. The minor term, or subject of the statement to be proved, is 'speech' (*śabda*) throughout and the first characteristic of a valid middle term, that it is a quality of the subject, is satisfied (otherwise there would be no argument). It can be seen that of the nine hypothetical arguments only two are valid: those at the top and bottom of the central column (Nos. 2 and 8). Those in the middle of the left and right columns (Nos. 4 and 6) are contradictory (*viruddha*). Those at the four corners (Nos. 1, 3, 7 and 9) are uncertain (?) (*aniścita* or *anaikāntika*), since the middle terms overlap into both kinds of example. The argument in the middle of the central column (No. 5) is also uncertain, since the middle term is not present in any example at all, of either kind (it is found only in the subject itself). The first argument will work out as follows: speech is eternal; because (of being) knowable; what(ever) is knowable is eternal, like space/what(ever) is not eternal is not knowable, like a pot. The middle term is false because both space and pots are knowable, i.e. it is present in both kinds of example. The third argument will be: speech is produced by effort; because non-eternal; whatever is non-eternal is produced by effort, like a pot, whatever is not produced by effort is not non-eternal, like lightning and space. Here the middle term is present in the agreeing example (a pot), but among different examples it may be present in some (e.g. lightning) but absent from others (e.g. space), thus the third characteristic is not satisfied (that the middle term must be absent from the different examples) and the middle term is false. The sixth argument will be: speech is eternal; because produced by effort; whatever is produced by effort is eternal, like space/whatever is not eternal is not produced by effort, like a pot and lightning. Here the middle term is absent from the agreeing example (space not being produced by effort) and present in one of the different examples (a pot), though absent from the other (lightning). Thus both the second and third characteristics are infringed and the middle term is contradictory. The seventh argument will be: speech is not produced by effort; because non-eternal; whatever is non-eternal is not produced by effort, like lightning and space/whatever is not not produced by effort is not non-eternal, like a pot. Here the middle term is present in some (lightning) but not in other (space) agreeing examples, which however would not invalidate the argument (the second characteristic is satisfied, according to Diṅnāga, if the middle term is present in at least some agreeing examples; it is a mistake to give space as an agreeing example but it does not invalidate the argument, it is simply irrelevant). What does invalidate the argument is that the middle term is present in the different examples (such as a pot, which is non-eternal as well as produced by effort).

The eighth argument will be: speech is non-eternal; because produced by effort; whatever is produced by effort is non-eternal, like a pot and lightning/whatever is not non-eternal is not produced by effort, like space. Here the second characteristic is satisfied because the middle term is present in some agreeing examples, its absence from others (lightning) being again irrelevant. The third characteristic is also satisfied because the middle term is absent from the different examples. The ninth argument will be: speech is eternal; because incorporeal; whatever is incorporeal is eternal, like space and the atom/whatever is not eternal is not incorporeal, like action and a pot. Here the middle term is again present in some (space) agreeing examples, although absent from others (it is worth noting that though the Buddhists did not admit that there were eternal atoms, other schools, such as the Vaiśeṣikas, did; though it is irrelevant here, it is sometimes necessary to bear in mind that a debater may argue against an opponent on the basis of something admitted by that opponent and so refute him on his own ground). The argument is invalid because the middle term is present in some (action) different examples, though absent from others (a pot).

A little study with this table will show that most of the sophistical refutations are attempts to overthrow a valid argument of the eighth variety. Here the examples of M are also examples of P (these are the 'some agreeing') and the examples of not P are also examples of not M (the different examples). But there are also examples of P which are not M (these are the 'other agreeing' examples, agreeing with P though not present in M). The proof is valid because whatever is M is P: it is not necessary that whatever is P should be M, that question is irrelevant to the proof, though it may be brought in as a sophistical argument to baffle a debater. The sophistical argument itself will usually be of the ninth variety (attempting to prove the contradictory of the eighth argument by means of a different middle term, thus the pot appears to be different from what is eternal and incorporeal and so to clinch the argument—'appearance of difference'—but the example 'action', also 'different', can be adduced to expose the sophistry).

Probably later than this analysis of middle terms is the *Nyāyamukha* ('Introduction to Method'), a comprehensive manual but still arranged in the traditional way, consisting of two sections, one on proof and one on refutation. Already, however, practically all the details, the definitions, etc., are different from Vasubandhu I's. The proof has three steps, as in Vasubandhu, but these are rearranged: (1) middle term, (2) example, (3) 'thesis' (*pakṣa,* replacing the 'statement' but equivalent to it). The means of knowledge are discussed at the end of the section on proof, and are sensation and inference, as in Vasubandhu, but their definitions are different. Sensation is knowledge (knowing, *jñāna*) without imagining. This means that there is no distinguishing or classification of objects through it and no naming or application of words. Inference is knowledge through a middle term. It cognises a subject as belonging to a class, to the class of things having that particular characteristic (the middle term). The subject will also belong to other classes if other characteristics are selected. Thus whereas inference cognises only characteristics of classes, sensation cognises only the 'characteristic' of the object by itself, not classified (classification is imagining). Classes are imagined by the intellect, they do not exist objectively.

Diṅnāga adds that there is nothing else knowable except these two: objects in themselves (through sensation) and classes (through inference). Each of the two kinds of knowable thing has its own separate means of knowledge and these two means of knowledge are completely distinct, they know two entirely different (and apparently unconnected) kinds of things. Sensation relates to objective reality but stops short at it because it cannot classify or even name its objects.

These (real) objects are just unclassified particulars. Inference for its part is restricted to imagining (with words and classifications or concepts) and deals in classes having no objective reality, it cannot reach real objects. Any other supposed means of knowledge, such as reliable authority or similarity, is, where true, covered by one or other of these and to be included in them: it rests on either a sensation or an inference.

For the characteristics of a valid middle term Diṅnāga follows his earlier table. A point which must be noted here is that for the first characteristic, that it should be a quality of the subject, he uses the term *pakṣadharma.* A curious ambiguity appears here, which presumably resulted from the use of traditional terms in the schools of logic and was consecrated by usage, so that Diṅnāga did not see fit to change it. At any rate he points it out in this Introduction to Method in order to avoid confusing the student: *pakṣa* ('thesis') in *pakṣadharma* means the subject only (whereas elsewhere it means the whole thesis to be proved, i.e. the subject as characterised by the predicate). The usage is said to be legitimate because a term for the whole of something may also be used for a part of it. The same term *pakṣa* may also be used for the predicate only. Moreover there are two synonyms for *pakṣa* here, namely *sādhya,* 'what is to be proved', and *anumeya,* 'what is to be inferred', and these similarly have three different meanings. There are, however, other terms available: *dharmin* for subject and *dharma* for predicate (though *dharma* means any predicate of the subject, for example the middle term). The agreeing examples are called *sapakṣa* (the different ones *asapakṣa*), and this evidently means agreeing with the predicate or among those things qualified by the predicate (i.e. *pakṣa* in *sapakṣa,* 'with the *pakṣa*', means the predicate). The example, in fact, is said to show that the middle term is followed by the predicate (the *sādhya*). Though there are two kinds of example, agreeing and different, there is only one middle term (in other words the method used is the single joint method of agreement and difference, not two separate methods). The example shows that the middle term is inseparably connected with the predicate to be proved: it is always followed by it, and wherever the predicate is absent the middle term also is absent. The use of an example which does not do this is a 'false example'. Diṅnāga further stresses the necessity of contraposition of the middle term and predicate in the different example part of the proof: in the case of the agreeing example we have, for instance, 'whatever is produced by effort is non-eternal, like a pot' (the middle term is followed by, accompanied by, the predicate, M is P); in the case of the different example we must have instead 'whatever is not non-eternal is not produced by effort, like space' (wherever the predicate is absent the middle term is absent, not P is not M). This formulation is necessary to ensure the absolute exclusion of the middle term from the different examples. (Diṅnāga is here criticising the Nyāya formulation of the different example, which is not contraposed, is 'not M is not P' which according to him leads to fallacies.) Both kinds of example are necessary, with this formulation, to avoid fallacious arguments.

The section on refutation (*dūṣaṇa*) explains that refutation is showing that the opponent's proof is in some way deficient with respect to the rules of proof set out in the first section. It deals in particular with the sophistical refutations, defined as attempts to refute a valid argument by breaking the rules of proof. Of course, if the original argument is really not valid it must be refuted by pointing out the fault in it, failure to point out such a fault being itself a defeat situation. The actual sophistical refutations discussed by Diṅnāga are the same as those in the **Tarkaśāstra* (which were also adopted by Vasubandhu), but he says that in fact sophistical refutations are infinite in number, mentioning a few more taken apparently from the *Nyāya Sūtra*, with the remark that they should be analysed in the same way as those he has discussed in detail. He does not follow the classification of the **Tarkaśāstra*. The analysis relates to the table of middle terms. It is incidentally remarked in the course of these discussions that sensation always overrides inference, an important principle of epistemology.

It is in Diṅnāga's final work, the *Pramāṇasamuccaya*, 'Compendium of the Theory of Knowledge', in which he collects and summarises the ideas scattered in his earlier writings, that he makes the great change of presenting his whole doctrine as a study of epistemology instead of as the theory of logic and debating. In this work the logical doctrines are not greatly modified, but the question of the two means of knowledge, the relationship between them, between the kinds of object they know, between words in particular and real objects, is elaborated with new theories (probably taken from some lost treatise on inference written previously) as the fundamental subject under investigation. The work is in six chapters: (1) sensation, (2) inference 'for oneself', (3) inference 'for another' (i.e. proof, which makes public an inference known to oneself), (4) the example, (5) the 'exclusion of what is other' (the nature of language and the relationship between words and objects), (6) sophistical refutations.

At the beginning of the first chapter Diṅnāga sums up his position: there are two means of knowledge, sensation and inference, because that which is to be known (*prameya*, the knowable) has two characteristics (*lakṣaṇas*), namely the 'own characteristic' (*svalakṣaṇa*) and the 'universal characteristic' (*sāmānyalakṣaṇa*, or 'class characteristic'). There is nothing else which can be known besides these two (in effect, 'particulars' and 'universals'): the 'own characteristic' is the object (*viṣaya*, 'scope', range, sense-object, datum; see 'Objects', p. 357) of sensation, the 'universal characteristic' is the object of inference. Nor is there any other means of knowledge for uniting the two kinds of knowledge in the mind (the relationship between them will be examined in the fifth chapter) (I.2 and Diṅnāga's *Vṛtti*).

Sensation is defined as excluding imagining (*kalpanāpoḍha*). This imagining which is excluded is connected with names, classes, qualities, actions and substances, it means using words of these five kinds. Sensation is (only) where this imagining is not. However, it is called 'sensation' (*pratyakṣa*, literally 'to the sense organ': so one must translate it 'sensation') because it is not common to the different senses but depends on each of them separately, it is of different kinds according to the senses. Therefore it is not called 'to the object' (*prativiṣaya*), since an object can be common to various senses, can appear in consciousness of mind (i.e. as an object, 'support', of which one becomes conscious) and also be common to different persons (literally to different series of consciousness). Diṅnāga then quotes the Sarvāstivāda *Abhidharma* (*Vijñānakāya* T. 1539, p. 559b; also *Abhidharmakośa Bhāṣya* p. 7: one is aware of a sense datum, not a 'substance') to the effect that 'one is conscious of blue' (for example), 'one is not conscious of "blue" ' (i.e. of 'blue' as a quality or predicate, *dharma*, of some object). One perceives just the object (*artha*) in the object, one does not perceive a quality (*dharma*), in an object (in other words the blue which one senses is itself the object, it is not a quality of some other object, of a 'substance'). The sense organ does not know a subject (*dharmin*, i.e. the object which possesses various predicates or qualities) completely, because the latter has many aspects, its scope is limited to an aspect or appearance (*rūpa* in its original meaning), which cannot be described (that would be to introduce 'imagining') and is an experience of just the 'own' (i.e. of a particular, of an 'own characteristic', of something not, as itself, classifiable) (I.5). Apart from the sensations of the five senses, Diṅnāga recognises mental sensation of an object in the mind, provided it is without imagining. It is 'own experience' (*svasaṃvitti*) in the mind, of desire, etc., independent of the senses (i.e. sensation of principles in one's own series of consciousness, introspection). Finally the intuition of a *yogin* (concentrator, in meditation), when simply of an object and independent of descriptions given by a teacher, is a kind of sensation. An illusion (*bhrānti*, error such as a mirage) is only a semblance of sensation (a false sensation, not a real one), it is obscure (a true sensation is vivid, clear). Similarly knowledge at the 'concealing' (*saṃvṛti*) level of truth (see XX above for a note on this), inference, anything inferred and wishing for something remembered are only semblances of sensation: knowledge at the concealing level involves superimposing something else, one's own supposed object, on the ultimate object (thus sensation is of ultimate reality). Knowledge occurs with two images (*ābhāsas*): the image of the 'own' (internal experience = knowledge of the knowledge) and the image of the object (knowledge of the datum). But when the object is external the means of knowledge is only the feature of the object (datum). The own experience is then only there being an image of the object, which is the means of knowledge, because through the image it is known (I.9 and *Vṛtti*; this seems to foreshadow, rather hesitantly, Dharmakīrti's pragmatic criterion of a true means of knowledge: it reaches a real object, which is known to be real because it produces effects). The means of knowledge, the feature (*ākāra*) of the object of knowledge and the result (effect, as experience in the series of consciousness) are not really three separate things (one might call any of them knowledge I.10).

Inference for oneself (*svārtha*) is knowledge of an object through a characteristic (*liṅga*, or 'middle term'), because of the three aspects (*trirūpa*, i.e. having the three characteristics of a valid middle term) (II.1). Inference is here separated from proof, and Diṅnāga is said (by Dharmottara) to have been the first to make the distinction between inference 'for oneself', which is inference proper, and inference 'for another', which is proof. The doctrine of the three aspects or characteristics is practically the same as in Diṅnāga's earlier works. Its details are left to the third chapter. Reliable authority, if not contradicted (by experience), is a kind of inference (not a separate means of knowledge), because it deals with universals. Inference infers the subject (*dharmin*) as characterised by (*viśiṣṭa*) the predicate (*dharma*) (*Vṛtti* on II.5). When the invariable concomitance (*avyabhicāra*) of the middle term with the major term (*dharma*, or 'predicate') is already known, one can conclude that the predicate is also present in the subject (*dharmin*) observed (in the present instance) to be connected with the middle term (II.11).

Inference for another (*parārtha*) is communicating an object (*artha*) already known to oneself to another (in other words formal proof set out in a debate; III.1). It is stating the middle term with its three aspects. Two steps only are necessary, the 'middle term' (here called *hetu*, to distinguish it as a step in proof from the *liṅga* as characteristic in inference proper) and the example (*dṛṣṭānta*). The thesis or statement, which is what is desired to be obtained as the conclusion, is not part of the proof (this is a revision of Diṅnāga's earlier theory). The middle term, in effect a minor premise, states that this middle term is a predicate of the subject. The example, in effect major premise, states that the middle term is pervaded (**vyāpta*) by the predicate. A subject cannot prove another subject or a predicate; only a predicate (*dharma*) proves another predicate (one predicate, that which is to be proved, is proved through another predicate, or quality of the subject, namely the middle term). The details concerning a valid middle term follow Diṅnāga's earlier table and the Introduction to Method. There are only two kinds of false middle term, the uncertain and the contradictory. 'Refutation' is simply pointing out that the opponent's middle term does not satisfy the three aspects.

The example (*dṛṣṭānta*, datum, evidence) shows that the middle term is followed by the predicate and that wherever the predicate is absent the middle term also is absent. Formally the example can be presented by agreement or by difference, but both these kinds of example are necessary: the agreeing example shows only that the middle term is present in the agreeing examples; the different example indicates the relation of pervasion (**vyāpti*) of the middle term by the predicate, or more strictly it excludes the possibility of non-pervasion, but even so is not adequate by itself to satisfy the conditions for a valid proof, because we may have a case of the middle term not being present in any example at all (i.e. of the argument in the middle of the central column of Diṅnāga's table, No. 5, which is uncertain and not valid). Diṅnāga again follows his Introduction in discussing 'false examples'.

The verbal (*śābda*) is not another means of knowledge, for it likewise is through inference: as in the case of 'artificiality', etc. (as middle terms), it expresses its meaning (object, *artha*) through the exclusion of what is other (V.1). A class-word does not refer to particulars (*bhedas*, the members of the class), because these are innumerable and variable (*vyabhicāratas*); nor is it an expression of a class plus its union (*yoga*, with the members), because the sound (*śruti*) is not many (*pṛthak*, capable of specifying the members separately, 2). What is true of class-words is also true of words for 'substances', 'qualities', 'actions' and union with these.

The existence-word (*sant*, a class) speaks of a 'substance' (etc., as members) as subordinate to the own-appearance (*svarūpa*, character) of the class, not that it is observed (by sensation). Because there is no indication (*ākṣepa*) of the members, 'pot', etc., included in it (the class), there being no actual mention of its members, there is no common location (*sāmānyādhikaraṇya*, of the class and the members, *Vṛtti* on 4). In speaking of the whiteness of jasmine or of oyster shell, a word simultaneously refers to a class and a member of it; but without understanding there may be excess (imposing a word on something outside its class) in referring to a substance because of a transferred quality. Thus a crystal may take on the quality red from some nearby lac (5 and *Vṛtti*). (7ff. are on transfer and on using compounds and suffixes in language to indicate relations.)

A sound makes an exclusion of what is other (*anyāpoha*, it does not refer positively); for example if it refers to a place as non-white, etc., that is not because of a class, because it is not a class, moreover there is uncertainty in indicating an object (*artha*, or 'meaning') (11). Also from speech there is no comprehensive access to what is to be expressed, which is manifold: it makes a meaning (object) by demarcation (*vyavaccheda*), conforming to its own relation (belonging to a class, 12). (Words) have different objects (meanings) because of difference of what is to be excluded, clumsy (*jaḍa*) in access to differences in their own objects, because of there being effects that are not different in the same place, they have (express the relation) 'distinction and distinguished' (*viśeṣaṇaviśeṣyabhāva*, 14). For that is not purely blue, nor is it purely a waterlily, because what is expressed is a combination (*samudāya*, 15). Many words may be used for one object to be expressed, but they do not exhaust it, their access is not comprehensive. The following *kārikās* are on such compounds, having a common location or a distinction and distinguished of the words composing them (up to 25ab).

Synonyms do not exclude each other's objects and a member does not exclude a class it belongs to. 'Tree' does not exclude 'solidity' (nor 'substance' nor 'existence'), because there is no contradiction (25cd, cf. 27 and 35). Lower classes do not exclude the higher classes to which they have an invariable relation (which include them). A member is not abandoned by its own 'universal' (class), because there is expectation of that only. (On the other hand) it is not specified by it because there is doubt (we saw in 2 above that a class does not refer to its members) (26). But a member excludes the object (meaning) of another member, because there is contradiction between them, like the sons of a king in their different domains or like the species of treeness. Likewise classes at the same level (members of a higher class) exclude one another and so on with reference to a higher class (28 and *Vṛtti*; as in 26).

There is facility (*saukarya*, easy understanding, glossed as conclusiveness, certainty, *ekānta*) in the relation of a sound (speech, to its object), and no variability, because it is not seen in the object of another speech and because it is seen in a part of its own object (34).

The knowables 'treeness', 'solidity', 'substance' and 'existence', if their order is reversed are a 'sign' (*nimitta*, of a concept, a 'sign' is perceived by the mind through perception, *saṃjñā*) of uncertainty whether they are included in each other, otherwise (not reversed) of certainty (35, summarising 25-6, 'treeness' implies 'solidity', etc., but 'existence' does not specify which lower classes are present on a particular occasion).

The non-difference of a pervasion which excludes another (object) through the objects of its members, if there is non-difference from an act of observation (sensation does not contradict it), is the establishing of a class-predicate (36). A class-predicate has the characteristic of comprehending any class such as oneness or permanence. From non-difference (means) from not being different from the support (projected into consciousness by a sense organ) which comprehends the whole of the object. Therefore speech speaks of existents distinguished only by exclusion of other objects (*Vṛtti*).

In using words we follow ordinary social conventions (37-8). (Presumably in the above discussion, since 'existence', 'existents' and the like would be questioned by Buddhist philosophers; but they held against the Mīmāṃsakas, etc., that language is established by convention, not by revelation, etc.) This is followed by a critique of Sāṃkhya (39-45).

At the end of chapter V Diṅnāga quotes some verses from Bhartṛhari's *Vākyapadīya* on linguistics (p.186 below). In analysis (*apoddhāra*), the object (meaning) of a word is discriminated from the sentence: therefore the object of the sentence, called 'intuition' (*pratibhā*), is produced first (46, cf. *Vākyapadīya* II.145ff.). An expression referring to 'water', for example, refers both to a drop and to a combination, it functions without regard to number, measure or shape (50=*Vākyapadīya* II.160). The function of speech which is used referring to that which is distinguished by shape, colour or parts is not perceived actually referring to a (particular) part (51=*Vākyapadīya* II.157). Thus speech approaches parts or particulars by means of exclusions, but it can never actually reach them, never reach the objects of sensation, because its meaning is always a class, however restricted. 'Intuition' is the understanding of the meanings of sentences by native speakers of a language, which resembles the instinct (also *pratibhā*) of birds, etc., and the intuition of genius; cf. 'intuition' (*pratibhāna*) above (p. 92).

'Similarity' (*upamāna*) is not a separate means of knowledge because it consists simply of speech plus inference (*Vṛtti* after 51).

The sixth chapter restates the doctrine of the Introduction to Method on sophistical refutations.

Thus of the six chapters the first is on sensation and the rest are all on various aspects of inference, which reduces to exclusion. Critiques of other schools are appended to each chapter. Sensation and inference are not absolutely separate, as inexpressible sense data and fictitious imaginings. Inference according to Diṅnāga is controllable by reference to sensation, though not directly. It can approximate to the truth, though it can never reach it.

XXV POST-DIṄNĀGA BRAHMANICAL PHILOSOPHY

It is not possible in a survey such as this to pursue in detail the very extensive contributions to philosophy of the various schools during the centuries following Diṅnāga. The main doctrinal positions of the schools were in fact established by his time. What followed consisted first of the greatly increased technical professionalisation of each school, second of a certain amount of influence of the new Buddhist ideas (the idealism of the Consciousness school and Diṅnāga's epistemological approach to philosophy) causing important modifications in the positions of certain other schools, third of the emergence of some hybrid schools attempting to combine the doctrines of two or more schools and fourth of the secondary development of philosophy as applied in the interests of theology by several schools of medieval religion. Thus each school sought rigorous definitions of all its concepts, and successive philosophers revised these definitions, engaging in minute polemics against predecessors in their own as well as in other schools, trying to secure all their positions against any possible criticism. A major branch of the Vedānta (that often known from the name of Śaṃkara) embraced idealism with an ultimate reality which is 'not a duality' (*advaya*, whence the school was also called Advaita), whilst later the Nyāya school (amalgamating with the Vaiśeṣika once more) reworked its whole doctrine as basically an epistemological enquiry and became the 'New Nyāya' (Navya Nyāya, see XXVII below). Besides this recombination of Vaiśeṣika and Nyāya, there developed hybrid Buddhist schools, particularly the attempt to combine Madhyamaka with the Pramāṇa doctrine. The Rāmānuja and Madhva (and other) schools of Vedānta are basically theological, being assimilated to the Vaiṣṇava faith (Viṣṇu=God), similarly there were (non-Vedic) Śaiva (Śiva=God) schools, notably the Pratyabhijñā school.

The new Buddhist ideas had a considerable impact on all the schools, so that Diṅnāga marks something like a turning point in the history of Indian philosophy, as well as a culminating point in the pioneering of new ideas. We can now review the main trends stemming from this point in history.

Praśastapāda (6th century A.D.?) reworked the Vaiśeṣika philosophy into what became its standard form. His *Padārthadharmasaṃgraha* is not really a commentary on the *Vaiśeṣika Sūtra,* though it is often referred to as such. Since his work gradually superseded all previous interpretations of Kaṇāda it has become very difficult to restore the original meanings of the *Sūtra,* disentangling them from the system of Praśastapāda and his successors. In order to provide the Vaiśeṣika with what he considered an adequate theory of knowledge and a strict doctrine of proof, Praśastapāda borrowed largely from Diṅnāga, with modifications of certain points. Thus he takes part of Diṅnāga's description of sensation from the *Nyāyamukha* (relating it to one or other of the senses, plus the mind) but adds that it can be either without imagining or with imagining (in the latter case it can be of universals, categories, etc.). On proof he adopts the Buddhist doctrine of the three characteristics of a valid middle term, but maintains the Nyāya method of five steps in the proof (with different names for some of them). Like Diṅnāga, he admits only two means of knowledge, with reliable authority included in inference.

Uddyotakara (later in the 6th century?) on the other hand, writing a sub-commentary to Vātsyāyana's Commentary on the *Nyāya Sūtra,* sought to refute all Diṅnāga's criticisms of Nyāya doctrine and maintain its positions rigidly. In doing so he rather often resorts to quibbles and sophistry. For example in order to attack Diṅnāga's table of middle terms he introduces various further distinctions, raising the possible cases from 9 to 2032, without bringing in any new logical principle but confusing matters in such a way as to produce a semblance of a refutation of Diṅnāga's doctrine.

The most important Sāṃkhya work after Īśvarakṛṣṇa's *Kārikās* is the anonymous *Yuktidīpikā* commentary on them, which discusses Diṅnāga's and other Buddhist views in establishing its epistemology (6th century?).

The history of the Vedānta school before the 7th century A.D. is very obscure. After the fixing of the *Brahman Sūtra c.* A.D. 200 a number of commentators wrote on it, but no commentaries earlier than the 7th century seem to survive (they have been superseded by newer commentaries of different trends). The Vedānta holds, as revealed knowledge, that *brahman* is the ultimate reality underlying the whole universe. This *brahman* is somehow transformed into all the things we experience in the universe. The early doctrine, and apparently that of the *Sūtra* itself, was that this transformation was real. The universe of our experience is real, the ultimate *brahman* also is real. In that case the universe is in a sense different (*bheda*) from *brahman* (as the reality we experience) but in another sense the same (*abheda*) as the *brahman* of which it is a transformation. This 'Different-Non-different Doctrine' (*bhedābhedavāda*) appears to have been that of the earlier commentators on the *Sūtra*.

Bhartṛhari, a senior contemporary of Diṅnāga or possibly a little earlier than him, occupies an independent position, which, however, throws light on the development of the Vedānta in his time. In principle he is a linguist rather than a philosopher, but he is concerned with the nature of language whilst accepting, as a Vedist, that the words of the *Veda* are eternal. He combines this eternal 'speech' (*śabda*) of the Mīmāṃsā with the *brahman* of the Vedānta and holds that this (*śabda* = *brahman*) is the ultimate reality. Perhaps this was an old Vedist view, preceding the division into Mīmāṃsā and Vedānta, or it may be Bhartṛhari's own attempt to reunite the two schools. Afterwards there came into existence, following his ideas, a separate school of linguistic philosophers who maintained that speech is the ultimate reality. It is clear that Bhartṛhari was influenced by the Madhyamaka and Vijñānavāda discussions about the nature of the ultimate reality and whether it is more real than the world of experience, or whether even the world of experience is not real at all, and he uses much of the same terminology as the Vijñānavāda. At the same time he does not accept Buddhism (though he seems to be on friendly terms with Buddhist philosophers and praises the work of one of them, Candragomin, who contributed to linguistics) but speaks as if he follows the Vedānta. For Bhartṛhari speech is eternal, is the ultimate reality, is the *Veda*, is *brahman*, moreover it is the only reality. The universe appears to evolve out of it, but this is mere imagining (*parikalpa*). (We do not know whether there was a Vedānta school at this time which held that *brahman* alone was real and the universe unreal.) The appearance of the universe in all its complexity is due to the various powers (*śaktis*) of the speech-*brahman*, namely existence, time, space, action, instrumentality, etc. Through these all the 'features' (*ākāras*) of the universe appear.

It was Gauḍapāda (6th century A.D.?) who effectively founded the Advaita ('Non-duality') Vedānta, by applying Vijñānavāda theories to the exegesis of one of the *Upaniṣads* (as part of the *Veda* revealing the nature of *brahman*) in his *Māṇḍūkya Kārikā.* Duality is an illusion, there is only the ultimate reality (*brahman*).

Śaṃkara (early 7th century ?) fully elaborated Gauḍapāda's Advaita as an idealist Vedānta by writing commentaries on most of the early *Upaniṣads* as well as on the *Brahman Sūtra* (and also the *Bhagavadgītā* out of the Epic *Mahābhārata,* which implies his adherence to the idea of fusing the Vaiṣṇava and Vedic traditions). In all these commentaries, regardless of the evident variety of opinions expressed in the texts he purports to explain, Śaṃkara claims to find the same teaching of strict non-dualism, with the universe an illusion.

Prabhākara (early 7th century) was considerably influenced by the Buddhist logicians in his systematisation of the Mīmāṃsā doctrine, which became the basis of a new Mīmāṃsā school (widely regarded among Brahmanical teachers as a somewhat unorthodox Mīmāṃsā). He still accepted five of the means of knowledge proposed in Mīmāṃsā tradition, but ruled out the sixth, non-existence, following Buddhist doctrine to the effect that negation (or non-existence) is only absence of something and not a positive thing, or means, in itself. His contributions to linguistics are important (for example that words have no meaning until they are combined in a sentence). He maintains the atheism of the Mīmāṃsā against Nyāya theism. (The *Veda* is eternal, was not created by God.)

Kumārila (early 7th century, his exact relationship to Prabhākara has been much disputed) represents a more orthodox Mīmāṃsā and effectively founded the major later school of that doctrine (often called Bhāṭṭa). Though generally more conservative than Prabhākara, he dealt with logic and epistemology at very great length, by way of expounding the doctrine of the *Vṛtti* (see XXIV above, beginning) on the means of knowledge. In logic he generally seems to follow Praśastapāda, with special additions (theory of the contradictory middle term, question of 'pervasion'). He accepts non-existence as a reality and as a sixth means of knowledge. In linguistics he holds, contrary to Prabhākara, that words have meanings and that the meaning of a sentence is the summation of the series of word-meanings in it.

Among later Nyāya philosophers of the 'Old' school the most important are probably Jayanta, who in the late 9th century wrote an extensive exposition of Nyāya doctrine (the *Nyāyamañjarī*), including polemics against opposed schools such as the Buddhists and Lokāyatikas, and Vācaspatimiśra (end of the 10th century). The latter took up the ancient battle against the Buddhist logicians, who had attacked all his predecessors from the time of the *Nyāya Sūtra* onwards. After Uddyotakara opposed Diṅnāga, he was in turn criticised by the Buddhist philosopher Dharmakīrti (see XXVI below). Vācaspatimiśra then attempted to revive the old Nyāya doctrines again by writing a sub-sub-commentary on Uddyotakara's sub-commentary on Vātsyāyana's commentary on the *Sūtra.* To do this he borrowed some points from Praśastapāda (two kinds of sensation, etc.) and some from the Mīmāṃsakas and Buddhists. This was practically the last defensive attempt on behalf of the obsolete *Sūtra* and afterwards the Naiyāyikas for the most part abandoned it and started out again from first principles, thus founding the 'New' school. (Udayana at the end of the 11th century, the founder of the New school, made the gesture of writing a sub-sub-sub-commentary on Vācaspatimiśra's sub-sub-commentary, which had been attacked by the Buddhist Jñānaśrīmitra, but his important works are all independent and constitute a fresh beginning in Nyāya, and Vaiśeṣika, theory.) Vācaspatimiśra is remarkable among Nyāya writers for his objectivity, moreover he wrote a series of works on the philosophies of other schools (Sāṃkhya, Yoga, Mīmāṃsā, Vedānta), showing an academic rather than a partisan interest in philosophical problems.

Vaiśeṣika writers after Praśastapāda include *Maticandra (6th century?), whose **Daśapadārthaśāstra* (which happens to have been preserved in a Chinese translation, used as a text book by Buddhist philosophy students) adds four new categories to Kaṇāda's six (power, non-power, universal-particular, non-existence—'universal-particular' means that which may be either a universal or a particular and not one of these only), and Śrīdhara (end of the 10th century), who wrote the standard commentary on Praśastapāda's work. There are also at least two commentaries on the *Vaiśeṣika Sūtra,* recently retrieved from total obscurity and published (see Bibliography to XVI). After Śrīdhara the school recombined with the Nyāya, mainly through the work of Udayana.

The Pratyabhijñā ('Recognition') school is in principle a system of theology revealed by Śiva to Vasugupta (8th century A.D.?) by way of explanation of the Śaiva scriptures (the school is also known as Trika and Spanda). The most important philosopher of the school is Abhinavagupta (fl. *c.* A.D. 1000), who amongst other things is perhaps the most prominent writer on aesthetics in India. The school is a 'non-duality' (*advaita*) school, in that its ultimate reality (in this case Śiva) is one and does not really divide into the multiplicity of the universe, nevertheless the universe is held to be real, in that it is actually Śiva. It is an appearance of Śiva, through his power. Our troubled state in the world is just part of this appearance, and liberation from it can be attained by 'recognition' that the individual soul is really identical with Śiva himself, it can then merge again with Śiva. Abhinavagupta brings in his aesthetic theories at this point: by going to the theatre and having aesthetic experience (*rasa*) there we are really training ourselves to see the world as Śiva sees it (the Indian audience traditionally consists of detached and contemplative spectators, forgetting their own limited individuality and acquiring a universal outlook), which is the best preparation for merging again with him. The Śaivas also hold that Śiva creates, or rather becomes, the world purely for sport: since he is already perfect no other purpose is conceivable, there can be no moral purpose, only an aesthetic one. The Recognition school seems to owe a good deal to the doctrines of Bhartṛhari, for example the conception of the 'powers' of the ultimate reality.

In the 11th century some Vaiṣṇava thinkers in South India, who were also Vedists and Vedāntins, reacted strongly against the Non-duality (Advaita) Vedānta of Śaṃkara, in effect reviving something like the earlier Vedānta of 'different-non-different'. Yāmuna at the beginning of the century argued that Śaṃkara's doctrine was contrary to all experience and also contrary to the *Upaniṣads:* these do not state that nothing except *brahman* exists, but that there is only one *brahman* as the basis of everything (not implying that everything except *brahman* is illusory). Rāmānuja, a follower of Yāmuna, afterwards established a school representing this trend of Vedānta, writing a commentary on the *Brahman Sūtra* from its standpoint. There exists only one all-embracing being = *brahman* = the ultimate soul (*ātman*) = God (Viṣṇu). This has all imaginable good qualities, especially consciousness. The plurality of the universe is real, individual pieces of matter, souls, etc., are all real as parts of the all-pervading *brahman*. 'God' thus pervades everything as the 'inner guide'. There are two states of the universe, unmanifest (*avyakta*) and manifest. In the unmanifest state all the qualities of *brahman* (including matter and souls) exist in a subtle state, the souls not being joined to bodies. From this initial state 'creation' takes place through the wish of *brahman*, matter becomes gross and the souls receive bodies. By means of knowledge the souls, after being involved in transmigration, can attain liberation and go to the 'world of *brahman*', where they become similar to *brahman* in all respects except that they cannot have the power of creating, guiding and dissolving the universe.

The Advaita school itself was defended in the 12th century by Harṣa, who adopted a method of dialectics similar to that of the Madhyamaka, incidentally admitting that the Madhyamaka itself is incontrovertible. He chiefly attacks the Nyāya. The dialectic is destructive of all possible systems, leaving (for Harṣa) only the pure, indefinable knowledge of *brahman*, which is just the fact of consciousness itself.

Madhva (13th century) opposed to the Advaita school and to the so-called 'Distinguished' (Viśiṣṭa) Advaita of Rāmānuja (the 'distinction' being that although *brahman* is one the universe is real also) a straightforward duality (*dvaita*) view of God (Viṣṇu, also *brahman*) on the one hand and souls and matter on the other. He thus founded a third main school of Vedānta. He expounded his doctrine in a series of commentaries on sacred texts and on the *Brahman Sūtra*. The evolution of the universe is real and there are five 'differences': between the souls and God, between one soul and another, between matter and God, between matter and matter and between souls and matter. It is self-contradictory to hold, as Rāmānuja does, that souls are both different from God and not different from God. The purpose of the *Veda* is the glorification of God (who is the same as all the Vedic gods) and the Vedic rituals should be performed because they are the commands of God (contrary to Śaṃkara, who held that the rituals are valueless and may be dispensed with). By devotion one can attain liberation, through the grace of God. The only evidence for the existence of God is the statements of the scriptures (these include the Vaiṣṇava *Pañcarātra* scriptures, the *Mahābhārata, Rāmāyaṇa,* some *Purāṇas* and other works of sages in so far as they are restatements of what is in the *Pañcarātra,* etc., and the *Brahman Sūtra* as well as the *Veda;* other alleged scriptures, such as the Śaiva *Āgama* and the Buddhist *Tripiṭaka,* were produced at the command of God only for the purpose of deluding the demons). The existence of God cannot be proved through inference. The scriptures as recognised by the Vaiṣṇavas are absolutely valid and authoritative, nothing else is and if they are not then nothing is. Madhva makes considerable use of logic, generally borrowed from the Nyāya, and also applies the Vaiśeṣika categories and several Sāṃkhya doctrines. He accepts three means of knowledge: sensation, inference and scripture.

Though basically a system of theology the Madhva or Dvaita school made substantial contributions to logic and epistemology. The most important writers here are probably Jayatīrtha (14th century) and Vyāsatīrtha (1460-1539). The latter, for example, studied the 'New' Nyāya, sometimes applying the doctrines of Gaṅgeśa and sometimes (e.g. the doctrine of inference) attempting to refute them.

Among later Bhāṭṭa Mīmāṃsaka writers, Śaṅkarabhaṭṭa (16th century) and the two Nārāyaṇas (17th century) composed concise but comprehensive manuals, on Jaimini's doctrine and on epistemology and ontology.

XXVI POST-DIṄNĀGA BUDDHIST PHILOSOPHY

Most of the numerous schools of Buddhism pursued their separate formulations of Buddhist doctrine until they were exterminated in India by the Muslim invaders around A.D. 1200 and afterwards, a few of them then continuing down to the present day in more fortunate countries. The Sthaviravāda flourished especially in Ceylon, hence has survived intact (alone among the early schools). Being extremely faithful to its earliest traditions it produced comparatively little new in philosophy after the ideas which appear in its commentaries in the 1st century A.D. (see XIV above). Buddhaghosa (5th century) translated and edited most of these in the form in which we now have them, in Pali, adding his *Visuddhimagga* as a comprehensive independent work on the complete system. His contemporary Buddhadatta wrote two introductory manuals of Abhidharma, one of which (the *Abhidhammāvatāra*, 'Introduction to Abhidharma') is remarkable as showing the writer's familiarity with the doctrines of the Madhyamaka, Vijñānavāda and possibly Sautrāntika—at least he uses some logical illustrations found also in Diṅnāga—, which he applies in his own presentation of the Buddhist doctrine of non-soul and the problem of the 'person' or 'agent'. The work of elaborating (in sub-commentaries) and polishing (in manuals) the Abhidharma was continued by a series of writers especially in the 8th or 9th century (Ānanda, Dhammapāla II) and 12th century (Anuruddha I and II, Sumaṅgala, Kassapa and others; their work was continued in the following centuries in Ceylon and Burma). Ānanda in his sub-commentary on the whole *Abhidhamma*, in clarifying concepts defines 'time' (*kāla*) as 'not occurring' (there is no reality corresponding to it) but being perceived as a locus in relation to the absences before and after of momentary events (*Atthasālinī Ṭ* p. 47). His student Dhammapāla II was the greatest author of sub-commentaries, also of a sub-sub-commentary on Ānanda's sub-commentary and a manual (*Saccasaṅkhepa*) on the two truths, the ultimate, which concerns the principles, and the concealing, which concerns concepts, which are unreal (*avastu*). In his sub-commentaries he adapts the epistemology of Diṅnāga: there are two means of knowledge, sensation, which excludes inference and knows the own-characteristic, and inference, which knows the universal-characteristic (e.g. *Dīgha Ṭ* Vol. I pp. 191-2). Tradition (*āgama*) is included in inference. He argues, following Buddhaghosa, that the Buddha had sensation of the past and future because his thought was undisturbed (Vol. III p. 119, quoting *Vākyapadīya* I.37 in support). The universal characteristics impermanent, etc., are not included in the groups because they are without own-beings, but they are not separate from them because they cannot be perceived apart from them, therefore they are concepts (*Visuddhimagga Ṭ* p. 825). The anonymous *Gaṇṭhipada* on the *Paṭisambhidāmagga* states that cessation (Nirvāṇa) is attained through the knowledge of the two characteristics, own and universal (55ff.). Anuruddha II (of Kāñcī) is one of the most interesting and original of these philosophers, with his *Paramatthavinicchaya*, which includes a study of different kinds of 'concept' (*prajñapti*). The most useful work is Kassapa's *Mohavicchedanī*, a masterly condensation of the contents of the entire seven books of the *Abhidhamma* of the school with their commentaries and some additional explanations, in the guise of a commentary on the *Mātṛkā* (see XIII above, but extended to cover all the seven books of this school) which is supposed to form the basic statement of the whole system. He offers some interesting new definitions, modifying the theory of 'own–being' in a way which seems to meet Nāgārjuna's criticisms.

The Sarvāstivāda system of Abhidharma seems to have been finalised in probably the 5th and 6th centuries by Skandhila, Saṃghabhadra and Vimalamitra. The first wrote an 'Introduction' (*Avatāra*). The other two defended the system against its wholesale revision by the Sautrāntika school, which had broken away from the Sarvāstivāda by criticising its *Abhidharma.* The *Abhidharmadīpa*, apparently by Vimalamitra, has survived incomplete in a single Sanskrit manuscript as the most comprehensive and detailed Sarvāstivāda manual.

The Tibetan historian Tāranātha tells us that six other early schools of Buddhism flourished in India alongside these until the 12th century (including the Mahāsaṅghika, Kaurukullaka, Prajñaptivāda, Vātsīputrīya and Saṃmitīya). Practically nothing is known of them and nothing seems to have survived of their philosophical activities.

Tāranātha also makes the interesting remark that as late as the 12th century the majority of Buddhists in India still followed the early schools, not the Mahāyāna.

Among Mahāyāna philosophers after Asaṅga the first to note is Buddhapālita of the Madhyamaka school (probably 5th century), who adhered rigorously to Nāgārjuna's purely critical method of the 'necessary consequence' (*prasaṅga*) of an opponent's position, without adding independent arguments. He is thus regarded as having established the Prāsaṅgika (from *prasaṅga*) school with his commentary on the *Mūlamadhyamakakārikā*.

Bhāvaviveka (late 5th century?), on the other hand, who also wrote a commentary on Nāgārjuna's major work, criticised Buddhapālita and adopted the new logical doctrines of Diṅnāga, arguing that it was legitimate for the Madhyamaka to advance independent proofs of Madhyamaka doctrines. He thus became the founder of the Svātantrika ('Independent') school. He wrote a number of other works expounding Madhyamaka doctrine and criticising other schools, including the idealist Buddhists as well as those of the early schools and the Brahmanical schools. He pays particular attention to distinguishing the Mahāyāna idea of ultimate reality (the 'thusness', *tathatā*, of the Perfection of Understanding) from the *brahman* of the *Veda*. The Vijñānavāda is criticised for its conception of the 'dependent' (*paratantra*) characteristic in principles as some kind of reality. Bhāvaviveka's position was defended by Avalokitavrata (probably 8th century), in a vast subcommentary, from the attacks of the rival Prāsaṅgika school.

It was Candrakīrti (end of the 6th century) who was the greatest Prāsaṅgika philosopher and critic of Bhāvaviveka. There are to be no concessions to the Buddhist epistemologists (Sautrāntikas), who would confuse the strict two levels of truth. Principles 'exist' at the 'concealing' level, not at the 'ultimate' level. The Vijñānavāda also is thoroughly criticised. Later Prāsaṅgika writers include Śāntideva (early 8th century, mainly ethics at the 'concealing' level) and Prajñākaramati (11th century).

In the Vijñānavāda school meanwhile Vasubandhu's (I) summary of Asaṅga's doctrine, the Treatise of Thirty Verses (*Triṃśikākārikāprakaraṇa*), was generally taken as the basic text. There were ten celebrated commentators on it by the first half of the 7th century (including Sthiramati II, Paramārtha, Dharmapāla and Asvabhāva), whose work was paraphrased in Chinese in a single comprehensive version and became the textbook of the flourishing idealist school in China. After that the Vijñānavāda in India is known only through Jñānaśrīmitra, etc., chiefly because the school did not become established in Tibet (which has practically always been Madhyamaka) and its tradition has not survived except in the Far East as a continuation of the Indian school of the 7th century.

The Sautrāntika school far surpasses all these others in philosophical interest, moreover it interacted with the Svātantrika Madhyamaka of Bhāvaviveka to produce further hybrid developments. Fortunately it became established in Tibet, as a department of study within the philosophical faculty of a liberal Madhyamaka, consequently many of its important texts have been preserved there for us. After Diṅnāga, Śaṅkarasvāmin wrote an elementary manual, following the *Nyāyamukha* rather than the *Pramāṇasamuccaya,* which is useful only because it happens to have survived in the original Sanskrit. Much more interesting, though on the periphery of the history of philosophy, is the literary critic Bhāmaha's work (*Kāvyālaṅkāra*), which has a chapter on logic and epistemology applied to literature. He quotes both Vasubandhu I and Diṅnāga but goes his own way, adopting Diṅnāga's conception of the two means of knowledge and their two (particular and universal) objects but rejecting the 'exclusion of what is other'. The logic of literature has to follow the conventions of poetry, however, so that the 'poetic fallacy' (poet's imaginary cause) ceases to be fallacious although the writer must generally be guided by actual sensation and valid inference. Īśvarasena carried on the study of the more advanced parts of Diṅnāga's work, but was completely eclipsed by Dharmakīrti.

Dharmakīrti (7th century) so dominated the Sautrāntika school as almost to supersede Diṅnāga himself. His seven works on epistemology, though conceived as explanations of and supplements to the *Pramāṇasamuccaya,* came to be looked upon as a sort of canon of the science on which all study should be based. On a number of points they do modify Diṅnāga's definitions slightly, in order to make them secure from the criticisms of other schools; they also add much that is new by way of expansion and development of the theory and on one or two fundamental matters they either adopt positions a little different from Diṅnāga's or else take up a definitive position where Diṅnāga appears to have left a question open.

Dharmakīrti's fundamental work is taken to be the *Pramāṇa-vārttika,* which is offered as a kind of explanation of Diṅnāga's work, though not a clause by clause commentary on it. It is in four chapters, usually read in the order (1) inference for oneself, (2) establishment of the means of knowledge, (3) sensation, (4) inference for another. Alternatively the second of these is read first, then the third, then the first and the fourth, which may appear to be more straightforward (following Diṅnāga). The first order may be explained either as indicating that inference (for oneself) is a prerequisite for any discussion on epistemology or as an accidental sequence arising from the fact that Dharmakīrti himself wrote a commentary (*Vṛtti*) on it alone of the four chapters (because it is the most difficult or because it stood first and he did not live to write commentaries on the rest?—as a matter of fact the fourth chapter ends rather abruptly, leaving some topics undiscussed which one might expect to be treated; thus this may be Dharmakīrti's last work and unfinished).

All inferences (Dharmakīrti adds to Diṅnāga's doctrine) are based on either 'own-being' (*svabhāva,* in effect identity of reference of the predicates M and P) or 'effect' (*kārya,* from which one can argue to a cause) or else on 'non-perception' (*anupalabdhi,* or 'not finding', i.e. they are negations of the first two kinds). One might interpret this as that all inferences are either 'analytic' (identity of reference, or M indicates part of what P indicates) or 'synthetic' (M and P indicate different objects, but M as effect is inseparable from P). Dharmakīrti's discussion on identity leads naturally into the problem of the meaning of words and the 'exclusion of what is other', which accordingly is dealt with in this same chapter. Inference involves the concept of a universal (or class), such as all the objects qualified by the predicate. This has no real existence: only the particular objects are real, and they are all different from one another. By 'concealing' (*saṃvṛti,* as in the 'concealing' level of truth) differences the intellect makes 'existents' appear as a class without differences, though this has no reality. This 'universal' (*sāmānya*) is precisely the 'exclusion of what is other' (*anyāpoha*) (I.70 [or 68]ff. and *Vṛtti*). The characteristic (*liṅga,* or middle term) in an inference likewise refers to exclusion as its object (*viṣaya*) (I.49). The discussion on the meaning of words (I.94ff.) brings in the point that although the use of words is a matter of convention, depending on the wishes of speakers rather than on real objects, there is some check on both using words and making inferences (which are really the same activity), namely the purpose of successful action (*arthakriyā*) and avoiding what is undesirable. The purpose of inference is thus practical, to attain desired objects, and there is a pragmatic test of its correctness: it is not completely separated from the real world of particulars, it can move towards them though in principle it can never reach them.

A (true) means of knowledge (*pramāṇa*) is knowing (*jñāna*) which is not contradicted (by experience): that it is not contradicted is established by successful action.

Sensation is defined (III.123) as excluding imagining, as in Diṅnāga, with the remark that this is established (as true) by sensation itself: if one excludes all reflection (imagining) from the mind, by concentration with the eyes on some object, one will have a kind of mental experience (*mati*) which is simply produced by the sense (of sight); then if one starts to imagine again one will have the imagining that one was aware of something in that former state but that it was not then in the intellect (understanding, i.e. not registered as an idea) but remained just in the sense organ (III.124-5). The varieties of sensation are the same as in Diṅnāga, but there is further discussion about the nature of illusion in connection with sensation. Sensation relates to the 'own characteristic' (the particular) (III.75), which is the ultimate reality (III.3).

Inference for another is generally as in Diṅnāga, allowing for the middle term (*hetu*) being of two kinds (own-being and effect), or negative, according to the kinds of inference explained earlier (IV. 195).

The *Pramāṇavārttika* is not systematic in its presentation, nor does it cover the whole of the theory. It is really a series of subsidiary discussions arising from various points in Diṅnāga's work, showing links between different topics rather than separating the topics and dealing with each in a simple and regular manner. More systematic and more comprehensive is Dharmakīrti's other very long work, the *Pramāṇaviniścaya.* This is a regular treatise in three chapters in the straightforward order sensation, inference for oneself and inference for another. Unlike the *Pramāṇavārttika* it has a commentary (*Vṛtti*) by Dharmakīrti himself on all its chapters (the text proper in both works is in *kārikā* verses). In its last chapter it goes far beyond the other work by covering the example step of the proof, false middle terms (barely touched on in the other), refutation and sophistical refutations. A concise and very convenient manual of the theory by Dharmakīrti is his *Nyāyabindu*, in three chapters like the *Pramāṇaviniścaya* but limited to the basic essentials and without digressions. It provides students with a regular and compact series of definitions. On 'non-perception' or negative inference, however, it introduces distinctions (sub-classes) not mentioned in the *Pramāṇavārttika*: besides negation of identity (own-being) or of effect we can have negation of a cause or of combinations of these three, we can also have negation of an 'inclusive term' (altogether there are eleven kinds of negative proof depending on these). Clearly this work is designed more as a manual of logic and debating than of epistemology. It opens, however, with the statement that the accomplishment of all human ends is preceded by right knowledge, which accordingly will be investigated, proceeding then to the mention of the two means and the definition of sensation. (This adds 'not illusory' to the definition in the *Pramāṇavārttika*.)

The other four works of Dharmakīrti are all monographs on special subjects. The *Hetubindu* is a manual on the middle term, covering in a more elementary and regular manner much of the same ground as the first chapter (inference for oneself) of the *Pramāṇavārttika*. The *Sambandhaparīkṣā* ('Critique of "Relation"') is a brief study subsidiary to inference, which is based on 'relations' (such as effect and cause). None of these exist in reality (as already maintained by Diṅnāga) and Dharmakīrti's critique is intended to prove this. The method is not unlike Nāgārjuna's: if the 'related' entities are different by nature they cannot really be related, if a related entity really exists it cannot be related (because it is independent), if it does not exist it cannot be related; if the 'relation' is present in either of the 'related' entities (separately) then it cannot be a relation, and so on. The critique is directed mainly against Vaiśeṣika concepts. The conclusion is that all 'existents' are by nature unrelated (i.e. ultimate reality is the unrelated particulars, the 'own characteristic'). (Relations are only imagined by the intellect, they can be used in inference but are not real and do not reach real objects.) The *Vādanyāya* ('Method of Debate') is a study of the 'defeat situations', a routine part of debating not covered in any of Dharmakīrti's (or Diṅnāga's) other works. It is quite elementary and self-explanatory and so presumably intended for beginners in debating. Dharmakīrti holds that really there are only two kinds of defeat situation: stating a fallacious proof and criticising a sound proof.

The *Santānāntarasiddhi* ('Proof that there are Other Series [of Consciousness]') is a monograph on the problem of the existence of other minds. That other minds exist is known by inference (not by sensation): given that our own purposive actions are preceded by intelligence or consciousness, when we observe similar purposive actions other than our own (not resulting from our own volition) we can infer that these are preceded by an intelligence other than our own. Dharmakīrti holds that this argument is conclusive from the point of view of idealist as well as materialist philosophy.

Dharmakīrti was followed by a group of Buddhist writers, some of whom were his own students, who undertook to expound his doctrines further. Probably at about the same time (but the date has not yet been worked out) lived Jinendrabuddhi, who wrote a great commentary on Diṅnāga's *Pramāṇasamuccaya* which became the standard explanation of that basic work, at least in Dharmakīrti's school (Jinendrabuddhi seems to interpret Diṅnāga in accordance with Dharmakīrti's views, sometimes probably straining the position of the text in order to do so).

Dharmakīrti's works are difficult in style, often unstraightforward in presentation and full of possible implications inviting further thought. As a result we find two quite different kinds of commentary produced on his works. First there is the very welcome series of simple explanations of Dharmakīrti's texts, enabling students to get to grips with them. The 7th century commentators of this type are Devendrabuddhi and Śākyabuddhi, followed in the 8th century by the Mahāyānist Vinītadeva. These commentaries seem to be preserved only in Tibetan, but we have a simple commentary available in Sanskrit on the *Pramāṇavārttika* (on the *kārikā* text of the four chapters), by

Manorathanandin, who is much later in date (probably 12th century). Also available in Sanskrit is Karṇakagomin's (7th century) commentary on Dharmakīrti's *Vṛtti* to *Pramāṇavārttika* I, which explains Dharmakīrti but adds some rather difficult extensions of the discussions as well.

On the other hand we have 'advanced' commentaries, which like Dharmakīrti's own *Vṛtti* just mentioned are not commentaries in the sense of explaining the statements of the text by paraphrasing them, etc., but are further philosophical discussions arising from points in the text, workings out of its implications which may even depart from Dharmakīrti's intentions. They also undertake polemic against other schools. The first of these is the Madhyamaka(?) Prajñākaragupta's (7th century), who followed Dharmakīrti's example of writing a *Vṛtti* to extend the discussions of *Pramāṇavārttika* I by writing an advanced, and very extensive, commentary of this kind on chapters II to IV of that work. This *Bhāṣya* or *Alaṅkāra* (it has both names) by Prajñākaragupta was itself found so important and difficult that it generated a succession of sub-commentaries from somewhat different points of view which developed later: Ravigupta's and Jinamitra's in the early 8th century and a much more elaborate one by Yamāri in the 9th century (who was a Sautrāntika like Dharmottara, see below).

In the 8th century two philosophers of the Svātantrika Madhyamaka school, Śāntarakṣita and Kamalaśīla, wrote commentaries on works of Dharmakīrti (Śāntarakṣita on the *Vādanyāya*), which indicates the trend towards fusion of the two schools: their more independent work will have to be noted below. Much more important Sautrāntika writers of the 8th century are Arcaṭa, Śubhagupta (or, probably incorrectly, Kalyāṇarakṣita) and Dharmottara. Arcaṭa wrote an 'advanced' commentary on the *Hetubindu* and monographs on the question of the means of knowledge being precisely two and on the problem of momentariness (*kṣaṇabhaṅga*), or the infinitesimal persistence of principles in time. His contemporary Śubhagupta wrote a series of monographs on such problems as the exclusion of what is other, omniscience, revelation (a critique), 'God' (a refutation) and the external object (proving that it exists).

Arcaṭa's pupil Dharmottara is the most outstanding of this group and wrote 'advanced' commentaries on the *Pramāṇaviniścaya* and

Nyāyabindu (the latter is not too advanced, however, being on an introductory manual, but it is much more than an explanation of the text: it has been one of the most popular works of the school). He also wrote monographs on the means of knowledge (critiques of the views of other schools), the exclusion of what is other, the 'other world' (this is established in its Buddhist sense) and momentariness. Dharmottara is one of the most original of Dharmakīrti's successors and is sometimes regarded as more 'critical', but might rather be seen as in the true Sautrāntika tradition. Thus he holds that the available means of knowledge do not enable us either to affirm or to deny the existence of an 'omniscient being' (i.e. a *buddha*) or an 'absolute' (ultimate reality). He further maintained the theory that knowledge is 'without features' (*nirākāra*), i.e. it does not have the shape (features) of its object.

Jñānaśrībhadra following him wrote a sub-commentary on his *Pramāṇaviniścaya* commentary and later Durvekamiśra (*c.* 1000) provided detailed sub-commentaries on the commentaries of Dharmottara and Arcaṭa on the *Nyāyabindu* and *Hetubindu* (at least four other works by Durvekamiśra seem to have been lost but his sub-commentaries are both available in Sanskrit). Yamāri already mentioned was apparently a pupil of Jñānaśrībhadra.

Also associated with the Sautrāntika school in the 9th century was Śaṅkarānanda, who wrote a commentary on the *Sambandhaparīkṣā* and began an 'advanced' commentary on Dharmakīrti's *Vṛtti* to *Pramāṇavārttika* I on a vast scale. He did not finish it but it was nevertheless accepted as a classic study (for Sautrāntikas it seems to have superseded Karṇakagomin's work). He also wrote two important monographs, proving the exclusion of what is other and on 'inseparability' (*pratibandha*, the inseparable connection of the middle term with the predicate to be proved which is the basis of inference).

Jitāri (late 10th century), the teacher of Durvekamiśra, may also be loosely associated with Dharmottara, though he basically follows the earlier writer Śaṅkarasvāmin rather than Dharmakīrti, whilst revising the system of Śaṅkarasvāmin to agree better with Dharmakīrti, thus arriving in fact at a position intermediate between Diṅnāga and Dharmakīrti. His *Hetuttattvopadeśa* is a short introduction to logic (mainly proof, with very little epistemology), following the outline and sometimes the wording of Śaṅkarasvāmin's manual *Nyāyapraveśa.* He wrote at least six other works on logic, including another introductory manual, a study of predicate and subject (*Dharmadharmiviniścaya*), a proof of 'non-soul', a work on debating and a treatise on knowledge being limited to the range of perception (*sahopalambha*, or perhaps the range of 'cognition' in some more general sense—the treatise has not yet been published).

The Yogācāra is represented especially by Jñānaśrīmitra in the 11th century. His position seems to be clearly idealist though he wrote on epistemology (he may be taken as representing the Vijñānavāda in the obscure later phase of its history and this may account for his works not being popular in Tibet—only one seems to have been translated). This differentiates him not only from Dharmottara but also from Diṅnāga and Dharmakīrti, who were realists though aiming to be convincing to the idealists as well as to non-idealists. He refers to the *Sandhinirmocana Sūtra* as well as to Asaṅga and other idealist philosophers. Criticising Dharmottara, he maintains that knowledge is 'with features' (*sākāra*), has the shape or peculiarities of its object. At the same time he claims to be establishing clearly the doctrine of Dharmakīrti and Prajñākaragupta, with their real intentions. He is not known to have written any commentaries, but instead produced a long series of monographs on the difficult problems, frequently quoting Dharmakīrti and explaining what he believes to be the implications of the text. He criticises Dharmottara on particular points but perhaps was content to accept his interpretations otherwise (and also Arcaṭa's). Most of Jñānaśrīmitra's criticisms are directed at the Nyāya school, the main opponents of all Buddhist philosophers, especially Vācaspatimiśra (see XXV above) and his contemporaries. His longest work is an elaborate treatise on momentariness, opposing the Nyāya doctrines. Whatever 'exists', which means that it produces effects, cannot be eternal, since an eternal entity cannot produce any effects, cannot participate in a causal or any other process. (This of course is the original Buddhist position against theories of an eternal soul, etc.) Also very long is the *Sākārasiddhiśāstra* establishing the 'with features' doctrine and elaborating the theory of consciousness. In this work Jñānaśrīmitra attempts to harmonise idealism with the Madhyamaka philosophy. Another fairly substantial work is the *Īśvaravāda* criticising the concept of 'God', with special reference to the Nyāya school. The other monographs are short, dealing with causality (this seems to be the only one translated into Tibetan), pervasion (*vyāpti*, the basis of inference), 'difference and non-difference' (a critique of some special doctrine of another school relating to perception, which does not seem to have been traced), non-perception (*anupalabdhi*, as basis of Dharmakīrti's negative inference), one of the sub-varieties of this, the exclusion of what is other, the intuition of a *yogin* (as a kind of sensation) and the relationship between consciousness and external objects (to the idealist these are not a duality, *advaita*). His proof of the possibility of an omniscient being (*buddha*) seems to have been lost.

Jñānaśrīmitra's pupil Ratnakīrti continued his work, but chiefly by writing concise summaries of some of his monographs, apparently as introductions for students. Among these the *Sarvajñasiddhi* on the omniscient being may serve to replace Jñānaśrīmitra's lost work. More original, perhaps (we do not know for certain that Jñānaśrīmitra did not write on these subjects), are the *Pramāṇāntarbhāvaprakaraṇa*, proving that all valid means of knowledge are included in sensation and inference, and the *Santānāntaradūṣaṇa*, 'Refutation of Other (than the) Series', which is apparently not intended as a refutation of Dharmakīrti's argument about other minds; partly because it is concerned with the idealist position that external objects (generally, not just other minds) do not exist independent of the mind (Dharmakīrti himself holds that they do, but the idealists interpret this in a special way); partly because Ratnakīrti applies the theory of two levels of truth (ultimately there is no duality, but other minds could exist at the 'concealing' level). Two other writers of this idealist school are Ratnākaraśānti (a pupil of Ratnakīrti who produced monographs on pervasion and proving 'only makings of consciousness') and Aśoka (who produced critiques of Nyāya doctrines).

Two late writers who appear to follow the Sautrāntika school of Dharmottara are Mokṣākaragupta (*c.* 1100) and Vidyākaraśānti (early 12th century?). Mokṣākaragupta's *Tarkabhāṣā* is an introduction to epistemology in three chapters (sensation, inference for oneself, inference for another). It criticises and rejects the doctrines on means of knowledge of the various other schools of Indian philosophy, from

Cārvāka to the linguists (Bhartṛhari, quoted as holding only two means, sensation and speech; he is in fact criticial of logic). Mokṣākaragupta also criticises the Nyāya theories (Vācaspatimiśra) when dealing with inference and discusses such topics as momentariness and God. He takes from Durvekamiśra sixteen kinds of negative proof. At the end he briefly reviews the positions of the main schools of Buddhist philosophy in northern India in his time on the nature of ultimate reality—the Sarvāstivāda, Sautrāntika, Vijñānavāda and Madhyamaka—and criticises the idealist 'with features' (*sākāra*). Vidyākaraśānti's *Tarkasopāna* is a somewhat similar manual closely following Dharmakīrti's *Nyāyabindu* with Dharmottara's commentary on it, but incorporating all sixteen kinds of negative inference given by Mokṣākaragupta (in a slightly different order). There is very little polemic, though the views of other schools are sometimes noted, and there is no discussion of the views of the schools on ultimate reality. The work is a simple introduction (not too concise, which the *Nyāyabindu* is) to the epistemology and logic of Dharmakīrti and Dharmottara. It is worth noting that the later activity of the Sautrāntika school included the writing of commentaries on important monographs of the school, for instance Muktākalaśa's commentary on Dharmottara's work on momentariness is of about this period.

We have finally to discuss the development of the hybrid Madhyamaka-Prāmaṇa trend which became increasingly important in the later history of Indian Buddhism and has dominated Buddhist philosophy in Tibet. Bhāvaviveka, whom we have already discussed, went some way in this direction by adopting Diṅnāga's methods of proof, but he did not take over the special doctrines of the Sautrāntika school concerning epistemology. It was Śāntarakṣita in the 8th century who adopted the new epistemology (from Dharmakīrti), whilst still remaining a Madhyamaka fundamentally. He rejects the idealist explanation of the nature of ultimate reality and adopts Dharmakīrti's doctrine that sensation relates to ultimate reality. The Madhyamaka conception of the two levels of truth has to be modified to fit Dharmakīrti's view: instead of taking the principles of ordinary experience as real at the concealing level only and regarding everyday popular epistemology and logic, such as the Nyāya, as good enough for everyday purposes, though having no bearing on ultimate reality, we are to sense ultimate reality in the 'own characteristic' of these principles and to correct our philosophical concepts and our language in an attempt to make them correspond better to it, though the correspondence can never be exact. Besides his commentary on one of Dharmakīrti's works, Śāntarakṣita wrote an exposition of the Madhyamaka (the *Madhyamakālaṅkāra*) and a kind of critical encyclopaedia of philosophy, the *Tattvasaṃgraha*. This remarkable work is a series of 26 critiques of the 'realities', i.e. supposed ultimate realities, first causes, categories and the like as variously conceived by practically all the schools of philosophy, leaving unscathed only conditioned origination as understood by Nāgārjuna, along with Dharmakīrti's epistemology. Śāntarakṣita's pupil Kamalaśīla wrote commentaries on the *Madhyamakālaṅkāra* and *Tattvasaṁgraha*, a kind of commentary on Dharmakīrti's *Nyāyabindu* (refuting the views of opponents which might stand in the way of accepting its doctrines), some other works on Madhyamaka and three celebrated manuals under the title *Bhāvanākrama*, '(Gradual) Course of Development'. These last are in origin pamphlets directed against the Chinese 'Meditation' (Dhyāna, Ch'an, Zen) school of Buddhism, with which the Indian Madhyamakas were engaged in an intellectual war of debates, etc., for the domination of Tibet. The 'Meditation' school was an offshoot of the Vijñānavāda in China (it seems never to have existed in India), whose characteristic doctrine (distinguishing them from other Mahāyānists, though not from the Sthaviravāda) is that long study and training is not necessary to attain enlightenment, but only a sudden flash of insight through which enlightenment came 'all at once' (*yugapad*). The Madhyamaka school taught on the contrary, following their interpretations of the Perfection of Understanding *Sūtras* as expounding the long way of the *bodhisattva* (propounded in a work called the *Abhisamayālaṅkāra* ascribed to 'Maitreya'), that enlightenment had to be approached 'gradually' (*kramaśas*) through a series of stages. Kamalaśīla's manuals summarise the gradualist doctrine, criticising the Vijñānavāda in general as well as the 'All at Once' school in particular.

Both Śāntarakṣita and Kamalaśīla visited Tibet. There had been attempts to establish Buddhism in Tibet before the 8th century, but it was Śāntarakṣita who first succeeded in founding a lasting school there, by training Tibetan students. The result of this has been that Tibetan Buddhism ever since has been basically Śāntarakṣita's Buddhism in its philosophy, with Madhyamaka and Pramāṇa studies flourishing side by side. Kamalaśīla went to Tibet later, in response to the threat of a 'schism' resulting from the arrival of 'All at Once' Meditation teachers from China. An assembly was convened and a decisive debate took place under royal patronage, in which Kamalaśīla was declared victorious. As a result his views became orthodox for Tibet.

The consolidation of this syncretistic, but basically Madhyamaka, trend was carried to its final stage by Haribhadra, another pupil of Śāntarakṣita (not to be confused with a Jaina philosopher Haribhadra, also 8th century). His professed aim is the proper interpretation of the Perfection of Understanding *Sūtras*, as a system of moral and intellectual training explained in the *Abhisamayālaṅkāra* (the outlook of which is similar to that of Sthiramati I in the *Ratnagotravibhāga*, see XXII above, and it is probably of about the same date, but Haribhadra interprets it as definitely Madhyamaka and not idealist). Accordingly we have a subject of study known as Pāramitā, 'Perfection' (from *Prajñāpāramitā*), which is also a name of the syncretistic school of Haribhadra. The intellectual equipment necessary for the difficult task of understanding the Perfection of Understanding *Sūtras* includes a knowledge of Abhidharma (for which the Sautrāntika Vasubandhu's critical *Abhidharmakośa* is adopted as the textbook), Madhyamaka (Nāgārjuna and his commentators) and Pramāṇa (Diṅnāga and especially Dharmakīrti). Consequently all these branches of philosophy were cultivated in India and Tibet under the auspices of the Madhyamaka-Pāramitā outlook. Haribhadra criticises the Vijñānavāda doctrine of an ultimate reality eternally pure and without duality. If it were really pure already, it would not be possible to get rid of the 'imaginings' or 'defilements' in it. Or if it were possible to get rid of them it would not now be completely pure. As for the three 'characteristics' of principles, they are all unreal—the 'perfected characteristic' has no own-character (*svarūpa*) and therefore is 'not perfected', unreal, not an ultimately real and existent absolute consciousness. The basis of interpretation of the Perfection of Understanding *Sūtras* is the distinction of the two levels of truth (and of statement in the *Sūtras*). The training laid down is at the concealing level, at the ultimate level it is a 'non-training' (*ayoga*). Enlightenment is attained only at the concealing level and good and bad actions exist only there. At the ultimate level all beings are pure by nature (cf. XVIII above for some of the statements of the *Sūtras*). The 'non-perception' of principles is stressed, i.e. not perceiving them as separate principles, since in ultimate reality there is no duality. Haribhadra's doctrine is expounded in a series of commentaries on the *Abhisamayālaṅkāra* with reference to different recensions of the Perfection of Understanding or none of them.

His studies were continued by a long series of writers in India down to the 12th century, and afterwards in Tibet. They include his pupil Buddhaśrījñāna, Dharmamitra (9th century), Ratnākaraśānti (11th or 12th century, Tāranātha says there were two writers of this name, so that this one may be different from the Yogācāra writer already mentioned) and Abhayākaragupta (early 12th century).

From the 13th century onwards, with the suppression of Buddhism in northern India, it is the Buddhism of Tibet which is the direct, though only partial, continuation of the Indian tradition of Buddhist philosophy. In southern India, Ceylon, Burma and South-East Asia the various Buddhist trends all become assimilated to the dominant Sthaviravāda after the 12th century. China and Japan remained the strongholds of idealism, divided into several sub-schools, the early schools and the Madhyamaka gradually disappearing.

XXVII NAVYA NYĀYA

The Navya Nyāya was started by Udayana, already mentioned in XXV above, at the end of the 11th century, whose major works constitute a new beginning in Nyāya philosophy and remained standard texts of the school throughout its history. (Nevertheless the term 'Navya' is sometimes restricted to Gaṅgeśa, 14th century, and his successors, though they continued to regard Udayana's works as fundamental texts and to write commentaries on them.) Udayana secured the patronage of the king of Tīrabhukti (now part of the state of Bihar) and established a school in Mithilā, the capital. The kingdom of Tīrabhukti succeeded in maintaining its independence, almost alone of the countries of northern India, through the period of Turkish Muslim domination, escaping the holocaust of literature and the massacres and dispersal of scholars perpetrated by the fanatical invaders, as well as the continuing persecution of intellectual activity connected with Brahmanism or Buddhism which everywhere accompanied Islamic rule. Mithilā preserved a small part of the Indian heritage during this dark age, though it does not seem to have been a major cultural centre in the preceding centuries (it did not have libraries comparable with those which had been destroyed at Nālandā, Vārāṇasī, Vikramaśilā, Jagaddala, Śrīnagarī, Kānyakubja, Valabhī, etc.), including Udayana's school.

Udayana aimed to repel the Buddhist critiques of Nyāya doctrines and attack the Buddhists in turn, just as most of his predecessors of the 'Old' school had done. He usually takes the works of Jñānaśrīmitra (see XXVI above) as a basis for these polemics, in other words some of the latest works of Buddhist epistemology. In his *Ātmatattvaviveka* he produced a famous defence of the doctrine of an eternal soul against the Buddhist critiques. The *Nyāyakusumāñjali* is a major and most original work on Nyāya philosophy, written from the standpoint of the means of knowledge as fundamental to the enquiry, though the aim proposed at the beginning is knowledge concerning heaven and release from transmigration (cf. the *Vaiśeṣika Sūtra*). Moreover as a theist (Śaiva) Udayana throughout attempts to make the philosophical problems a basis for establishing the existence of God. His arguments for the existence of God remained classical for the school. Udayana upholds the traditional Nyāya four means of knowledge. At the same time, or at least in the latter part of his career, Udayana took up the study of the Vaiśeṣika system, with the result that the Nyāya and Vaiśeṣika schools became reunited in the Navya Nyāya. His *Kiraṇāvalī* is a commentary (unfinished, probably interrupted by his death) on Praśastapāda's *Padārthadharmasaṃgraha* (see XXV above). Afterwards the Navya Nyāya philosophers mostly followed the Vaiśeṣika system of categories. The *Kiraṇāvalī* takes up the problem of 'class' (*jāti*), seeking to overcome the difficulties of the theory of universals. A 'class' must satisfy certain conditions: Udayana lays down six impediments to the setting up of a class (*jātibādhakas*), as follows. (1) A class must have more than one member. (2) Synonymous names for the same class do not constitute different classes. (3) A group of members cannot belong as a whole to two different classes unless one of those classes includes the other wholly. (4) Classes do not imply further classes as abstractions of themselves, as classnesses, which would lead to an infinite regression. (5) The ultimate particulars being by definition absolutely distinct from one another cannot be taken together as a class: this illustrates contradiction of nature between the proposed members of a class. (6) There is no class where there is no relation which could account for the residence of the class character in a member, for example 'combinationness' could not reside in combination (cf. No. 4). An apparent 'class' which fails to satisfy any of these conditions is called an *upādhi* (this topic was afterwards fully elaborated by Gaṅgeśa and his followers). Through studies like this the Nyāya and Vaiśeṣika doctrines were reworked and made very precise and systematic. In connection with the Vaiśeṣika categories it may be noted that Udayana, and following him the Navya Nyāya school, recognises 'non-existence' (*abhāva*) as a kind of category, as the negative category whereas the other six are positive or existent. He also divides non-existence into four types. In giving non-existence as a kind of seventh category Udayana was supported by the Vaiśeṣika philosopher Śivāditya (12th century?), who did the same in his *Saptapadārthī* (there is a controversy as to how far back in Vaiśeṣika tradition non-existence was looked upon as a 'category', and whether

Praśastapāda, and even Kaṇāda, recognised it in practice though not enumerating it in the list of categories; at any rate *Maticandra (6th century?) gives it among his ten categories, whereas the more standard writers of the school ignore the question). On the other hand in the Nyāya tradition 'non-existence' had been regarded as a category, in the sense of something real, as early as Vātsyāyana. See his commentary on *Nyāya Sūtra* II.2.8ff.

Udayana's studies were continued by a number of writers both in Mithilā and elsewhere (in the 13th century there were Navya Nyāya philosophers at Devagiri in Mahārāṣṭra and from there the school spread further south and became established in Vijayanagara). In the 12th and 13th centuries we may note Varadarāja, Vallabha and Vādīndra, of whom Vallabha (or Śrīvallabha) stands beside Udayana as one of the great teachers of the school. His *Nyāyalīlāvatī* (on Vaiśeṣika, taking Praśastapāda as the basis and studying the categories, adding special doctrines of his own) was several times commented on later as a classic. Keśavamiśra's (12th century) introductory manual *Tarkabhāṣā* follows the outline and topics of the *Nyāya Sūtra,* but inserts the Vaiśeṣika categories and several times follows Udayana's interpretations. Maṇikaṇṭha (*c.* 1300) carries further the study of such problems as the universal' (*sāmānya*) in his *Nyāyaratna.*

The most famous philosopher of the Navya Nyāya is Gaṅgeśa (14th century, Mithilā). In his *Tattvacintāmaṇi* he carried out much more thoroughly the reworking of the Nyāya theory attempted by Udayana. The subject of the work is epistemology and Gaṅgeśa follows Diṅnāga's example in the *Pramāṇasamuccaya* in taking the means of knowledge as the primary topics. Accordingly there are four chapters, on the four means accepted by the Naiyāyikas, sensation, inference, similarity and speech. The work is extremely detailed and largely preoccupied with definitions. For each term which comes up Gaṅgeśa discusses a series of definitions which have been proposed and finds most, if not all, of them imprecise. Most definitions are either too wide or too narrow and thus fail to delimit exactly what is intended. For example inference is defined as knowledge produced by the fact of there being present in the subject something distinguished by a 'pervasion' (*vyāpti*). This is a restatement of the old idea of a 'characteristic' or middle term pervaded by a predicate which can be inferred from its presence. The term 'pervasion' had been used earlier, for example by Diṅnāga, in explaining the inseparable connection between the middle term and the predicate, but Gaṅgeśa finds it extremely hard to define satisfactorily. He analyses a long series of attempts to define it before offering one he thinks acceptable. In this connection the problem of what is meant by a 'class' (*jāti*) arises. The old concept of a universal had been thoroughly demolished by the Lokāyatikas and Buddhists, so the Naiyāyikas reworked their theory in such a way as to eliminate it and substitute something more satisfactory. Udayana had already contributed some of the basic ideas for setting up 'classes' not requiring metaphysical assumptions. Gaṅgeśa now defines 'class' either simply as a characteristic of a particular or as the generic character which it has. Thus instead of a concept such as 'all pots' suggesting the old universal we have the characteristic or property 'pot-ness': an abstraction, not an implied enumeration of an endless number of objects. A 'class' (*jāti*) is related to its members by 'combination' (*samavāya*). An *upādhi* is not related by combination but by e.g. *svarūpa* (own character), i.e. not by a 'relation' or a 'class' but simply in the (own) appearance of the subject (*āśraya*) itself. The problem of pervasion thus becomes that of the pervasion of such a character, or class, as pot-ness by some predicate. Another approach to the problem, presumably derived ultimately from Diṅnāga's exclusion of what is other, is the double negation, such as 'not not-pot'. Another technique used in description and inference is that of the 'delimitor' (*avacchedaka*), e.g. 'pot' delimited by 'pot-ness'.

Under 'speech' as a means of knowledge Gaṅgeśa includes any speech which can produce knowledge (not simply scripture or other authority). Here he discusses a number of linguistic doctrines derived largely from the Mīmāṃsakas, though in general as a Naiyāyika he is critical of Mīmāṃsā metaphysics. On the meaning of words Gaṅgeśa holds, contrary to the old Nyāya and in agreement with his doctrine of class or character, that words refer to particulars (*vyaktis*) only, but as distinguished by their characters (classes), such as 'pot-ness', through the relation of 'combination'. The meanings of words are purely conventional.

The principle of economy (*lāghava*) is very important methodologically for Gaṅgeśa. One must make use only of the simplest possible assumptions necessary to account for the data.

Gaṅgeśa's son Vardhamāna carried on the work of the school at a high level by writing commentaries on Udayana's works (especially the *Nyāyakusumāñjali* and *Kiraṇāvalī*, also the *Nyāyanibandha* or sub-sub-sub-commentary on the *Nyāya Sūtra*) and on Vallabha's *Nyāyalīlāvatī*. In addition he wrote a refutation of the Advaita Vedāntin Harṣa's *Khaṇḍanakhaṇḍakhādya*: the Vedāntins were now the main opponents of the Naiyāyikas. Vardhamāna was regarded as practically the equal of his father and his commentaries became standard works studied in the school.

Among the commentators of the 15th century who continued these analytical studies the two Pakṣadharas (often confused), Yajñapati and Śaṅkaramiśra are the most noteworthy. Pakṣadhara I wrote sub-commentaries on Vardhamāna's commentaries on the *Kiraṇāvalī* and *Nyāyalīlāvatī*, but his works (also a commentary on Gaṅgeśa) seem soon to have been superseded by more elaborate ones by later scholars. Śaṅkaramiśra wrote a series of works, several of which remained at least minor classics dealing with branches of Navya Nyāya study: an early work commenting on Gaṅgeśa has not found much favour (Yajñapati's *Prabhā* also was eclipsed); the *Bhedaprakāśa* is a refutation of the Advaita Vedānta, establishing duality (*bheda*='difference'); the *Khaṇḍanaṭīkā* explains and refutes Harṣa's *Khaṇḍanakhaṇḍakhādya*; the *Vādivinoda* is an independent treatise on debating; the *Upaskāra* has remained the best known commentary on the *Vaiśeṣika Sūtra*, superseding any earlier Vaiśeṣika commentators known among Navya Nyāya philosophers though hardly very faithful to the original (apart from later Vaiśeṣika interpretations he inserts Navya Nyāya doctrines), the aim clearly being to assimilate the venerable *Sūtra* to the New school; lastly the *Nyāyalīlāvatīkaṇṭhābharaṇa* is a commentary on Vallabha's work, in which Śaṅkaramiśra frequently criticises Vardhamāna who had commented on it previously. Pakṣadhara II (Jayadeva) has generally been recognised as the greatest Naiyāyika of this period, on account of his *Āloka* commentary on the *Tattvacintāmaṇi*.

Pakṣadhara II's pupil Rucidatta (early 16th century) wrote elaborate sub-commentaries on Vardhamāna's commentaries on the *Nyāyakusumāñjali* and *Kiraṇāvalī*, also a commentary on Gaṅgeśa. Equally elaborate and apparently better known are his fellow pupil Bhagīratha's set of three sub-commentaries on Vardhamāna's commentaries on the

Nyāyakusumāñjali, Kiraṇāvalī and *Nyāyalīlāvatī.* Bhagīratha's brother Maheśa wrote a sub-commentary on Pakṣadhara's *Āloka.*

In the 16th century the Navya Nyāya began (with Vāsudeva Sārvabhauma) to be taught in Bengal, where Brahmanical scholarship led a precarious existence under the persecutions of Muslim governors. In this period Bengali scholars are regularly found taking refuge in neighbouring Orissa, which was still ruled by Indian kings (it was also a centre of Vaiṣṇavism and Vedānta, a stronghold of religion rather than of philosophy), nevertheless a Navya Nyāya tradition was gradually established in Navadvīpa (Akbar's policy of religious toleration later in the 16th century for a time moderated the Muslim persecutions). The greatest Naiyāyika of the 16th century (or later) is universally agreed to be Raghunātha. He wrote a commentary on the *Tattvacintāmaṇi* (called the *Dīdhiti,* but several of his other works are also called *Dīdhiti,* this being a kind of general title, just as Bhagīratha's commentaries are all called *Jalada* and Vardhamāna's *Prakāśa*), one on Udayana's *Ātmatattvaviveka* and sub-commentaries on Vardhamāna's commentaries on the *Kiraṇāvalī* and *Nyāyalīlāvatī.* Most original are two monographs, the *Padārthatattvanirūpaṇa* on categories and the *Nañvāda* on negation (negative words). In the first of these he institutes a critique of the Vaiśeṣika system of categories, usually accepted in the Navya Nyāya school, and also of its lists of substances, qualities, etc. He accepts 'substance' but reduces the number of substances, thus space, time and position are identical with 'God', the supreme soul (added to the Vaiśeṣika system by its later philosophers). The qualities also are reduced and Raghunātha seems to doubt the validity of such a category, finding its definition unsatisfactory. 'Universal' had already been completely revised in the school and replaced by 'class'. 'Particular' is rejected by Raghunātha. He then adds a series of new categories to the theory, including 'power' (*śakti,* cf. *Maticandra), the 'moment' of time and 'number', in an attempt to make the system more coherent. There are similar discussions in Raghunātha's sub-commentary on the *Kiraṇāvalī,* which of course deals with Vaiśeṣika categories.

Of other later writers of importance we may note first Madhusūdana (Mithilā, 16th century), whose sub-commentary on the *Tattvacintāmaṇi* and Pakṣadhara's *Āloka* claims to meet all the criticisms that had been made, including Raghunātha's. Jagadīśa (Navadvīpa, 17th century) wrote a famous sub-commentary on Raghunātha's *Tattvacintāmaṇi* commentary and a sub-sub-commentary on his *Nyāyalīlāvatī* sub-commentary. Mathurānātha (Navadvīpa, 17th century) produced a long series of commentaries, sub-commentaries and sub-sub-commentaries on major works of the school, distinguished for minute analysis even in a school dedicated to minute analysis (he commented on Udayana's *Ātmatattvaviveka* and *Kiraṇāvalī*; Vallabha's *Nyāyalīlāvatī*; Gaṅgeśa's *Tattvacintāmaṇi*; Vardhamāna's commentaries on the *Kiraṇāvalī* and *Nyāyalīlāvatī*; Pakṣadhara's *Āloka*; and Raghunātha's commentary on the *Tattvacintāmaṇi*, sub-commentaries on the *Kiraṇāvalī* and *Nyāyalīlāvatī*, and *Nañvāda*; it will be noticed that the works here commented on seem to form a kind of canon of basic texts of the Navya Nyāya; the commentary on Gaṅgeśa, or rather certain key parts of it, is widely used for introductory courses). Gadādhara (Navadvīpa, 17th century) commented on Udayana's *Nyāyakusumāñjali*, Pakṣadhara's *Āloka* and Raghunātha's commentaries on the *Ātmatattvaviveka* and *Tattvacintāmaṇi* and *Nañvāda*, he also wrote a large number of short monographs on Navya Nyāya topics. Viśvanātha (Navadvīpa, 17th century) achieved great popularity with an introductory manual of Navya Nyāya, the *Bhāṣāpariccheda*, and wrote a commentary on the *Padārthatattvanirūpaṇa* of Raghunātha and other works.

From South India in the later period we may note two useful manuals: Annambhaṭṭa's (17th century) *Tarkasaṃgraha* based on the Vaiśeṣika system incorporating the Nyāya theory of knowledge (and the New techniques) and the anonymous *Maṇikaṇa* (18th century) summarising the *Tattvacintāmaṇi*.

SELECTED BIBLIOGRAPHY

III

Veda—Ṛgvedasaṃhitā ed. Aufrecht, Bonn (Marcus), 2nd. edn. 1877 (2 vols.); translated by Griffith, Varanasi (Chowkhamba Sanskrit Studies), 4th. edn. 1963.

—*Sāmavedasaṃhitā* ed. Sāmaśramin (Kauthuma recension), Calcutta (Bibliotheca Indica), 1871; ed. Caland (Jaiminīya recension), Breslau (*Indische Forschungen*), 1907.

—*Yajurvedasaṃhitā* Vājasaneyin recension ed. Weber (including the *Śatapathabrāhmaṇa*), Berlin/London (Williams and Norgate), 1852-9 (3 vols.); translated by Griffith, Varanasi, 1899.

—*Atharvavedasaṃhitā* ed. Roth and Whitney (Śaunaka recension), Berlin, 1856ff.; translated by Griffith, Varanasi (Lazarus), 1895-6 (2 vols.).

—*Śatapathabrāhmaṇa* of the *Yajurveda* (see above under *Yajurveda*); translated by Eggeling, London (Oxford University Press, Sacred Books of the East), reprinted Delhi (Motilal Banarsidass), 1963 (5 vols.).

—*Taittirīyabrāhmaṇa* of the *Yajurveda* (Taittirīya recension), Calcutta (Bibliotheca Indica), 1855-90.

(For Vedic science see under *Vedāṅgas* in XII below.)

IV and V

Upaniṣads of the *Veda*—see Ruben, *Die Philosophen der Upanishaden*, Bern, 1947.

Aitareya Upaniṣad ed. Böhtlingk, Leipzig, *Berichte über die Verhandlungen der Königl. Sächsischen Gesellschaft der Wissenschaften* (Philol.-histor. Klasse), 1890.

Bṛhadāraṇyaka Upaniṣad ed. Böhtlingk, St. Petersburg, 1889.

Chāndogya Upaniṣad ed. Böhtlingk, Leipzig (Haessel), 1889.

Kauṣītaki Upaniṣad ed. and translated by Cowell, Calcutta (Bibliotheca Indica), 1861.

Taittirīya Upaniṣad ed. in Ānandāśrama Sanskrit Series, Poona, 5th edn. 1929.

Radhakrishnan has given a text and translation of these and some later *Upaniṣads* in *The Principal Upaniṣads*, London (Allen and Unwin), 1953. (His translations should be used with caution, checking against the original text.)

Hume's *Thirteen Principal Upaniṣads*, OUP, 1931, is better.

VII

Arthaśāstra (see under Kauṭalya in XI).

Āryadeva (see under XX).

Aśvaghoṣa (see under XV).

Basham: *History and Doctrines of the Ājīvikas*, London (Luzac), 1951.

Bhagavatī (see under XVII).

Bhāskara: *Brahmasūtra Bhāṣya* ed. Vindhyeśvarī, Varanasi (Chowkhamba), 1915.

Candrakīrti (see under XXVI).

Dīgha Nikāya (see under VIII).

Guṇaratna (see Haribhadra).

Haribhadra: *Ṣaḍdarśanasamuccaya* ed. with Guṇaratna's commentary by Suali, Calcutta, 1905.

Kāmasūtra (of Mallanāga Vātsyāyana) ed. Dāmodara, Varanasi (Kashi Sanskrit Series), 1929.

Mādhava: *Sarvadarśanasaṃgraha*, ed. Īśvaracandra, Calcutta (Bibliotheca Indica), 1858; translated by Cowell and Gough, London (Trübner), repr. 1914.

Mahābhārata ed. Sukthankar and others, Poona (Bhandarkar Oriental Research Institute), 1933-66; translated by Roy, Calcutta, 1884.

Nettippakaraṇa ed. Hardy, London (Pali Text Society), 1902.

Nīlakaṇṭha: *Bhāvadīpikā* commentary on the *Bhagavadgītā*=part of his commentary on the *Mahābhārata* (*Bhāratabhāvadīpikā*), ed. Kinjawadekar, Poona, 1929-33.

Nyāya Sūtra (see under Akṣapāda in XXI).

Patañjali: *Mahābhāṣya*, Harayāṇā Sāhitya Saṃsthāna edn., Rohataka, 1962 (Vol. V).

Sadānanda: *Advaitabrahmasiddhi*, Calcutta (Bibliotheca Indica), 1890.

Saṃghadāsa: *Vasudevahiṇḍi* ed. Caturavijaya and Puṇyavijaya, Bhāvanagara (Ātmānanda Series), 1930-31.

Saṃyutta Nikāya (see under VIII).
Sarvadarśanasaṃgraha (see Mādhava).
Śīlāṅka: Commentary on the *Sūtrakṛtāṅga*, ed. Suracandra, Bombay, 1917.
Somadeva: *Yaśastilaka*, ed. Śivadatta, Paṇaśīkar and Parab, Bombay (Kāvyamālā), Vol. 1, 2nd. edn. 1916, Vol. II 1st. edn. 1903.
Śukra Nītisāra, ed. Oppert, Madras, 1882.
Sūyagaḍa (see *Sūtrakṛtāṅga* in IX).
Śvetāśvatara Upaniṣad, ed. S.V. Shastri, Allahabad, 1916.
Tattvasaṃgraha (see under Śāntarakṣita in XXVI).
Tattvopaplavasiṃha (see under Jayarāśi in XVII).
Uvāsaga Dasāo, ed. and translated by Hoernle, Calcutta, 1889-90 (2 vols.).
Vaṃsatthappakāsinī, ed. Malalasekera, London (Pali Text Society), 1935 (2 vols.).
Vinaya (see under VIII).

VIII

On Buddhism generally see A.K. Warder, *Indian Buddhism*, Delhi (Motilal Banarsidass), 2nd. edn. 1980 repr. 1991.
Tripiṭaka consists of *Sūtrapiṭaka*, *Vinayapiṭaka* and *Abhidharmapiṭaka* (on the last see under XIII and XIV below).
Sūtrapiṭaka includes:

Dīgha Nikāya (Pali), ed. Rhys Davids and Carpenter, London (Pali Text Society), 1890-1911 (3 vols., since reprinted); translated by Rhys Davids as *Dialogues of the Buddha*, London (PTS), 1899-1921 (3 vols., since reprinted); Chinese version of another (Dharmaguptaka?) recension, Taishō 1 in Vol. I of the Taishō *Tripiṭaka* or *Taishō Issaikyō, Canon Bouddhique de l'ère Taishō*, ed. Takakusu and Watanabe, Tōkyō, 1924ff. (see Index in *Hōbōgirin*, Fascicule Annexe, ed. Demiéville, Tōkyō (Maison Franco-Japonaise), 1931); other Chinese versions of the *Mahānidāna* from this collection are Taishō 14 and 52.

Majjhima Nikāya (Pali), ed. Trenckner and Chalmers, London (PTS) 1888-99 (3 vols., since reprinted); translated by I.B. Horner as *Middle Length Sayings*, London (PTS), 1954-59 (3 vols.); Chinese (Sarvāstivāda) Version Taishō 26.

Saṃyutta Nikāya (Pali), ed. Feer, London (PTS), 1884-98 (5 vols., reprinted 1960); translated by C.A.F. Rhys Davids and Woodward as *Kindred Sayings*, London (PTS), 1917-30 (5 vols., since reprinted); Chinese (Sarvāstivāda) version Taishō 99; Sanskrit fragments (Sarvāstivāda) of the *Nidānasaṃyukta* ed. Tripāṭhī, Berlin (Deutsche Akademie der Wissenschaften zu Berlin, Institut für Orientforschung), 1962.

Aṅguttara Nikāya (Pali), ed. Morris and Hardy, London (PTS), 1885-1900 (5 vols., since reprinted and partly re-edited); translated by Woodward and Hare as *Gradual Sayings*, London (PTS), 1932-36 (5 vols., since reprinted); Chinese (Dharmaguptaka?) version Taishō 125.

Vinayapiṭaka (Pali), ed. Oldenberg, London, 1879-83 (since reprinted by the PTS, 5 vols.); translated by I.B. Horner as *The Book of the Discipline*, London, (PTS), 1938-66 (6 vols., but Vol. I of Oldenberg's text becomes, as it should be, Vol. IV of the translation); there are several different recensions in Chinese (Taishō 1435-37, 1441, 1442-51; 1454-55; 1428-31, 1421-24, 1463, 1425-27) and extensive texts in Sanskrit.

Mahāvastu (part of the *Vinaya* of the Lokottaravāda Mahāsaṃghika school), ed. Senart, Paris, 1882-97 (3 vols.); translated by Jones, London (PTS), 1949-56 (3 vols.).

Śikṣāsamuccaya (see under Śāntideva in XXVI).

IX

Ācārāṅga, ed. Jacobi, London (Pali Text Society), 1892; translated by Jacobi, London (Oxford University Press, Sacred Books of the East, Vol. XXII), 1884.

Sūtrakṛtāṅga (*Sūyagaḍa*), ed. Suracandra, Bombay, 1917; translated by Jacobi, London (Sacred Books of the East, Vol. XLV), 1895.

X

Sāṃkhya—See Johnston, *Early Sāṁkhya*, London (Royal Asiatic Society, Prize Publication Fund), 1937.

Brahman Sūtra (see under XV).

Kaṭha Upaniṣad, ed. Böhtlingk, Leipzig, *Berichte über die Verhandlungen der Königl. Sächsischen Gesellschaft der Wissenschaften* (Phil.-histor. Klasse), 1890.

Mahābhārata (see under VII).
Majjhima Nikāya (see under VIII).
Mīmāṃsā Sūtra (see under XV).
Upaniṣads (see under IV).
Vedāṅgas—Kalpasūtras, consisting of *Śrautasūtras* (which include *Śulvasūtras*), *Gṛhyasūtras* and *Dharmasūtras*, for the bibliography see Ram Gopal, *India of Vedic Kalpasūtras*, Delhi (National Publishing House), 1959, pp. 488-91. Ram Gopal's book is an excellent monograph on the ritual of the Vedic schools.
Yoga Sūtras with Vyāsa's commentary, ed. Bodas, Bombay (Sanskrit Series), 1892.

XI

Dharmaśāstras—e.g. *Mānava Dharmaśāstra*, ed. Deslongchamps, Paris (Levrault), 1830; translated by G. Bühler as *The Laws of Manu*, London/Oxford (Sacred Books of the East, Vol. XXV), 1886; in due course 36 such books of 'institutes' were recognised as authoritative (outstanding is Yājñavalkya, later than 'Manu' and much more systematic, also somewhat revised to accommodate social changes in the 'feudal' period) and these naturally were followed by commentaries and digests (by Medhātithi, Bhoja, Vijñāneśvara, Lakṣmīdhara, etc.); for the earlier *Dharmasūtras* of the Vedic schools (not yet a universal law) see under X (*Vedāṅgas*).
Kauṭalya: *Arthaśāstra*, ed. and translated by Kangle, Bombay (University 'Studies'), 1960 (text) and 1963 (translation).

XII

Science—see R. Billard: *L'Astronomie indienne*, Paris (Adrien-Maisonneuve: ÉFEO), 1971; A.K. Warder, 'Prolegomena to a History of Indian Science' in *New Paths in Buddhist Research*, Durham N.C. (Acorn Press), 1985.
Āryabhaṭa: *Āryabhaṭīya*, ed. Kern, Leiden, 1874; translated by W.E. Clark, Chicago (University Press), 1930.
Astronomy (*jyotiṣa*, see under *Vedāṅgas* for the early period).
Bhāskara: *Siddhānta Śiromaṇi*, ed. Bāpu Deva Śāstrin, Varanasi, 1866; the section on arithmetic (*pāṭīgaṇita*, called *Līlāvatī*) and some parts of algebra translated by Colebrooke, 2nd. ed. Calcutta (The Book Company), 1927, with a text; the *Golādhyāya* translated by

Wilkinson and Bāpu Deva, Calcutta, 1861-62.
Bījagaṇita (on parts of algebra and trigonometry), ed. Ekendranath Ghosh, Lahore (Motilal Banarsidass), 1926.
Karaṇakutūhala, ed. Sudhākara, Varanasi, 1881.
Brahmagupta: *Brāhmasphuṭa Siddhānta,* ed. Sudhākara, Varanasi 1902.
Khaṇḍakhādyaka, ed. B. Misra, Calcutta, 1925; translated (from manuscripts) by Sengupta, Calcutta (University), 1934.
Caraka: *Carakasaṃhitā,* ed. with Cakrapāṇi's commentary Vidyāsāgara, Calcutta, 1896.
Gārga (see Weber's study of *Jyotiṣa* under *Vedāṅgas* below).
Geometry (see *Śulvasūtras* under *Vedāṅgas*).
Mahāvīra: *Gaṇitasārasaṃgraha,* ed. and translated by Rangacarya, Madras, 1912.
Mathematics—see Datta and Singh, *History of Hindu Mathematics,* new edn. Bombay (Asia Publishing House), 1962.
Pāṇini: *Aṣṭādhyāyī,* ed. and translated by S.C. Vasu, reprinted Delhi (Motilal Banarsidass), 1962 (2 vols.).
Vācaspatimiśra (see under XXV, the reference is to pp. 550f. of the Varanasi edn. of the *Nyāyavārttikatātparyaṭīkā*).
Vasumitra (II) and Pārśva: *Mahāvibhāṣā,* Chinese translation (the original seems to be lost) Taishō 1545-47.
Vedāṅgas—traditionally there are six of these:

(1) Phonetics (*śikṣā*) on which see W.S. Allen, *Phonetics in Ancient India,* London (Oxford University Press), 1953.
(2) Linguistics or grammar (*vyākaraṇa,* 'analysis'), see under Pāṇini.
(3) Lexicology (*nirukta*), *The Nighaṇṭu and the Nirukta,* ed. and translated by L. Sarup, reprinted Delhi (Motilal Banarsidass), 1967.
(4) Metrics (*chandas*), Piṅgala: *Chandaḥsūtra,* ed. Kedāranātha, Bombay (Nirnaya Sagara Press), 3rd edn. 1938.
(5) Astronomy (*jyotiṣa*), see Weber, *Uber den Vedakalender namens Jyotisham,* Berlin (Abhandlungen der Akademie der Wissenschaften), 1862; *Yājuṣa* and *Ārca Jyotiṣa,* ed. Sudhākara, Varanasi, 1908; *Atharvan Jyotiṣa,* ed. Datta, Lahore, 1924, Shamasastry, Mysore, 1936.
(6) Ritual (*kalpa*), which includes geometry (*śulva*) in its

Śulvasūtras (cf. under *Vedāṅgas* in X); *Āpastamba Śulva Sūtra*, ed. Srinivasachar and Narasimhachar, Mysore (University Sanskrit Series), 1931; *Baudhāyana Śulva Sūtra*, ed. and translated by Thibaut, Vạranasi, in *The Pandit*, 1874-77 (these two are perhaps the oldest *śulva sūtras*).

XIII

Abhidharma—the earliest *Abhidharma* may be studied through and reconstructed from the following works of the schools now extant (see *Indian Buddhism* 218ff.):

Śāriputrābhidharmaśāstra (of the Dharmaguptaka school?), Chinese translation Taishō 1548.

Vibhaṅga (Sthaviravāda), Pali ed. C.A.F. Rhys Davids, London (Pali Text Society), 1904.

Puggalapaññatti (Sthaviravāda), Pali. ed. Morris, London (PTS), 1883.

Dhātukathā (Sthaviravāda), Pali ed. Goonaratne, London (PTS), 1892; translated by Nārada, London (PTS), 1962.

Paṭṭhāna (Sthaviravāda, see under XIV).

Dharmaskandha (Sarvāstivāda), Chinese translation Taishō 1537.

Dhātukāya (Sarvāstivāda, Chinese translation, Taishō 1540.

Vijñānakāya (Sarvāstivāda), Chinese translation Taishō 1539.

F. Watanabe: *Philosophy and its Development*, Delhi (MB), 1983.

Kathāvatthu, ed. Taylor, London (PTS), 1894-97 (2 vols.); translated by Aung and C.A.F. Rhys Davids as *Points of Controversy*, London (PTS), 1915 (since reprinted).

Mātṛkā, see A.K. Warder, 'The Mātikā', in *Mohavicchedanī*, ed. A.P. Buddhadatta and A.K. Warder, London (PTS), 1961.

XIV

Schools of early Buddhism—Buddhaghosa's commentary on the *Kathāvatthu* notes the schools which maintained the controversial propositions in the text, this information from the commentary has been included in the translation, *Points of Controversy* (see under XIII), the commentary itself has been edited by Minayev, London (*Journal of the Pali Text Society*), 1889; a Sarvāstivādin work on the schools is Vasumitra's *Samayabhedoparacanacakra*, Chinese version Taishō 2031 (also in Tibetan in the Tibetan

Tripiṭaka reprinted in Kyōto, Otani University, ed. Suzuki, 1957), translated by Bareau, Paris (*Journal Asiatique*), 1954, pp. 235ff.; a Mahāyānist account of the subject is found in Demiéville, 'L'origine des sectes bouddhiques d'après Paramārtha', in *Mélanges Chinois et Bouddhiques* (Louvain and elsewhere) I, 1931-32, pp. 15ff.

Adikaram: *Early History of Buddhism in Ceylon,* Migoda (Puswella), 1946.

Bahuśrutīya school—Harivarman's *Tattvasiddhiśāstra* (Chinese version Taishō 1646) see S. Katsura: *A Study of Harivarman's Tattvasiddhi,* Univ. of Toronto PhD thesis 1974.

Dhammasaṅgaṇi, ed. Müller, London (Pali Text Society), 1885; translated by C.A.F. Rhys Davids as *A Buddhist Manual of Psychological Ethics,* London (Royal Asiatic Society), 2nd. edn. 1923 (recently reprinted by the PTS).

Commentary on the *Dhammasaṅgaṇi—Atthasālinī,* by Buddhaghosa, ed. Müller, London (PTS), 1897; translated by Tin as *The Expositor,* London (PTS), 1920-21 (2 vols., since reprinted).

Commentary on the *Puggalapaññatti,* ed. in *Journal of the Pali Text Society,* 1914.

Paṭisambhidāmagga, ed. Taylor, London (PTS), 1905-07 (2 vols.); translation by Ñāṇamoli London (PTS), 1982, on Sthaviravāda see A.K. Warder's Introduction.

Paṭṭhāna, 2nd. Bangkok edn. 1927 (6 vols.) (the PTS has published only excerpts, which moreover cannot be relied on for the text).

Peṭakopadesa, ed. Rangoon 1917 and 1956, and by A. Barua, London (PTS), 1949; translated by Ñāṇamoli as the *Piṭaka-Disclosure,* London (PTS), 1964.

Saṃmitīya school—**Āśrayaprajñaptiśāstra,* Chinese version Taishō 1649; translated by K. Venkataramanan in *Viśvabhāratī Annals* V, 1953.

Sarvāstivāda school—their basic *Abhidharma* work is the *Jñānaprasthāna* by Kātyāyanīputra, Chinese version Taishō 1543-44; Stcherbatsky has surveyed their doctrine in his *Central Conception of Buddhism,* London (Royal Asiatic Society), 1923, but indirectly through a Sautrāntika (see XXIV) source, the *Abhidharma Kośa.*

Yamaka, ed. C.A.F. Rhys Davids, London, (PTS), 1911-13 (2 vols.).

XV

Aśvaghoṣa: *Buddhacarita*, ed. and translated by Johnston, Sanskrit text of I.8 to XIV.31, Calcutta (Panjab University Oriental Publications), 1935, translation of I to XIV ibid, 1936, translation of XV to XXVIII (from Tibetan and Chinese) in *Acta Orientalia* (Leiden/Copenhagen), 1937.

Brahman Sūtra of Bādarāyaṇa, ed. Poona (Ānandāśrama Sanskrit Series), 1890-91; translated by Thibaut with two commentaries in Sacred Books of the East Vols. XXXIV, XXXVIII and XLVIII, reprinted Delhi (Motilal Banarsidass), 1962.

Johnston: *Early Sāṁkhya* (see under Sāṃkhya in X).

Mīmāṃsā Sūtra, of Jaimini, ed. with Śabarasvāmin's commentary in the Ānandāśrama Sanskrit Series, Poona, 1929-34; also with Mārūlakara Narahari Śāstrin's *Vṛtti* (modern) *Bhāvabodhinī*, Kolhāpūra (Dhārmika Granthāvali 10), 1951; translated by Ganganatha Jha, Allahabad (Sacred Books of the Hindus), 1910, Baroda 1933-34.

Stcherbatsky: *Central Conception of Buddhism* (see under Sarvāstivāda in XIV).

Śvetāśvatara Upaniṣad (see under VII).

XVI

Vaiśeṣika—see Faddegon, *The Vaiçeṣika-System*, Amsterdam (Müller, Verhandelingen der Koninklijke Akademie van Wetenschappen), 1918.

Caraka (see under XII).

Mahābhāṣya, by Patañjali (see under VII), also ed. Kielhorn, Bombay, 1880-85, re-edited (Abhyankar) at Poona (Bhandarkar Oriental Research Institute), 1962ff.; see also H. Scharfe, *Die Logik im Mahābhāṣya*, Berlin (Akademie-Verlag, Deutsche Akademie der Wissenschaften, Institut für Orientforschung), 1961.

Praśastapāda (see under XXV).

Vaiśeṣika Sūtra, of Kaṇāda, ed. and translated by Nandalal Sinha, Allahabad (Sacred Books of the Hindus), 1911 (the translation follows the misinterpretations of the later commentators); also ed. Anantalal Thakur with an anonymous commentary, Darbhanga (Mithila Institute), 1957; also ed. Jambuvijaya with the commentary of Candrānanda, Baroda (Gaekwad's Oriental Series), 1961.

XVII

Aruṇandi: *Civañāṉacittiyār*, ed. Aḻagappa, Madras, 1911; translated by Nallaswami Pillai, Madras, 1913 (title transliterated as *Śivajñāna Siddhiyār*).

Bhadrabāhu: *Daśavaikālika Niryukti*, ed. with the text by Leumann, Leipzig (*Zeitschrift der Deutschen Morgenländischen Gesellschaft*), 1892, pp. 581ff.

Bhagavatī (*Vyākhyāprajñapti*), ed. Bombay (Āgamodaya Samiti), 1918-21 (3 vols.).

Candrakīrti (see under XXVI).

Civañāṉacittiyār (see Aruṇandi).

Dīgha Nikāya (see under VIII).

Gaṅgeśa (see under XXVII).

Haribhadra: *Ṣaḍdarśanasamuccaya* (see under VII).

Jayanta (see under XXV).

Jayarāśi: *Tattvopaplavasiṃha* ed. Sanghavi and Parikh, Baroda (Gaekwad's Oriental Series), 1940.

Kamalaśīla: *Tattvasaṃgraha Pañjikā* (see under XXVI).

Maṇimēkalai (see Śāttanār).

Nīlakeci (anon.), ed. A. Chakravarti, Madras, 1936.

Sarvadarśanasaṃgraha (see under Mādhava in VII).

Śāttanār: *Maṇimēkalai*, ed. Swaminath Aiyar, Madras, 1898; see also the study by Krishnaswami Aiyangar, *Maṇimēkalai in its Historical Setting*, London (Luzac), 1928.

Siddhasena Divākara: *Sanmatitarkaprakaraṇa*, ed. Sanghavi and Doshi, Ahmedabad (Gujarat Puratattva Mandira Granthavali), 1922.

Sthānāṅga, ed. Suracandra, Bombay, 1918-20 (2 vols.).

Uttarādhyayana, ed. Vijayomaṅga, Bombay, 1937; translated by Jacobi, London (Sacred Books of the East, Vol. XLV), 1895.

Vādideva: *Syādvādaratnākara*, ed. Bombay (Nirnaya Sagara Press), 1914.

XVIII

Mahāyāna—for its origins see Tāranātha's history translated by Schiefner as *Geschichte des Buddhismus in Indien*, St. Petersburg, 1869, especially Chapter 13; Lamotte in *Asiatica*, p. 387; Sthaviravāda traditions in *Kathāvatthu* and its commentary (see under XIII and XIV), e.g. on Caitikas, and in Adikaram (see under XIV), p. 100 (*Ratnakūṭa* an Āndhra text); Candrakīrti, *Madhyamakāvatāra* pp. 134f. and *Prasannapadā* p. 548 (see under XXVI) on Pūrva Śaila verses teaching the new doctrine; *Aṣṭasāhasrikā Prajñāpāramitā Sūtra* (see *Prajñāpāramitā*) p. 225 (will be known in the South at first); Demiéville from Paramārtha (see under XIV), pp. 19ff. on Mahāsaṃgha as predecessor of Mahāyāna.

Early Mahāyāna *sūtras*, e.g. the (small) *Ratnakūṭa* (*Kāśyapaparivarta*), ed. von Staël-Holstein, Shanghai, 1926; *Rāṣṭrapālaparipṛcchā*, ed. Finot, St. Petersburg (Bibliotheca Buddhica), 1901 (reprinted in Indo-Iranian Reprints, 'S—Gravenhage, 1957); *Ugraparipṛcchā* (T 322) trs. N. J. (Barnes) Schuster, University of Toronto PhD thesis, 1976.

Jātaka (Pali), ed. Fausbøll, London 1877-96 (recently reprinted by the Pali Text Society); translated by Cowell and others, Cambridge, 1895-1907 (reprinted PTS 1957).

Prajñāpāramitā—Aṣṭasāhasrikā Prajñāpāramitā, ed. R. Mitra, Calcutta (Bibliotheca Indica), 1888; ed. Vaidya with Haribhadra's *Āloka* and the *Abhisamayālaṅkāra* (see under Haribhadra in XXVI).

Vimalakīrtinirdeśa, L'Enseignement de Vimalakīrti, É. Lamotte, Université de Louvain, 1962.

XIX

Caraka (see under XII).

Mahāvibhāṣā (see under Vasumitra in XII).

Nyāya Sūtra (see under Akṣapāda in XXI).

* *Upāyahṛdaya*, translated from Chinese into Sanskrit by Tucci in *Pre-Diṅnāga Buddhist Texts on Logic from Chinese Sources*, Baroda (Gaekwad's Oriental Series), 1929 (from *Fang pien sin louen*, Taishō 1632).

XX

Āryadeva: *Catuḥśataka*, Sanskrit fragments ed. Haraprasād, Calcutta, 1914; partial (VIII-XVI) reconstruction and translation by Vaidya (not very successful), Paris, 1923; more successful reconstruction by Bhattacharya, Calcutta (Viśvabhāratī), 1931.

Śataśāstra, translated from Chinese by Tucci in *Pre-Diṅnāga* (see under XIX) (Taishō 1569, only the first half of the text is available).

Bu-ston: *Chos-ḥbyung* (=*Dharmodbhava*, 'Production of the Doctrine'), translated by Obermiller, Heidelberg (Materialien zur Kunde des Buddhismus), 1931-32 (a Tibetan history of Buddhism and introduction to the *Tripiṭaka*, see Vol. II pp. 122ff. on Nāgārjuna).

Nāgārjuna: *Mūlamadhyamakakārikā*, ed. La Valleé Poussin, St. Petersburg (Bibliotheca Buddhica), 1903-13, with Candrakīrti's commentary *Prasannapadā*; translated by Stcherbatsky (Chapters 1 and 25) in his *Conception of Buddhist Nirvāṇa*, Leningrad (Academy of Sciences of the USSR), 1927 (reprinted in Indo-Iranian Reprints, The Hague, 1965); May (2-4, 6-9, 11, 23-24 and 26-27), Paris (Maisonneuve), 1959; Schayer (5 and 12-6), Krakow (Polska Akademja Umiejçtności), 1931 and (10) in *Rocznik Orjentalistyczny*, 1931, pp. 26ff.; Lamotte (17) in *Mélanges Chinois et Bouddhiques*, Vol. IV, 1936; and de Jong (18-22), Paris (Geuthner, Buddhica), 1949 (this complete but patchwork translation includes Candrakīrti's commentary).

Vigrahavyāvartanī and *Vṛtti*, ed. Johnston and Kunst in *Mélanges Chinois et Bouddhiques*, Vol. IX, 1951.

Śūnyatāsaptati and *Vṛtti* (only in the Tibetan *Tripiṭaka*).

Yuktiṣaṣṭikā, translated from the Chinese by Schaeffer, in Materialien zur Kunde des Buddhismus, 1923.

Vaidalyaprakaraṇa, ed. in Tibetan by Kajiyama, Kyoto (University, *Miscellanea Indologica Kiotiensia*), 1965.

Suhṛllekha, translated from the Tibetan by Wenzel, London (*Journal of the Pali Text Society*), 1886.

Ratnāvalī, Sanskrit partly ed. and translated by Tucci, London (*Journal of the Royal Asiatic Society*), 1934 and 1936.

Catuḥstava (*stotras*), Sanskrit of the *Niraupamya* and *Paramārtha* ed. and translated by Tucci, London (*Journal of the Royal Asiatic Society*), 1932.

Tāranātha (see under XVIII).

XXI

Akṣapāda: *Nyāya Sūtra*, ed. and translated by Vidyabhusana and Nandalal Sinha, Allahabad (Sacred Books of the Hindus), 1930; ed. and translated by Ruben, Leipzig (*Abhandlungen für die Kunde des*

Morgenlandes), 1928 (reprinted Liechtenstein, Kraus, 1966).

**Tarkaśāstra*, translated from Chinese into Sanskrit by Tucci in *Pre-Diṅnāga* (see under XIX) from *Jou che louen*, Taishō 1633).

Vātsyāyana: *Nyāya Bhāṣya*, ed. Gaṅgādhara, Varanasi (Lazarus, Vizianagram Sanskrit Series), 1896.

XXII

Candrakīrti (see under XXVI).

Gaṇḍavyūha Sūtra, ed. Suzuki and Idzumi, Kyoto (the Sanskrit Buddhist Texts Publishing Society), 1934-36; ed. Vaidya, Darbhanga (Mithila Institute, Buddhist Sanskrit Texts), 1960; see Suzuki, *Essays in Zen Buddhism, Third Series*, London (reprint, Rider), 1953.

Laṅkāvatāra Sūtra, ed. Nanjio, Kyoto, 1923; ed. Vaidya, Darbhanga (Mithila Institute, Buddhist Sanskrit Texts), 1963; translated by Suzuki, London (Routledge), 1932.

Sandhinirmocana Sūtra, Tibetan text ed. and translated by Lamotte, Louvain (Université, Recueil de travaux. .2e série, 34e fascicule), 1935.

Śrīmālā Sūtra, Tibetan text in the (Great) *Ratnakūṭa* of the *Tripiṭaka*; Chinese also in the Great *Ratnakūṭa*, in Taishō 310 and also 353; Sanskrit quotations in the *Ratnagotravibhāga* of Sthiramati.

Sthiramati (I, or Sāramati): *Ratnagotravibhāga Mahāyāna Uttaratantra Śāstra*, ed. Johnston, Patna (Bihar Research Society), 1950; translated (from the Tibetan, the Sanskrit text not having been then recovered) by Obermiller as 'The Sublime Science' (i.e. *Uttaratantra*) in *Acta Orientalia*, Vol. IX, 1931.

XXIII

Asaṅga: *Sandhinirmocanabhāṣya* (in the Tibetan *Tripiṭaka*).

Abhidharmasamuccaya, ed., in part reconstructed, by Pradhan, Santiniketan (Viśvabhāratī), 1950.

Madhyāntavibhaṅga, ed. Yamaguchi, Nagoya, 1934; first part translated by Stcherbatsky, Moscow/Leningrad (Academy of Sciences, Bibliotheca Buddhica), 1936.

Dharmadharmatāvibhaṅga (in Tibetan *Tripiṭaka*), Sanskrit unpublished (manuscript in Spos-khang, Tibet, see *Journal of the Bihar and Orissa Research Society* XXIV. 4, p. 163).

Mahāyānasaṃgraha, Tibetan text ed. and translated (along with a reprint of the Chinese, Taishō 1594) by Lamotte, Louvain (Muséon), 1938-39 (4 parts).

Yogācārabhūmiśāstra, Sanskrit MS in Patna (Chinese T. 1579); V. Bhattacharya has edited *Bhūmis* 1-5 of the *Bahubhūmikavastu,* Calcutta (University), 1957; Wogihara has edited the 'Bodhisattvabhūmi' (No. 15) of the *Bahubhūmikavastu,* Tokyo, 1930-36. Chinese, Taishō 1579.

[Tucci has given some account of Asaṅga's logic, in comparison with some other writers, in his article 'Buddhist Logic before Diṅnāga' in the *Journal of the Royal Asiatic Society,* London, 1929, and also in his *Pre-Diṅnāga* (see under XIX), which must be revised in the light of publications since then.]

Mahāyānasūtrālaṅkāra, ed. and translated by S. Lévi, Paris (Champion, Bibliothèque de l'école des hautes études, fasc. 159 and fasc. 190), 1907 and 1911.

Vasubandhu (see under XXIV).

XXIV

Bodhāyana (?): *Mīmāṃsā Vṛtti* is known only in the extract quoted by Śabarasvāmin in his *Bhāṣya* commentary (ed. and translated with the *Sūtra,* see under XV).

Brahman Sūtra (see under XV).

Diṅnāga: *Hastavālaprakaraṇa,* Tibetan text ed. Frauwallner in *Wiener Zeitschrift für die Kunde Süd—und Ostasien* (Österreichische Akademie der Wissenschaften), 1959, pp. 152ff.; Sanskrit reconstructed and translated by F.W. Thomas and Ui, London (*Journal of the Royal Asiatic Society*), 1918.

Ālambanaparīkṣā, Tibetan text ed. and translated by Frauwallner in *Wiener Zeitschrift für die Kunde des Morgenlandes* (Hölder), Vol. 37, 1930, 174ff.; also translated by Yamaguchi, Paris, *Journal Asiatique,* 1929; summary by Stcherbatsky in *Buddhist Logic* (see under Dharmakīrti, *Nyāyabindu,* in XXVI), I, 518ff.

Sāmānyaparīkṣā, according to Kitagawa, *A Study of Indian Classical Logic—Diṅnāga's System* (see under *Pramāṇasamuccaya*), pp. 430f., there is a Chinese version extant (Taishō 1623), the *Kuan-tsung-hsiang-lun-sung* (='*Sāmānyalakṣaṇaparīkṣā-*

prakaraṇakārikā').

Hetucakraḍamaru, Tibetan text ed. Frauwallner in *Wiener Zeitschrift für die Kunde Süd—und Ostasien*, 1959, pp. 161ff.; Sanskrit reconstructed and translated by D. Chatterji, Calcutta (*Indian Historical Quarterly*), 1933.

Nyāyamukha, translated from the two Chinese texts (*Taishō* 1628-29) by Tucci in Materialien zur Kunde des Buddhismus, 1930.

Pramāṇasamuccaya, there are two Tibetan texts in the *Tripiṭaka* (see the works of Kitagawa and Hattori for detailed information), with Diṅnāga's *Vṛtti*; Kitagawa has translated parts of Chapters 2-4 and 6 into Japanese and also collected the Sanskrit fragments from these parts in his *A Study of Indian Classical Logic—Dignāga's System* (*Indo Koten-Ronrigaku no Kenkyū*), Tokyo, 1965; Hattori has translated Chapter 1 (into English) and collected its Sanskrit fragments in *Dignāga on Perception*, Cambridge Massachusetts (Harvard Oriental Series), 1968; for Chapter 5 see Jinavijaya: *Dvādaśāram Nayacakram*, Bhāvanagara, Part II, 1976, pp. 607-729 and S. Katsura, 'The Apoha Theory of Dignāga', in the *Journal of Indian and Buddhist Studies* XXVIII, 1979, pp. 489ff.

Īśvarakṛṣṇa: *Sāṃkhyakārikā*, ed. Ramesh Chandra, Calcutta (Sanskrit Series), 1935; ed. and translated by Colebrooke, London, 1837.

Jinendrabuddhi: *Viśālāmalavatī Pramāṇasamuccayaṭīkā* in the Tibetan *Tripiṭaka*.

Ṣaṣṭitantra, fragments collected by Frauwallner, *Wiener Zeitschrift für die Kunde Süd—und Ostasien*, 1958, pp. 1 ff.

Vasubandhus: *Vādavidhāna* (II) and *Vādavidhi* (I), for fragments see Frauwallner, *Wiener Zeitschrift Für die Kunde des Morgenlandes*, Vol. 40, 1933, pp. 281ff. and *Wiener Zeitschrift für die Kunde Süd—und Ostasien*, Vol. I, 1957, pp. 1 ff.

Abhidharmakośa and *Bhāṣya* (II) ed. Pradhan, Patna, 1967.

A.K. Warder: 'Objects', in *Journal of Indian Philosophy* III, 1975, pp. 355 ff.

XXV

On (Old) Nyāya and Vaiśeṣika logic see Randle, *Indian Logic in the Early Schools*, Oxford, 1930.

Abhinavagupta: *Abhinavabhāratī*, ed. M.R. Kavi, K.S. Ramaswami and J.S. Pade, Baroda (Gaekwad's Oriental Series), 1926-64 (4 vols., of which the 2nd. edn., 1956, of Vol. I should be used); see Gnoli, *The Aesthetic Experience according to Abhinavagupta*, Rome (Serie Orientale Roma), 1956.

Īśvarapratyabhijñāvivṛtivimarśinī, Srinagar (Research Department, Kashmir State, Kashmir Series of Texts and Studies), 1938-43 (3 vols).

Tantrāloka, Srinagar (Kashmir Series of Texts and Studies), 1918-38 (12 vols).

Bhartṛhari: *Vākyapadīya, kāṇḍa* I ed. Cārudeva Śastrin, Lahore (Ramlal Kapur Trust Society), 1934; also Raghunātha Sharma, Varanasi (Sarasvatī Bhavana Granthamālā), 1963; *kāṇḍa* II ed. Gaṅgādhara Śāstrin, Varanasi (Benares Sanskrit Series), 1887; *kāṇḍa* III. 1-7 ed. Subramania Iyer, Poona (Deccan College Monograph Series), 1963; *kāṇḍa* III. 8-14 ed. Sāmbaśiva Śāstrin and Ravi Varma, Trivandrum (Sanskrit Series), 1935 and 1942 (2 vols.); for a good study see Gaurinath Sastri, *The Philosophy of Word and Meaning*, Calcutta (Sanskrit College Research Series), 1959.

Gauḍapāda: *Kārikās* on the *Māṇḍūkya Upaniṣad*, Mysore (Rāmakṛṣṇa Āśrama), 1936 (with Śaṃkara's commentary).

Harṣa: *Khaṇḍanakhaṇḍakhādya*, ed. Lakshmana Shastri, Varanasi (Chowkhamba Sanskrit Series), 1914.

Jayanta: *Nyāyamañjarī*, ed. Gaṅgādhara Śāstrin, Varanasi (Vizianagram Sanskrit Series), 1895.

Jayatīrtha: *Vādāvalī*, ed. and translated by Nagaraja Rao, Madras (The Adyar Library), 1943.

Pramāṇapaddhati, Madras (Modern Printing Works), 1917; the *Pramāṇacandrikā* of Śalāriśeṣa, ed. and translated by S.K. Maitra as *Mādhva Logic*, Calcutta (University), 1936, is a summary of the doctrines of the *Pramāṇapaddhati*.

Kumārila: *Mīmāṃsāślokavārttika*, Varanasi (Chowkhamba Sanskrit Series), 1898-99; translated by Ganganatha Jha, Calcutta (Bibliotheca Indica), 1900-08.

Tantravārttika, Varanasi (Benares Sanskrit Series) translated by Ganganatha Jha, Calcutta (Bibliotheca Indica), 1903-24.

Tupṭīkā, ed. by Gaṅgādhara Śāstrin, Varanasi (Benares Sanskrit Series), 1903-4.

Madhva: *Brahmasūtrabhāṣya*, ed. Raghavendracharya, Mysore, 1911-22 (4 vols.); translated by Subba Rao, Madras, 1904.

Commentaries on *Chāndogya* and *Bṛhadāraṇyaka Upaniṣads*, Allahabad (Sacred Books of the Hindus, Vols. III and XIV).

[On Madhva and his school see Dasgupta, *A History of Indian Philosophy*, Vol. IV, Cambridge (University), reprinted 1955.]

*Maticandra, see Ui, *The Vaiśeṣika Philosophy*, London (Royal Asiatic Society), 1917.

Nārāyaṇa and Nārāyaṇa: *Mānameyodaya*, ed. and trs. C.K. Raja and S.S. Sūryanārāyaṇa, Adyar, 1933.

Prabhākara: *Bṛhatī*, Varanasi (Chowkhamba Sanskrit Series), 1929-33.

[On Prabhākara see Ganganatha Jha, *The Prābhākara School of Pūrva Mīmāṃsā*, Allahabad, 1911; also his comparative study *Pūrva-mīmāṃsā in its Sources*, Varanasi (Benares Hindu University), 1942.]

Praśastapāda: *Padārthadharmasaṃgraha*, ed. Ḍhuṇḍhirāja, Varanasi (Haridāsa Saṃskṛta Granthamālā), 1923; also ed. Kālīpada, Calcutta (Sanskrit Sahitya Parishat), no date; translated by Ganganatha Jha, Varanasi (*The Pandit*), reprinted 1916.

Rāmānuja: *Brahmasūtrabhāṣya* (*Śrībhāṣya*), ed. Abhyankar, Bombay, 1915; translated by Thibaut, London (Oxford University Press, Sacred Books of the East, Vol. XLVIII), 1904 (reprinted Delhi, Motilal Banarsidass, 1962).

Vedārthasaṃgraha, ed. and translated by van Buitenen, Poona (Deccan College Monograph Series), 1956.

[On Rāmānuja and his school see also Dasgupta, *A History of Indian Philosophy*, Vol. III, Cambridge (University), reprinted 1952.]

Śaṃkara: *Brahmasūtrabhāṣya*, ed. N.R. Acarya, Bombay 1948; translated by Thibaut, London (Oxford University Press, Sacred Books of the East, Vols. XXXIV and XXXVIII), 1904 (reprinted Delhi, Motilal Banarsidass, 1962).

Upaniṣadbhāṣya, ed. Bhagavat, Poona, 1927-28.

[On Śaṃkara's school see Dasgupta, *A History of Indian Philosophy*, Vol. II, Cambridge (University), reprinted 1961.]

[N.B. Though Dasgupta gives useful general surveys he is not to be relied on for details, which should always be checked against the original sources before being used as a basis for study.]

Śaṅkarabhaṭṭa: *Mīmāṃsābālaprakāśa,* Chowkhamba Sanskrit Series, 1902.

Śrīdhara: *Nyāyakandalī,* ed. Vindhyeśvarīprasād, Varanasi (Vizianagram Sanskrit Series), 1895; translated by Ganganatha Jha, Varanasi (*The Pandit*), reprinted 1916.

Udayana (see under XXVII).

Uddyotakara: *Nyāyavārttika,* ed. Vindhyeśvarīprasād, Varanasi (Kashi Sanskrit Series), 1916.

Vācaspatimiśra: *Nyāyavārttikatātparyaṭīkā,* ed. Rājeśvara, Varanasi (Kashi Sanskrit Series), 1925-26.

Vaiśeṣika commentaries (see under XVI).

Vasugupta: *Śivasūtra,* Srinagar (Kashmir Series of Texts and Studies), 1916.

Vyāsatīrtha: *Tarkatāṇḍava,* ed. Srinivasachar and Madhwachar, Mysore (University, Sanskrit Series), 1932.

Yāmuna: *Siddhitraya,* ed. Rama Misra, Varanasi (Chowkhamba Sanskrit Series), 1904; on the understanding of Yāmuna and Rāmānuja and Vedānta theology generally see van Buitenen's monograph under Rāmānuja, *Vedārthasaṃgraha.*

Yuktidīpikā, ed. R.C. Pandeya, Delhi (Motilal Banarsidass), 1967.

XXVI

Abhayākaragupta: *Marmakaumudī* (commentary on the *Abhisamayālaṅkāra*), in the Tibetan *Tripiṭaka.*

Munimatālaṅkāra, in the Tibetan *Tripiṭaka.*

Abhisamayālaṅkāra, of 'Maitreya', ed. Stcherbatsky and Obermiller, Leningrad (Bibliotheca Buddhica), 1929; also printed in Vaidya's edn. of the *Aṣṭasāhasrikā Prajñāpāramitā* (see under XVIII); for studies see Obermiller, *The Doctrine of Prajñāpāramitā as exposed in the Abhisamayālaṅkāra,* Acta Orientalia, 1932-33, and Obermiller, *Analysis of the Abhisamayālaṅkāra,* Calcutta (Oriental Series), 1933-43 (3 parts, not completed).

Ānanda (I): *Abhidhamma Mūlaṭīkā,* Burmese edn. of the Pali text 1924-26 (3 vols.) and new edn. 1960.

Atthasālinī Ṭīkā, Colombo (Hewavitarne) 1938.

Anuruddha I (of Ceylon): *Abhidhammatthasaṅgaha,* ed. Rhys Davids, London (*Journal of the Pali Text Society*), 1884; translated by

C.A.F. Rhys Davids as *Compendium of Philosophy*, London (Pali Text Society), 1910 (reprinted 1957).

Nāmarūpapariccheda, ed. A.P. Buddhadatta, London (*Journal of the Pali Text Society*), 1914.

Anuruddha II (of Kāñcī): *Paramatthavinicchaya*, ed. A.P. Buddhadatta, London (*Journal of the Pali Text Society*), 1983; see A. K. Warder: 'The Concept of a Concept' in *Journal of Indian Philosophy* I, 1971, pp. 181 ff.

Arcaṭa: *Hetubinduṭīkā*, ed. Sanghavi and Jinavijayaji, Baroda (Gaekwad's Oriental Series), 1949.

Aśoka: *Avayavinirākaraṇa* and *Sāmānyadūṣaṇadikprasāritā*, ed. A. Thakur, Patna, 1974.

Avalokitavrata: *Prajñāpradīpaṭīkā*, in the Tibetan *Tripiṭaka*.

Bhāmaha: *Kāvyālaṅkāra*, ed. Baṭukanāthaśarman and Baladevopādhyāya, Vārāṇasī (Kashi Sanskrit Series), 1928.

Bhāvaviveka: *Prajñāpradīpa*, Tibetan text (from the *Tripiṭaka*) ed. Walleser, Calcutta (Bibliotheca Indica), 1914; Chinese Taishō 1566; translation begun by Kajiyama, *Wiener Zeitschrift für die Kunde Süd— und Ostasien* VII-VIII, 1963-64.

Madhyamakahṛdaya and *Tarkajvālā* in the Tibetan *Tripiṭaka*, see Gokhale in *Indo-Iranian Journal* (The Hague), Vols. II and V.

Karatalaratna in the Tibetan *Tripiṭaka*; Chinese Taishō 1578; translated from the Chinese by Aiyasvami in *Viśvabhāratī Studies* (Santiniketan) 9, 1949.

Buddhadatta: *Abhidhammāvatāra*, ed. A.P. Buddhadatta, London (Pali Text Society), 1915.

Buddhadeva (only quotations in the *Abhidharmakośa*, see Vasubandhu II, and elsewhere).

Buddhaghosa: *Visuddhimagga*, ed. Warren and Kosambi, Cambridge Massachusetts (Harvard Oriental Series), 1950; translated by Ñāṇamoli as *The Path of Purification*, Colombo (Semage), 1956.

Commentaries including *Sumaṅgalavilāsinī* on *Dīgha Nikāya*, London (PTS) 1886-1932; *Sāratthappakāsinī* on *Saṃyutta Nikāya*, PTS 1929-37; *Atthasālinī*(see under XIV); etc.

Buddhapālita: *Mūlamadhyamakavṛtti* in the Tibetan *Tripiṭaka*, part ed. Walleser, St. Petersburg (Bibliotheca Buddhica), 1913-14.

Buddhaśrījñāna: *Prajñāpradīpāvalī Abhisamayālaṅkāravṛtti* in the Tibetan

Tripiṭaka.

Candrakīrti: *Madhyamakāvatāra,* Tibetan text, ed. La Vallée Poussin, St. Petersburg (Bibliotheca Buddhica), 1907-12; partly translated by La Vallée Poussin in *Le Muséon* (Louvain), 1907, 1910, 1911.

Prasannapadā Madhyamakavṛtti, ed. and translated along with the *Kārikās,* see under Nāgārjuna in XX.

Devendrabuddhi: *Pramāṇavārttikapañjikā,* in the Tibetan *Tripiṭaka;* see Frauwallner in *Wiener Zeitschrift für die Kunde Süd—und Ostasiens* IV, 1960.

Dhammapāla (II): *Anuṭīkā* (sub-sub-commentary to the Pali *Abhidhamma*) on Ānanda's *Mūlaṭīkā,* ed. with the latter (new edn.), see under Ānanda.

Paramatthamañjūsā (commentary on Buddhaghosa's *Visuddhimagga*), ed. Rangoon 1960 (2 vols.).

Līnatthappakāsinī (on Buddhaghosa's *Sumaṅgalavilāsinī*), ed. de Silva, London (Pali Text Society), 1970.

Saccasaṅkhepa ed. Dhammārāma JPTS 1917-19.

Dharmakīrti: *Pramāṇavārttika Kārikā* ed. with Manorathanandin's commentary by Sāṅkṛtyāyana, Patna (*Journal of the Bihar and Orissa Research Society,* Appendices to Vols. XXIV, XXV and XXVI), 1938-40.

Pramāṇavārttika I and *Vṛtti* ed. Mālavaṇiyā, Vārāṇasī (Hindu Vishvavidyalaya Nepal Rajya Sanskrit Series), 1959; also by Gnoli, Rome (Serie Orientale Roma), 1960; partly translated (from the Tibetan version) by Frauwallner in *Wiener Zeitschrift für die Kunde des Morgenlandes* Vols. 37, 39 and 40, 1930-33.

Pramāṇaviniścaya and *Vṛtti* in the Tibetan *Tripiṭaka;* partly translated by Vetter and Steinkellner Vienna, 1966, 1973.

Nyāyabindu ed. and translated by Stcherbatsky, Petrograd/Leningrad (Bibliotheca Buddhica), 1918 (text) and 1930-32 (in *Buddhist Logic,* which is a study of the entire Pramāṇa theory, reprinted The Hague, Indo-Iranian Reprints, 1958, also as a Dover paperback, New York); also ed. Mālavaṇiyā, Patna (Tibetan Sanskrit Works Series, Jayaswal Research Institute), 1955.

Hetubindu, Sanskrit text reconstructed from the Tibetan and Arcaṭa's commentary in the edn. of the latter, see Arcaṭa; Steinkellner, Vienna, 1967.

Sambandhaparīkṣā and *Vṛtti* in the Tibetan *Tripiṭaka;* the available

Sanskrit *Kārikās* are given by Sāṅkṛtyāyana in the Introduction to his edn. of the *Pramānavārttikabhāṣya*, see Prajñākaragupta; the Tibetan text ed. and translated by Frauwallner, *Wiener Zeitschrift für die Kunde des Morgenlandes* Vol. 41, 1934, pp. 261 ff.

Vādanyāya ed. Sāṅkṛtyāyana, Patna (*Journal of the Bihar and Orissa Research Society*, Appendix to Vols. XXI and XXII), 1935-36.

Santānāntarasiddhi, Tibetan text ed. Stcherbatsky, Petrograd (Bibliotheca Buddhica Vol. XIX) and translated by him as *Obosnovanie chuzhoi odushevlennosti*, Petrograd (*Pamyaniki Indiiskoi Filosofii* I), 1922, summary in *Buddhist Logic* I, 521ff.; English translation from the Russian by H.C. Gupta, Soviet Indology Series 2, Calcutta, 1969.

Dharmamitra: *Prasphuṭapadā* (commentary on Haribhadra's *Sphuṭārthā*) in the Tibetan *Tripiṭaka*.

Dharmatrāta (I) (only quotations in the *Abhidharma Kośa*, see Vasubandhu II, and elsewhere).

Dharmottara: *Pramāṇaviniścayaṭīkā* in the Tibetan *Tripiṭaka*.

Nyāyabinduṭīkā ed. and translated along with the *Nyāyabindu* in the works mentioned above under Dharmakīrti.

(*Anya-*) *Apohaprakaraṇa*, Tibetan text ed. and translated by Frauwallner in *Wiener Zeitschrift für die Kunde des Morgenlandes* Vol. 44, 1936, 233ff.

Kṣaṇabhaṅgasiddhi, Tibetan text ed. and translated by Frauwallner in *Wiener Zeitschrift für die Kunde des Morgenlandes* Vol. 42, 1935, 217ff.

Other monographs in the Tibetan *Tripiṭaka*.

Durvekamiśra: *Pradīpa* (on Dharmottara's *Nyāyabinduṭīkā*), ed. Mālavaṇiyā with the *Nyāyabindu*, see Dharmakīrti.

Āloka (on Arcaṭa's *Hetubinduṭīkā*), ed. Sanghvi and Jinavijayaji with Arcaṭa's work, see Arcaṭa.

Haribhadra: *Abhisamayālaṅkārāloka*, ed. Tucci, Baroda (Gaekwad's Oriental Series), 1932; ed. Wogihara, Tokyo, 1932-35; ed Vaidya, Darbhanga (Mithila Institute, Buddhist Sanskrit Texts), 1960.

Sphuṭārthā, manuscript in Rome.

Subodhinī Saṃcayagāthāpañjikā, manuscript in Ṣalu, Tibet.

Jina(mitra): *Pramāṇavārttikālaṅkāraṭīkā* in the Tibetan *Tripiṭaka*.

Jinendrabuddhi (see under XXIV).

Jitāri: *Hetutattvopadeśa*, ed. Tucci, Rome (Serie Orientale Roma), 1956.

Jātinirākaraṇa, ed. Tucci, Poona (*Annals of the Bhandarkar Oriental Research Institute*, Vol. XI), 1930.

Vādasthāna, ed. Aiyangar, Mysore, 1944.

Sahopalambhaprakaraṇa and *Nairātmyasiddhi*, manuscripts in Ngor and copies in Patna, Bihar Res. Soc.

Bālāvatāratarka and *Dharmadharmiviniścaya* in the Tibetan *Tripiṭaka*.

Jñānaśrībhadra: sub-commentary on Dharmottara's *Pramāṇaviniścayaṭīkā* in the Tibetan *Tripiṭaka*.

Jñānaśrīmitra: *Jñānaśrīmitranibandhāvali* (12 of his monographs) ed. A. Thakur, Patna (Tibetan Sanskrit Works Series), 1959.

Kalyāṇarakṣita: *Anyāpohavicāra, Sarvajñasiddhi, Śrutiparīkṣā, Īśvarabhaṅga* and *Bāhyārthasiddhi* in the Tibetan *Tripiṭaka*.

Kamalaśīla: *Nyāyabindupūrvapakṣasaṃkṣipti* in the Tibetan *Tripiṭaka*.

Tattvasaṃgrahapañjikā (ed. and translated with the text, see Śāntarakṣita).

Madhyamakālaṅkārapañjikā in the Tibetan *Tripiṭaka*.

Bhāvanākrama Nos. I-III, No. I ed. Tucci, Rome (Serie Orientale Roma), 1958; No. III ed. Tucci, Rome, 1971; No. II in the Tibetan *Tripiṭaka*; Chinese Taishō 1664.

Karṇakagomin: *Ṭīkā* on *Pramāṇavārttika* I with *Vṛtti*, ed. Sāṅkṛtyāyana, Ilāhābād, 1943.

Kassapa: *Mohavicchedanī* (see under *Mātṛkā* in XIII).

Manorathanandin (see under Dharmakīrti, *Pramāṇavārttika*).

Mokṣākaragupta: *Tarkabhāṣā*, ed. E. Kṛṣṇamācārya, Baroda (Gaekwad's Sanskrit Series), 1942; translated as *An Introduction to Buddhist Philosophy* by Kajiyama, Kyoto (University, Memoirs of the Faculty of Letters, No. 10), 1966.

Muktākalaśa: commentary on Dharmottara's *Kṣaṇabhaṅgasiddhi* in the Tibetan *Tripiṭaka*.

Prajñākaragupta: *Pramāṇavārttikabhāṣya* (or—*Alaṅkāra*), ed. Sāṅkṛtyāyana with *Pramāṇavārttika Kārikās* II-IV, Patna (Tibetan Sanskrit Works Series), 1953, Index Vol. 1959.

Sahāvalambanirṇayasiddhi in the Tibetan *Tripiṭaka*.

Prajñākaramati: *Bodhicaryāvatārapañjikā* (on Śāntideva) ed. La Vallée Poussin, Calcutta (Bibliotheca Indica), 1902-14; ed. Vaidya,

Darbhanga (Mithila Institute, Buddhist Sanskrit Texts), 1960.
Ratnākaraśānti: *Antarvyāptisamarthana*, ed. Haraprasād, Calcutta (Bibliotheca Indica), 1910.
Vijñaptimātratāsiddhi in the Tibetan *Tripiṭaka*.
Ratnākaraśānti (II ?): *Sāratamā Abhisamayālaṅkārapañjikā*, ed. P.S. Jaini, Patna (Tibetan Sanskrit Works Series), 1979.
Ratnakīrti: *Ratnakīrtinibandhāvalī* (10 of his monographs) ed. A. Thakur, Patna (Tibetan Sanskrit Works Series), 1957.
Ravigupta: *Ṭīkā* on *Pramāṇavārttikabhāṣya* III in the Tibetan *Tripiṭaka*.
Pramāṇavārttikavṛtti in the Tibetan *Tripiṭaka*.
Śākyabuddhi: *Pramāṇavārttikaṭīkā* in the Tibetan *Tripiṭaka*.
Saṃghabhadra: *Nyāyānusāra*, Chinese translation Taishō 1562.
Samayapradīpikā, Chinese translation Taishō 1563.
Śaṅkarānanda: *Pramāṇavārttikaṭīkā* in the Tibetan *Tripiṭaka*.
Anusāra Ṭīkā on *Sambandhaparīkṣā* in the Tibetan *Tripiṭaka*.
Sarvajñasiddhisaṃkṣepa, manuscript in Ngor and copy in Patna.
Apohasiddhi and *Pratibandhasiddhi* in the Tibetan *Tripiṭaka*.
Śaṅkarasvāmin: *Nyāyapraveśa*, ed. Dhruva, Baroda (Gaekwad's Oriental Series), 1927-30 (2 vols.).
Śāntarakṣita: *Vipañcitārthā* (on *Vādanyāya*, ed. with the text, see Dharmakīrti).
Tattvasaṃgraha, ed. E. Kṛṣṇamācārya, Baroda (Gaekwad's Oriental Series), 1926 (2 vols.); translated by Ganganatha Jha, Baroda (Gaekwad's Oriental Series), 1937-39 (2 vols.).
Śāntideva: *Bodhicaryāvatāra* (ed. with the commentary, see Prajñākaramati); translated by *La Vallée Poussin*, Paris, 1912.
Śikṣāsamuccaya, ed. Bendall, St. Petersburg (Bibliotheca Buddhica), 1897 (reprinted The Hague, Indo-Iranian Reprints, 1957); translated by Bendall and Rouse, London (Murray, Indian Texts Series), 1922.
Skandhila: *Abhidharmāvatāra* in the Tibetan *Tripiṭaka*; Chinese Taishō 1554.
Sthiramati II: commentary on Vasubandhu's *Triṃśikā*, ed. and translated by S. Lévi with the text, see Vasubandhu I.
Abhidharmasamuccayavyākhyā, manuscript in Ngor and photocopy in Patna.
Madhyāntavibhaṅgaṭīkā ed. Yamaguchi, Nagoya, 1934; part translated by Friedman, Utrecht (Utr. Typ. Ass.), 1937.

Śubhagupta (see Kalyāṇarakṣita).

Sumaṅgala: *Abhidhammatthavikāsinī* (commentary on Buddhadatta's *Abhidhammāvatāra*), ed. A.P. Buddhadatta, Ambalangoda, 1961.

Abhidhammatthavibhāvanī (commentary on Anuruddha's *Abhidhammatthasaṅgaha*), ed. Paññāsāra and Wimaladhamma, Colombo, 1933.

Commentary on Anuruddha's *Nāmarūpaparicheda*, manuscripts in Ceylon.

Tāranātha (see under XVIII).

Vasubandhu I: *Triṃśikākārikāprakaraṇa*, ed. and translated by S. Lévi, Paris (Bibliothèque de l'école des hautes études, Champion), 1925 and 1932 (with the *Viṃśikākārikāprakaraṇa* and *Vṛtti*).

see under XXIV for his work on logic.

commentaries on Asaṅga's *Dharmadharmatāvibhaṅga* and *Mahāyānasaṃgraha* in the Tibetan *Tripiṭaka.*

commentary on Asaṅga's *Madhyāntavibhaṅga*, manuscript in Ngor and copy in Patna.

[for the commentators on the *Triṃśikākārikāprakaraṇa* see Hsuan-tsang, Taishō 1585, translated by La Vallée Poussin as *Vijñaptimātratāsiddhi*: *La Siddhi de Hiuan-tsang* (sic), Paris (Geuthner, Buddhica), 1928-29, 1948 (2 vols. and Index).]

Vidyākaraśānti: *Tarkasopāna*, ed Tucci, Rome (Serie Orientale Roma), 1956.

Vimalamitra(?): *Abhidharmadīpa* and *Vibhāṣāprabhāvṛtti*, ed. Jaini, Patna (Tibetan Sanskrit Works Series), 1959.

Vinītadeva: commentary on *Santānāntarasiddhi*, Tibetan text ed. and translated by Stcherbatsky along with the text, see Dharmakīrti.

commentaries on *Nyāyabindu, Hetubindu, Sambandhaparīkṣā* and *Vādanyāya* in the Tibetan *Tripiṭaka.*

commentary on Diṅnāga's *Ālambanaparīkṣā* in the Tibetan *Tripiṭaka.*

Yamāri: *Supariśuddhā Ṭīkā* (on *Pramāṇavārttikabhāṣya*) in the Tibetan *Tripiṭaka.*

XXVII

On Navya Nyāya see Ingalls, *Materials for the Study of Navya-Nyāya Logic,* Harvard Oriental Series, 1951.

Annambhaṭṭa: *Tarkasaṃgraha,* ed. and translated by Foucher, Paris (Adrien-Maisonneuve), 1949.

Bhagīratha: *Kusumāñjaliprakāśikā*, ed. Varanasi (Kashi Sanskrit Series), 1957 (with the text and Vardhamāna's *Prakāśa*).

Kiraṇāvalīprakāśikā, manuscripts in Government Sanskrit Library, Varanasi.

Nyāyalīlāvatīprakāśikā, ed. Varanasi with the text, see Vallabha.

Gadādhara: *Gādādharī* (sub-commentary on Raghunātha's *Dīdhiti* on the *Tattvacintāmaṇi*), Varanasi (Chowkhamba Sanskrit Series), 1913-27 (with the *Dīdhiti*).

Nañvādaṭīkā, see Raghunātha.

monographs, e.g. *Vyutpattivāda*, Varanasi (Kashi Sanskrit Series), 1935.

Gaṅgeśa: *Tattvacintāmaṇi*, ed. Calcutta (Bibliotheca Indica), 1892-1900; also with *Āloka* and *Darpaṇa*, see Maheśa.

Jagadīśa: *Jāgadīśī* (sub-commentary on Raghunātha's *Dīdhiti* on the *Tattvacintāmaṇi*), Varanasi (Chowkhamba Sanskrit Series), 1906-08.

Keśavamiśra: *Tarkabhāṣā*, ed. Kulkarni, Poona (Oriental Series), 1953; translated by Ganganatha Jha, Poona (Oriental Series), 1949.

Madhusūdana: *Kaṇṭakoddhāra*, partly ed. Varanasi (Sarasvatī Bhavana Texts), 1939.

Maheśa: *Darpaṇa* (sub-commentary on Pakṣadhara Jayadeva's *Āloka* on the *Tattvacintāmaṇi*), ed. Umesha Mishra and Sasinatha Jha, Darbhanga (Mithila Institute), 1957 in progress.

Manikaṇa (anon.), ed. and translated by Sreekrishna Sarma, Madras (Adyar Library Series), 1960.

Maṇikaṇṭha: *Nyāyaratna*, ed. Subrahmanya and Krishnamacharya, Madras (Govt. Or. Ser.), 1953.

Mathurānātha: commentary on the *Tattvacintāmaṇi*, ed. with the text (Bibliotheca Indica), see Gaṅgeśa.

Pakṣadhara (II) Jayadeva: *Āloka* (commentary on the *Tattvacintāmaṇi*), ed. with the *Darpaṇa*, see Maheśa.

Raghunātha: *Dīdhiti* on the *Tattvacintāmaṇi*, ed. with its sub-commentaries, see Gadādhara and Jagadīśa.

Dīpikā on the *Ātmatattvaviveka* of Udayana, ed. Varanasi (Chowkhamba Sanskrit Series), 1925.

Kiraṇāvalīprakāśadīdhiti, ed. Badri Nath, Varanasi (Sarasvatī Bhavana Texts), 1932.

Padārthatattvanirūpaṇa, ed. Varanasi (*The Pandit*), 1903-05; translated by K.H. Potter, Cambridge Massachusetts (Harvard-Yenching Institute Studies), 1957.

Nañvāda, ed. in Bibliotheca Indica edn. of *Tattvacintāmaṇi* (Vol. IV), with Gadādhara's commentary, see Gaṅgeśa; translated by Matilal in *The Navya-Nyāya Doctrine of Negation*, Harvard, 1968.

Rucidatta: *Kusumāñjalimakaranda*, manuscript in Government Sanskrit Library, Varanasi; excerpts (only ?) in edn. of Vardhamāna's *Prakāśa*, see Vardhamāna.

Dravyaprakāśavivṛti (on *Kiraṇāvalī*), ed. with the *Prakāśa*, Calcutta, see Vardhamāna.

Cintāmaṇiprakāśa, manuscript in Calcutta Sanskrit College (cf. Peterson, *Sixth Report*, p. 76).

Śaṅkaramiśra: *Maṇimayūkha*, manuscript in Jammu (Stein, *Jammu Catalogue*, p. 144).

Bhedaprakāśa, ed. Varanasi (Sarasvatī Bhavana Texts), 1933 (under the title *Bhedaratna*).

Khaṇḍanaṭīkā, ed. Bhāgavatācārya, Varanasi, 1888.

Vādivinoda, ed. Ganganatha Jha, Allahabad, 1915.

Upaskāra, ed. Calcutta (Bibliotheca Indica), 1861; also ed. Varanasi (Chowkhamba Sanskrit Series), 1923.

Līlāvatīkaṇṭhābharaṇa, ed. Varanasi (Chowkhamba), 1934.

Śivāditya: *Saptapadārthī*, ed. Jetly, Ahmedabad (Lālbhāī Dalpatbhāī Institute of Indology), 1963.

Udayana: *Ātmatattvaviveka*, ed. Dhundhiraja, Varanasi (Chowkhamba Sanskrit Series), 1940.

Nyāyakusumāñjali, ed. and translated by Cowell, Calcutta (Bibliotheca Indica), 1864; also by Upadhyaya and Dhundhiraja, Varanasi (Chowkhamba), 1957, see Bhagīratha; also in other edns. of various commentaries (Vardhamāna, etc.).

Kiraṇāvalī, ed. Vindhyeśvarīprasāda, Varanasi (Benares Sanskrit Series), 1885-1919; also with Vardhamāna's commentary in the Bibliotheca Indica (part 1: 1911-12; 2: 1956), etc.

Nyāyavārttikatātparyapariśuddhi, ed. with Vardhamāna's *Nyāyanibandhaprakāśa* by Vindhyeśvarīprasāda and Dravida, Calcutta (Bibliotheca Indica), 1911-24.

Vādīndra: *Rasasāra* (commentary on *Kiraṇāvalī*, *Guṇa* part), ed. Varanasi (Sarasvatī Bhavana Texts), 1922.

Mahāvidyāviḍambana, ed. Telang, Baroda (Gaekwad's Oriental Series), 1920.

(Śrī) Vallabha: *Nyāyalīlāvatī*, ed. Harihara and Dhundhiraja, Varanasi (Chowkhamba), with the commentaries of Vardhamāna, Bhagīratha, etc., 1927-34.

Varadarāja: *Tarkikarakṣā*, ed. Vindhyeśvarīprasāda, Varanasi (*The Pandit*), 1903.

Vardhamāna: *Kusumāñjaliprakāśa*, ed. Candrakānta, Calcutta (Bibliotheca Indica), 1891-95; also Varanasi (Chowkhamba, Kashi Sanskrit Series, 1957), see Bhagīratha.

Kiraṇāvalīprakāśa, ed. Śivacandra, Calcutta (Bibliotheca Indica), 1911-12 and 1956; ed. Varanasi (Sarasvatī Bhavana).

Līlāvatīprakāśa, ed. Varanasi with the text, see Vallabha.

Nyāyanibandhaprakāśa, see Udayana.

Vāsudeva Sārvabhauma: *Sārāvalī* commentary on Gaṅgeśa, manuscript in Varanasi (Sarasvati Bhavan).

Viśvanātha Pañcānana: *Bhāṣāpariccheda*, ed. and translated by Roer, Calcutta (Bibliotheca Indica), 1850; ed. with other works of Viśvanātha, Varanasi, 1905, again Varanasi (Kashi Sanskrit Series), 1951.

Commentary on *Padārthatattvanirūpaṇa*.

Yajñapati: *Tattvacintāmaṇiprabhā*, manuscript in Darbhanga Raj Library.

[Several of the above editions do not appear to have been completed.]

INDEX

If a name appears in a chapter title it is usually not repeated here. Sometimes only the first reference is given or only the main one, to be understood with 'ff'.

object, 168, 177
object (*ālambana*, see 'support')
object (*viṣaya*), 177, 197
omniscient, 201
organisation (*nāma*), 19, 50
other minds, 199
other-being (*parabhāva*), 93
own characteristic, 163, 197, 199
own experience, 178
own-being (*svabhāva*), 32, 34, 93, 196

padasthāna (immediate cause), 94
pakṣa, 175
Pakṣadhara, 212
Pakṣadhara II (Jayadeva), 212
Pañcaśikha, 64
paradoxes, 127
Paramārtha, 195
Parāśara, 64
parokṣa, 115
particular, 177
particular (*bheda*), 180
particular (*viśeṣa*), 108
particular (*svalakṣana*, see own characteristic), 175
Paṭisambhidāmagga, 92
perception (*saṃjñā*), 182
person (*pudgala*), 86
pervaded (*vyāpta*), 179
pervasion (*vyapti*), 180, 182
Peṭakopadeṣa, 92
philosophy (*ānvīkṣikī*), 71
philosophy, birth of, 14
ponential, 83
Prabhākara, 187
pragmatic criterion of truth, 197
Prajñākaragupta, 200
Prajñākaramati, 194
Prajñaptivāda, 85, 97
prakṛti, 101, 156
prasaṅga, 139
Prāsaṅgika, 194
Praśastapāda, 185
Pratardana, 27
pratibandha, 201
pratibhā, 182
Pratyabhijñā, 189
pratyakṣa, 177
predicate, 175
principle (*dharma*), 56, 59, 86, 94, 125, 141, 145, 158, 161
probability (*sambhāvana*), 123
probabilities, 133
pronouns, 51
proof, 117, 162, 164, 174, 179
proposition, 117
Pūraṇa, 42
Purandara, 122
Pūrva Śaila, 124

quality (*dharma*), 103
quality (*guṇa*), 104
quantitative experiment, 23
quantity, 82

Rāhulabhadra, 138
Raikva, 21
Raghunātha, 213
Rāmānuja, 189
rational thinking, 17
Ratnagotravibhāga, 156
Ratnakīrti, 203
Ratnākaraśānti, 203, 207
Ravigupta, 200
real, 59, 96, 178
reality, 57, 122
rebirth, 26, 49
refutation, 83, 176
regularity, 59
regularity of principles, 56
relation, 198
resistance (*pratigha*), 51
ritual, 15, 17
Rogue Cārvākas, 121
Rohagupta, 116
ṛta, 15
Rucidatta, 213
rūpa, 19, 26, 178

śabda, 151, 181
śābda, 180
sādhya, 152, 175
sādhyasama, 153
sākāra, 212
Śākyabuddhi, 199
sāmānya, 108, 129, 170